'Race', Sport and British Society is the first book to fully explore the dynamics of racism within sport in Britain. Despite popular belief that sport is an arena free from the corrosive effects of racism, the reality presents a more complex and troubling picture. As we start the twenty-first century, racism is still evident in sport. Racism manifests itself from the playing fields and boardrooms, to the decisions of sports policy makers and media representations. Sport is also an arena that far-right nationalists have used in order to promote a xenophobic version of British identity that excludes Asian and black Britons. Yet, despite this, sport can also be used to show how Britain is slowly moving towards becoming a genuinely multi-cultural society.

'Race', Sport and British Society argues that until racism is eradicated sport's meritocratic ideals will remain unfulfilled. Moreover, the book discusses British nationalism and considers the increasing significance of the inter-relationship between 'race' and sport to nationalist ideologies. With chapters from some of Britain's leading sociologists, educationalists and journalists, it breaks new ground in showing how discourses of 'race' and nation continue to pervade the field of sports. Chapters cover a wide range of topics, including the manifestation of racism in football, cricket and rugby, the alleged innate and 'natural' sporting superiority of black athletes, the place of the law in regulating racism, and the importance of the media in perpetuating, and challenging, racial stereotypes. 'Race', Sport and British Society issues a timely and important challenge to those in positions of power to confront bigotry and discrimination so that sport becomes genuinely open to all.

Ben Carrington is a lecturer in Sociology at the University of Brighton, and Ian McDonald is a lecturer in Sports Policy and Politics at the University of Brighton.

'Race', Sport and British Society

Edited by

Ben Carrington
and Ian McDonald

London and New York

First published 2001
by Routledge
11 New Fetter Lane, London EC4P 4EE

Simultaneously published in the USA and Canada
by Routledge
29 West 25th Street, New York, NY 10001

Routledge is an imprint of the Taylor & Francis Group

© 2001 Ben Carrington and Ian McDonald

Typeset in Goudy by The Midlands Book Typesetting Company,
Loughborough
Printed and bound in Great Britain by MPG Books Ltd, Bodmin

British Library Cataloguing in Publication Data
A catalogue record for this book is available from the British Library

Library of Congress Cataloging-in-Publication Data
'Race', Sport, and British Society / edited by Ben Carrington and Ian
McDonald ;
foreword by Paul Gilroy.
     p. cm.
    Includes bibliographical references and index.
    ISBN 0-415-24629-6 – ISBN 0-415-24630-X (pbk.)
    1. Discrimination in sports–Great Britain. 2. Athletes, Black–Great
Britain. 3. Great Britain–Race relations. I. Carrington, Benjamin, 1972-
II. McDonald, Ian, 1965-
GV706.32 .R316 2001
306.4'83–dc21
                                 00-051782

ISBN 0-415-24630-X (phk)   0-415-24629-6 (hbk)

Contents

Figures

Contributors

Les Back is a Reader in Sociology at Goldsmiths' College, University of London. He has written extensively on racism and popular culture. He is the author of, amongst others, of *New Ethnicities and Urban Culture* (UCL Press, 1996), co-author (with John Solomos) of *Race, Politics and Social Change* (Routledge, 1995) and *Racism and Society* (Macmillan, 1996), and co-editor (also with John Solomos) of *Theories of Race and Racism: A Reader* (Routledge, 2000).

Ben Carrington teaches sociology and cultural studies at the Chelsea School, University of Brighton.

Tim Crabbe is Principal Lecturer in Sport Sociology at Sheffield Hallam University. He has published in a variety of academic and popular journals and has co-authored (with Les Back and John Solomos) *The Changing Face of Football: Racisms, Multiculture and Identity* (Berg, 2001). His research interests focus on sport, racism and identity and the relationship between sport and notions of deviance. He is also a former national chair of the Football Supporters' Association.

Paul Dimeo lectures in the Division of Sport Studies at University College Northampton. His doctoral research at the University of Strathclyde from 1995–2000 examined the relationship of football and racism in Scottish society. Since then he has been researching various aspects of the history and sociology of football in South Asia.

Gerry P.T. Finn is Reader in the Department of Educational Studies at the University of Strathclyde. His major research focus is on societal conflict in relation to sport, education and society. He co-edited (with Richard Giulianotti) *Football Culture: Local Contests and Global Visions* (Frank Cass, 2000). Recent publications on societal conflict outside sport include ' "Sectarianism" and Scottish Education', in *Scottish Education* (EUP, 1999) and 'A Culture of Prejudice: Promoting pluralism in education for a change' in *Scotland's Shame? Bigotry and Sectarianism in Modern Scotland* (Mainstream Press, 2000).

Scott Fleming is Head of the School of Sport at Cheltenham and Gloucester College of Higher Education. He has written widely on sport, physical education and ethnicity, and is the author of *'Home and Away': Sport and South*

Asian Male Youth (Avebury Press, 1995), and co-editor (with Alan Tomlinson) of *Ethics, Sport and Leisure: Crises and Critiques* (Meyer and Meyer, 1997)

Simon Gardiner is Director of the International Sports Law Centre at Anglia Polytechnic University. He is co-author of *Sports Law* (1998, Cavendish Publishing) and has published widely in the discipline of sports law. He is currently researching in areas of sports governance and legal issues surrounding European national identity and sport.

Sanjiev Johal is co-author of *Corner Flags and Corner Shops – The Asian Football Experience* (Phoenix, 1999). Having completed his doctoral research which examined the South Asian experience of sport in Britain, at the University of Warwick, he has returned to the world of sports journalism with *The Observer*.

Emma Lindsey is an award-winning journalist who was born in London but spent her formative years flitting between the West Coast of America and London. She has written extensively about sport and other issues for a variety of publications including the *Observer*, the *Guardian*, the *Independent on Sunday*, the *Sunday Express,* and *Arena Magazine*.

Mike Marqusee is the co-author of *Defeat from the Jaws of Victory: Inside Kinnock's Labour Party* (Verso, 1992), and author of *Anyone but England: Cricket and the National Malaise* (Verso, 1992, shortlisted for the 1994 William Hill Sports Book of the Year, reprinted by Two Heads in 1998), *War Minus the Shooting: A Journey through South Asia during Cricket's World Cup* (Heinemann, 1996) and *Redemption Song: Muhammad Ali and the spirit of the sixties* (Verso, 1999, shortlisted for the 1999 William Hill Sports Book of the Year). He has also contributed articles on sport and politics to the *New Statesman*, *Esquire Magazine*, the *Guardian*, *Race and Class*, *India International Quarterly*, *Indian Express*, and many other periodicals. Mike is the founding member and current chairman of Hit Racism for Six.

Ian McDonald teaches politics and policy in sport and physical education at the University of Brighton.

Sheila Scraton is Professor of Leisure and Feminist Studies at Leeds Metropolitan University. She began her career as a PE teacher and has taught in schools, further education and higher education. She is UK co-ordinator of a major European research project on women's experiences of sport (highly competitive and recreational) and is involved in research exploring difference and identity in relation to women, leisure and the city. She has published extensively in the areas of gender and physical education, women, sport and leisure, leisure and the post-modern city.

Chris Searle is a lecturer in education at Goldsmiths' College, University of London. He is the author of numerous books on teaching and language. His study of language in the Caribbean, *The Forsaken Lover: White Words and*

Black People (Penguin, 1972) won the Martin Luther King Prize in 1973. He continues to write regularly on cricket for the *Morning Star*, *Race and Class*, and the *Observer*.

John Solomos is Professor of Sociology in the Faculty of Humanities and Social Sciences at South Bank University. His many publications include *Black Youth, Racism and the State* (Routledge, 1988), *Race and Racism in Britain* (Palgrave, 2001), and he is co-editor (with Martin Bulmer) of *Racism* (Oxford University Press, 1999).

Karl Spracklen is a Development Officer for the Sporting Equals project, and is a member of the Rugby League Supporters Association. Until recently he was at Leeds Metropolitan University, where he was awarded his PhD, which examined the social construction of community and masculine identity in rugby league. He also co-authored the report on racism in rugby league entitled *What's the Difference?* (LMU, 1995).

Roger Welch is a Senior Lecturer in law at the University of Portsmouth. He researches and writes on employment law issues and how they pertain to sport. He is a co-author of *Sports Law* (Cavendish Publishing, 1998) and a regular contributor to *Sports Law Bulletin*. Other recent work includes *Trade Union Rights in South Africa: The Labour Relations Act 1995* (Institute of Employment Rights, 2000).

Foreword

For the last three decades or so, the brash motto of 'true brit' nationalism has been supplied by a curious boast: 'two world wars and one world cup, doo dah, doo dah'. Future historians will puzzle over that odd phrase which, as it echoed around many British sports venues, became an ugly, almost musical chant. They will probably scratch their heads trying to make sense of the strange symbolic system in which it circulated and the warped patriotisms to which it gave such disturbing expression. The visceral ideas and feelings which it conjured up have acquired a continuing appeal, but they have slipped past most academic analyses of popular nationalist politics. For the most part, the full historic force of this fraternalistic and class-bound braggadocio has not been registered in the beleaguered places where the sociology of British sporting cultures is still being invented. Sociology is culpable here for its failures of imagination and principle and for its persistent, symptomatic refusal to address the interconnection of nationalism, racism and popular culture. Those words form an important, telling phrase that should not be set aside embarrassedly or passed over because it appears initially to be trivial. The intellectual commitment to taking these sentiments seriously, to making them worth understanding and unpacking, involves recognizing the dignity and value of the worthy lives that motto has helped to lead astray or divert into the arid lands of nationalist fantasy. For anyone willing to dig a little past the bright, clean surface of its red, white and blue wrapping, that phrase will supply not only an overall rationale for this worthwhile book but a wealth of other valuable insights into the morbid culture of a once-imperial nation that has not been able to accept its inevitable loss of prestige in a determinedly post-colonial world. Rather like the epochal phrase, 'There ain't no black in the Union Jack' which served a similar orienting function in various British sports grounds for a while, these words provide a rare window from which all the remorseful processes of Britain's vanished imperial status can be observed.

In this light, the phrase 'two world wars and one world cup' becomes a valuable means through which to consider the bewildering effects of England's post-colonial melancholia even where they have been intermittently offset by the compensations of the country's rare but nonetheless significant sporting successes. The words furnish the truly committed investigator with a compressed but still priceless history of post-war class relations in what is harder these days to call the United Kingdom. All the latent violence, all the embittered machismo, all the introjected class warfare articulated by defeated victors (mostly men and boys who were baffled and bewildered by a new post-war world that refused to recognize their historic manly qualities) is coded here in a dynamic and still explosive form. Historians and sociologists should not then turn away from that extraordinary phrase too swiftly. When it loses all its medieval power, England, and the Britain it has recently but comprehensively subsumed, really will have changed for the better.

Those words and sounds: 'two world wars and one world cup, doo dah, doo dah' suggest firstly, and most disturbingly, that war is a sport. Secondly, they introduce the possibility that sport, particularly football, has the same value as war in the indices of a distinctive national axiology. This twist is a local 'post-colonial' peculiarity of English life and it demands detailed historical con-sideration. It is not only that the two fields, war and sport, are adjacent in the metonymic chain of Britain's reluctantly-post-imperial nationalisms. We are being told that they should be understood as intimately connected areas of the country's national consciousness. Once they have been rendered equivalent and perhaps even interchangeable, we can see that war and sport generate many of the same emotions and libidinal investments, that they articulate the same intense and highly-prized forms of fraternal solidarity. The surrogate wars that were previously enacted only on the playing field, become a better, more exciting game when they are extended after the sporting formalities have been dispensed with. Opposing fans, foreign police and any 'aliens' unlucky enough to get in the way have all contributed to the body count of these excursions. Thirdly, this absurd phrase contains a deeply and spontaneously conservative assertion of national continuity. It expresses not national history but an anti-history governed by the familiar amnesiac principles by which deluded nations live. The boast these words articulate is also an integral part of a bigger denial. It announces that nothing significant changed during the course of Britain's downwardly-mobile twentieth century. Under a tattered flag, the precious thin red, white and blue line remains unbreached just like the crumbling, chalky frontier down at Dover. We are then required to admit that the nations which triumphed in 1918 and 1945 live on, unmodified and for the most part unre-marked upon. An implicit challenge invites us to discover their untimely, con-tentious definitions of nationality again today as a lingering, gritty presence inside the glittery but battered package of Britain's perennially suspended mod-ernization. Fourthly, those words testify to the continuing power of a class-based political language. In a stroke, they repudiate the fashionable notion that casual and informal status hierarchies have now replaced the destructive architecture of an obviously class-divided nation with a more appealing new arrangement in which class and regional divisions are more evenly blended or perhaps altogether dispersed. Tony Blair and his cronies may cynically dream of making populist politics out of lowering the exorbitant price of replica football kits. He may even appear in his best referee's shorts and profess undying support for Newcastle

United, but no matter where his own constituency is located, he is nowhere near to being a Geordie. Indeed, his brazen, utterly implausible claim to belong to the political body of that slumbering colossus, has, like Paul Gascoigne's boozy antics further south, thrown the shifting dynamics of what we should probably call Geordie 'ethnicity' into sharp relief. Post-industrial Britain's class divisions adhere stubbornly to the regional and geo-political patterns of its ebbing industrial phase. They are clearly alive and well. Particularly while inequality is intensified and recreated, sport and its various spectator cultures are producing, reproducing and channelling nationalist and absolutist identifications and identities in acute but attractive forms.

Those historic chanted words have another disturbing dimension: their perlocutionary power. This atavistic force is little understood. It produces the artificially whitened, comprehensively armoured national community to which the phrase casually refers. It demonstrates that there are still many courageous and willing working-class hearts beating around here. The martial, I am tempted to say Churchillian, performances in which they are incanted, communicate another significant hint. They reveal that there is a sense in which those brave but confused souls prefer an ordered past in which they were exploited and pauperized but knew who they were, to a chronically chaotic present in which even those limited certainties have been stripped away by the new corporate mandate of interminable, regressive change. In Britain's mud-and-blood-spattered past, heroic lions were led to ignominious slaughter by posh donkeys. Today at last, their belated but incomplete redemption is finally at hand. It is to be accomplished not so much by any occasional national victories on the sports field but by another characteristic national accomplishment: unblinking and unthinking pride in those performances which is indifferent as to whether the worthy lions in question are ultimately victorious. The gentlemen have died out or moved on to more remunerative pastures leaving the sportsfield in the horny hands of the players. We are confronted by one worthwhile international competition in which 'true brits' will not be bested by wily, elegant wine-drinking 'eyeties' and girly, shampoo-selling 'frogs' or shamed by the over-disciplined ranks of mechanical, unfeeling 'krauts' who don't know the volkish meanings of a warm pint let alone the traditional joys of a kebab or an extra bag of chips. England's traditional foolhardiness and 'up and at 'em' daring combine with a monstrously exaggerated sense of the country's importance to ensure that they will triumph in the national pride stakes every time. That triumphant conquest entails a more profound and total victory than any merely sporting contest can contain.

The same sinister phrase reveals its more melancholy aspects once the adrenaline begins to subside. It is deployed (but inevitably fails) to block consciousness of the irreversible fact that the carnival of Britain's imperial potency is now over for ever. Any residual celebrations to which those words contribute, help to constitute not the final stages of that stirring jubilee but the protracted process of cleaning-up that has followed it. They supply an appropriate vernacular soundtrack to the overdue task of taking down the bunting. The party is certainly over, but 'Two world wars and one world cup' can be articulated as an overdue invitation as well as a battle cry. Come and celebrate, it says, come to the national necropolis. Come and drink and shout and fight. Johnny foreigner needs a lesson in patriotism and we will be handing it out – doo dah doo dah. We may not win many games but we do know how to support our side – doo dah doo dah.

The historical record of England's belligerent fans 'on tour' is dismal and well known. But there is still a great deal of reluctance to identify these recurrent and depressing symptoms as part of the country's wider topography of ultra-nationalist race-consciousness. We need to understand that this refusal compounds the injuries involved in exclusion. Those of us who have had to run for our lives from vicious drunken crowds intent on a different, bloodier sport from the one they pay to see on the terraces, have always been able to know where nationalist sentiments were wired in to the raciological circuitry of the British nation and where Brit racisms and nationalisms were fused together as something like a single ethnic gestalt. This ready intermingling is not only an issue for English fans whose fears and conceits have a wider resonance in the nationalist aspirations of the United Kingdom's minor nations. Even when defined explicitly against Imperial England, their dreams of nationality have been enhanced by the ideal of purity and fantasies of homogeneity. This book makes it clear that the serious study of British sport cannot sanction the luxury of believing that 'race', nation and ethnicity can be readily or easily disentangled. Nationalism cannot be purged of its racialized contents any more easily than a body can be purged of the skeleton that supports it. Doubtless, the full implications of that realization will one day transform the conduct of British political life. Let us hope that many more people will not have to die before the penny finally drops. In the meantime, here is more proof that English nationalism remains volatile material. Manipulative politicians should not play with it thinking that they can easily harness its populist potency to exclusively benign and wholesome ends. Where it is politically engaged, all the violent perversities of race-thinking will not be far behind.

This collection encompasses a number of histories and angles of vision. It promotes an understanding of the relationship between 'race', nationalism and politics that shows the centrality of football without becoming football-centred. That game is itself changing as national and local leagues decline as part of a wider transition towards supra-national audiences and global branding. Though, as we have seen, absolute nationalism is openly expressed in that space, we must thank the likes of Alan Sugar, Ken Bates and Rupert Murdoch for the fact that an emergent cosmopolitanism is now, tentatively, evident there too. Real-time encounters in the stadium are increasingly becoming the preserve of the wealthy while the television transmissions are sold to Murdoch's empire. Under these unprecedented conditions it is by no means clear which of those cultural tendencies will eventually triumph. It may take the formation of a pan-European super league to consolidate a new set of regional ties and trans-local loyalties that could make the option of absolute ethnicity less attractive than it appears to be at present. Pending that outcome, different patterns of marketing and visibility are evident in other sports and spectacles. The same historic chemistry of 'race', ethnicity and national belonging has certainly touched them too but the effects have not always been destructive. Men's cricket is in what appears to be terminal decline as a national spectator sport. Its old imperial logics lost and its civilizing codes increasingly anachronistic and unmoving in a world sharply and permanently divided into the two great camps: a select group of winners and an ever-expanding legion of losers. Few state schools have the time or the facilities to maintain teams. Tall boys want to play basketball rather than bowl and the fundamental idea that a wholly satisfying contest can endure for five days and yet produce no result, increasingly defies comprehension. Meanwhile, the dead weight of a corrosive class culture prevents the decomposing game from re-inventing itself. Rugby Union on the other hand has accomplished exactly that next to impossible mission and now exists on a more modest, but apparently sustainable scale. The unhealthy, damaging expectation that England could be a spontaneous and casual world-beater was purged from that sporting arena long ago by decades of ruthless dominance by the 'old commonwealth' countries of the southern hemisphere. With its amateur rules rewritten, the game has recently hosted a novel and strange tradition in which the newly com-mercialized national team is cheered on by well-heeled fans who have made the old slave hymn 'Swing Low Sweet Chariot' into their post-colonial alternative to the national anthem. The appeal of 'Rule Britannia' and 'God Save The Queen' has apparently been exhausted. It is at Twickenham rather than in the knowing, post-modern efforts of Fat Les and co., that we can locate a resentful acknowledgement of how the country has been compelled by its reduced cir-cumstances to change for the better. Blake would no doubt have approved.

This welcome anthology accomplishes a number of other important and diver-gent tasks. It inquires from a historical perspective into the distinctive pattern of sporting events that has accented the rhythm of Britain's racialized politics during the second half of the twentieth century. These episodes: among them, that watershed world cup victory, Virginia Wade's Jubilee-year win at Wimble-don, the 'blackwash' cricket series of the eighties, Diego Maradona's 'hand of God goal', the tearful exit from Italia 90, the riots of Euro 96, the deaths at Heysel and Hillsborough, might productively be seen as staging posts en route to a more complex sense of Englishness and English culture, particularly as they bear upon changing relations between women and men and the ways that mas-culinity and femininity are experienced. The same historical sequence invites us to ask what the fame of Daley Thompson, Frank Bruno and Linford Christie and the ephemeral celebrity of Denise Lewis, Sonia Lannaman, Fatima Whit-bread, Tessa Sanderson, Zola Budd and many, many others long forgotten, tell us about the nation that we live in. By revealing the nation's heroes and mani-festing its more fantastic desires, this patriotic pantheon asks us systematically to reconsider the significance of the misty evening on which Viv Anderson made his international debut. We must ponder again the joyous moment when Arsenal's Paul Davies broke Glenn Cockerill's jaw, recall other better-organized fights between Cooper and Clay, Minter and Hagler, Bruno and Tyson and to retrieve the unforgettable occasion on which Jack Charlton, the original Geordie 'backwoodsman' of English football and perhaps of England itself, cheerfully killed that poor stag for the benefit of an unforgettable Channel 4 programme.

Of course, overt, respectable politics seldom intrudes into this avowedly un- and emphatically anti-political mediascape apparently populated by greying and balding ghosts and other more tragic alcoholic shadows of vanished greatness. Deprived of a political compass to orientate us, we are required to explore the strange meaning of John Barnes' appearance on an overcrowded platform supporting Margaret Thatcher's Conservative party and to understand how his recently-publicized authoritarian inclinations could combine with great dignity and exemplary sensitivity in comforting the relatives of ordinary Scouse people whose lives had been lost, whilst police officers allegedly laughed, at Hillsborough. Away from Merseyside, where 'You'll Never Walk Alone' would always eclipse the strains of 'Abide With Me', never mind the pieties of 'God Save The Queen', Barnes was never a hero. Greavsie and company made his exclusion from the inner circle of British sporting greatness a matter of national honour. Barnes' private education made him a marked man but he could never really be one of them/us while he retained a Jamaican passport. All the historic perfidies of the post-war race relations industry were laid on his shoulders and then made incarnate in the dazzling image of that afro-haired traitor in a white shirt streaking past those gobsmacked Brazilian defenders in the Maracana. A cat can be born in a kipper box but that, as we've been sagely told in a cynical echo of neo-fascist discourse, will never make it into a kipper. His successors have had to adopt different tactics which, where they have been successful, and I have the belligerent career of Paul Ince in mind, have had the additional virtue of underlining the insubstantiality of racial difference.

All these sorry tales might be orchestrated so as to culminate in the recent controversial visits of Mike Tyson to Britain's wretched inner cities. His rapturous reception by poor and marginal men, both black and white, suggests that there is plenty of life left in the patterns of identification, desire and connection originally established early in the last century by sporting figures whose unassailable heroism first defined the era of mass culture and showed the way towards the globalization of sporting spectacle. Appreciating the novelty of this pattern and its links to new kinds of commerce and capital also requires that we grasp another discomforting possibility. It is not primarily class that is at stake here but the trans-local integrity both of the male body and the appeal of the idea of manliness which has become such an ambiguous and contested factor in the cultural economy of 'race' and nation. Here perhaps are the deepest, latent meanings of the national family romance, of poor falsetto Becks dressed up in Posh's expensive underwear. The lost key to all those puzzling layers of over-sentimental Hornbyism that have recently saturated the political landscape can now be discovered hidden in Linford's lunchbox. Once again, spectator sport is the fitting cipher in which these big historic confrontations are knowingly transmitted and unknowingly received.

The essays that follow also pursue a number of useful quarrels with the sociologies of 'race' and of sport. These sub-disciplines are struggling to adapt their practice so that they can function in novel post-Cold War circumstances and to recognize how the increasingly desperate obligation to produce national solidarities and pleasures, reflects a new geometry of power even as the old imperial super-nation breaks apart. Though they certainly disagree among themselves, these writers ask us to move far beyond the obvious response, namely that sporting activities and achievements have been integral to the consolidation of Britain's black communities. This cultural shift requires more from us than just tracking the lives and histories of black sportswomen and men. It is ultimately about seeing them and their increasingly active and sometimes prestigious bodies in new ways that do not endorse the racialization of action, conflict, skill and embodiment. Here is an opportunity to make this overdue initiative into a noisy cue for revaluing sport and its cultures. We can begin to appreciate them for the fleeting, prefigurative glimpses of a different nation that they have unwittingly provided.

Paul Gilroy
Professor of Sociology and African American Studies
Yale University

Preface

Students have often complained to us about a lack of appropriate resources when they have wanted to research issues surrounding 'race', racism and sport. Articles have appeared, albeit disparately, but there is, as we write, no academic text within the social sciences that deals directly with issues of racism in British sport. '*Race*', *Sport and British Society* seeks to address this absence. However, in addition to providing a much-needed student resource, our aim in producing this book is also to raise the quality of analysis on 'race' issues prevalent in the sociology of sport. This means, for example, developing and testing the discussions about 'race', nation and sport beyond the sometimes insular disciplinary world of sport sociology. It means challenging those in positions of power in the world of sport who complacently see the superficial racial integration of some sports as demonstrating the 'no problem here' position. In seeking to advance the understanding of 'race', racism and sport in Britain amongst students, participants and policy makers, our goal is to create a climate conducive to informed debate, with a view to stimulating change.

In putting this collection together, and in line with our aims set out above, we sought out a rich mix of different authors. The contributions range from the more orthodox academic theoretical explications of Fleming and Scraton, to the engaging polemics of Johal and Marqusee, to the semi-autobiographical and critical essays of Lindsey and Searle. Collectively, the authors – sociologists, educationalists and journalists – provide a challenge to those within academia, the sports policy world and in politics to start taking racism in sport seriously.

Inevitably, there are omissions. We do not attempt to provide a historical survey of the changing nature of racism in British sport, though many of the chapters, such as Johal's and Searle's, do place their accounts in historical perspective. Such work urgently needs to be done as a way of challenging myths about the lack of presence of Asian and black communities within British history. The exemplary work of Phil Vasili in recovering the hidden histories of radical black working-class sporting heroes from the Victorian and Edwardian periods has been crucial in redressing this historical imbalance, but much more work, particularly concerning the place of Asian and black female athletes, still needs to be done. Such work is important, not only for recovering the hidden histories of the black presence in Britain which stretches back nearly five hundred years, but as a way of challenging some of the anodyne historical accounts concerning the development of Western sport which often fail to acknowledge how slavery, colonialism and certain modes of raciological thinking have been central to Modernity, and the place of sport within this. As Scraton argues (this volume), although 'we have some knowledge about the historical development of sport as an institution producing and reproducing patriarchal relations of domination . . . there is an absence of historical material that considers sport as inherently racialized as well as gendered'.

There are also very few young Asian and black female scholars researching the social significance of sport within British higher education. In trying to solicit chapters by or on the experiences of Asian and black women in sport for this collection we found virtually no work being done within the UK. Whilst there are numerous explanations for this – the lack of Asian and black PhD students generally within the social sciences; the marginalization of 'race' and sport as an area of critical inquiry within sociology – it does mean that even a comprehensive collection like this leaves huge areas uncovered. Whilst all contributors remained tuned to the gender specificity of their arguments most still focus on male sports with the regrettable result that women's participatory involvement is, to a degree, further marginalized.

We would argue that those currently working within higher education in Britain, and particularly those within sports studies departments – where the majority of work on 'race' and sport is still likely to come from – have to take seriously their responsibility for this situation. Whilst the entrance of Asians and blacks into higher education is determined and constrained by external structural factors – funding implications, personal choices of students, opportunities to receive quality secondary school education etc. – senior lecturers could clearly do much more than they currently do in terms of outreach work to young college students in getting them into HE in the first place. Those students, currently grossly under-represented at postgraduate level, that do make it into the system need to be encouraged and given the confidence and opportunity to pursue higher degree work. A cursory examination of PhD scholarships advertised in the last few years by most of the higher education sports departments – with one or two notable exceptions – clearly demonstrate that racial inequality is still not considered an area worthy of investigation by many within sports sociology. This must change. Only then we will see more Asian and black (female and male) scholars emerging and therefore able to contribute to these debates.

The collection also demonstrates the need for more scholarship on 'race' and sport outside England. The experience of Asian and black communities in Wales has had some reportage, but very little and even less so in Northern Ireland. For a number of years Dimeo and Finn's work has been important in addressing these issues as regards Scotland, and their contribution here further establishes their expertise. That said, all contributors critically interrogate notions of Englishness and Britishness where appropriate and provide insights for work to be carried out in other locations to test the validity of some of the arguments presented here.

Finally, a number of sports were not addressed, particularly those sports, such as hockey and netball that are often associated with high female participation and individual sports such as tennis and golf. Other team sports such as basketball have had some analysis but the work has generally been piecemeal and lacking in general theoretical sophistication. Whilst both editors have supervised numerous undergraduate dissertations that have shown widespread racial discrimination, especially in many private tennis and golf clubs, postgraduate research has yet to be fully undertaken in these areas. It needs to be, not only to test the hypotheses and arguments developed in the 'major' sports of rugby, cricket and football, but also because different analyses of the articulation of racism will emerge in sports which have distinct moral and ethical codes, and differing class and gender configurations.

These caveats aside, we still strongly believe that the current collection presents an important moment in theorizing sport and racism, which we hope will further inform and influence some of the ongoing policy debates occurring within several sports bodies.

The opening introductory chapter sets out the editors' theoretical and political position and should be read as a chapter in its own right. It also engages with the issues raised by each chapter and refers to each one in turn. Though the chapters can, and should, be read as complete in their own right, their cohesion centres on their attempts to critically interrogate our taken-for-granted and common-sense understandings about the relationship of 'race' to sport, set within the context of contemporary British society. As we state in our introduction, the complacency and lack of importance previously attributed to these issues by those within the sports industries and within academia itself has for too long gone unchallenged. The book's modest aim is to begin to challenge such attitudes.

Ben Carrington and Ian McDonald
University of Brighton, September 2000

Acknowledgements

Ben and Ian would like to thank their colleagues at the Chelsea School, University of Brighton, who have helped to provide a productive working environment.

We would both like to acknowledge the professional support and guidance of Mari Shullaw and Simon Whitmore at Routledge. Thanks to Steve Wagg, who suggested that we should work together on a book about racism and sport, and was very helpful in the early stages of the book's development. Finally, the contributors themselves also deserve our sincerest thanks, all of whom worked to tight deadlines and produced work of high quality.

Any errors, oversights or omissions that remain in the text we readily attribute to each other.

1 Introduction

'Race', sport and British society

Ben Carrington and Ian McDonald

Introduction: 'race', sport and the changing discourses of racism

There is a general argument within sociology that since the second world war –
when the full horrors of raciological thinking reached their climax with the
Holocaust – the discourse of racism has shifted from a crude biological racism,
based on the mistaken belief in biologically discrete 'races' each having their
own innate characteristics, towards a cultural racism, based on notions of
absolute cultural difference between ethnic groups (see Barker 1981; Gilroy
1987). Cultural racism posits that although different ethnic groups or 'races'
may not exist in a hierarchical biological relationship, they are nevertheless culturally distinct, each group having their own incompatible lifestyles, customs
and ways of seeing the world. So distinct in fact, that any attempt to 'mix
cultures' is doomed to failure, 'inevitably' leading to 'race riots' and 'rivers of
blood' flowing through the streets.[1] Thus signifiers such as language, dress,
musical preferences, sporting identifications and religion become key cultural
markers of distinguishing 'insider' and 'outsider' groups (Bauman 1990). Within
Britain, this 'new' racism claimed that it was not against Asians or blacks *per se*
entering into mainstream society, but only against those migrants unwilling to
disown any referents to a cultural heritage not defined as British. This British
heritage tended, of course, to be defined in very narrow and limited ways which
actually spoke more to an imagined sense of white middle-class Englishness than
it did to the contemporary realities of a multi-cultural, racial and urban Britain.
Crucially, as we discuss in more detail below and throughout this volume, sport
has been, and continues to be, used to articulate these tensions over the liminal
spaces between 'race' and nation.

It is important however not to overstate this transition to a new more subtle
form of coded racism based on cultural rather than crude biological difference.
In reality, the two forms can co-exist and often inter-penetrate. Further, in the
eyes of many racists the fact that someone may or may not have accepted
the cultural norms, conditions and ascriptions of national inclusion demanded
by the political right is irrelevant. The murderers of Rolan Adams, Rohit
Duggal and Stephen Lawrence (to name but three examples during the 1990s
from South London alone) did not stop to ask whether their victims defined

themselves as 'British' before attacking them. Skin colour and the logic of centuries-old European racism, shored up by bogus science, racist popular beliefs, and self-promoting political leaders, created the justification and climate for the murderers' actions. Indeed, the belief that blackness and Britishness are mutually exclusive categories is still firmly embedded within the British psyche. As Enoch Powell put it, in a public speech in Eastbourne in 1968, 'A West Indian or an Asian does not by being born in England become an Englishman. In law he becomes a United Kingdom citizen by birth; in fact he is West Indian or an Asian still.' Or in the words of his contemporary, 'comedian' Bernard Manning, speaking at a police function in the early 1990s when talking about blacks, whom he repeatedly referred to as niggers, 'they think they are English just because they were born here. That's like saying just because a dog is born in a stable, it must be a horse' (both quoted in Malik 1996: 143–144).

We argue in this chapter that sport is a particularly useful sociological site for examining the changing context and content of contemporary British racisms, as it articulates the complex interplay of 'race', nation, culture and identity in very public and direct ways. In a sense, this is the greatest paradox about sport's relationship to racism. It is an arena where certain forms of racism, particularly cultural racisms, have been most effectively challenged. Yet, at the very same time, it has provided a platform for racist sentiments to be most clearly expressed, revealing how not only British sport, but British society itself, is still a long way off from being truly equal to all.

As the chapters in this volume demonstrate there is no single, unidimensional relationship between 'race' and sport. By its very nature, sport is a complex protean cultural formation. It is too simplistic to argue that sport improves 'race relations', just as it is to say that sport can only reproduce racist ideologies. Sports racism, and its relationship to wider society, needs to be carefully studied in specific historical periods in particular social contexts, which is one of the reasons why informed sociological research is so important in challenging mis-placed common-sense assumptions about 'race' and sport. Given its ability to both produce and counter contemporary racisms, sport needs to be analysed and understood more fully than has tended to be the case hitherto by many of those engaged in countering racism in British society. This book is an attempt, then, to provide the beginnings for such analysis.

Sport, nationalism and multiculturalism

Recent decades have witnessed a number of extraordinary achievements by Asian and black athletes. There have now been black captains of the men's England football and Great Britain rugby league teams, black females have represented England at rugby union and football, Asian players have represented England in rugby league, and most sports now have large numbers of Asian and particularly black players involved in the game, at both the recreational and top-performance levels. Even Britain's sporting bastions of white colonial power and privilege are being changed from within. In the summer of 1999, twenty-year-old, Hitchin-born Arvind Parmar became the first British Asian to compete at the All England Club's annual tournament, Wimbledon, whilst Nasser Hussain became the first cricketer of South Asian descent to captain England. Arguably, such achievements have had a powerful ideological and symbolic effect in challenging common-sense racisms that have tried to argue that Asians and blacks do not quite fully belong to the nation (cf. Gilroy 1987: 62). Thus the far-right chant of the 1970s and 80s, that 'there ain't no black in the Union Jack', loses its populist hold every time we see Denise Lewis or Naseem Hamed wrapped in the colours of the Union Flag. As Stuart Hall has observed, in discussing some of the shifts concerning the visibility of blacks within the British popular consciousness during the 1980s and 1990s:

> Take sport in Britain. Nothing is closer to the heart of the average Englishman – as opposed to the fields where classically blacks have been outstanding, such as cricket or boxing – than the heartland of soccer. There isn't an occasion when you can pick up a decent Sunday paper, with its photos of Saturday's matches, and not see black faces.
>
> (Hall 1998b: 43)

However, Hall is also sensitive to the fact that sport is a complex and inherently contradictory cultural arena that simultaneously serves to both challenge and confirm racial ideologies. Hall (1998b: 43) thus continues:

> Are blacks in the boardrooms of the clubs? Of course not. Are they relatively powerless in the institutions which organize the game? Of course. The question is whether they have any currency, any visibility in the culture of sport where the nation's myths and meanings are fabricated. The answer must be 'yes', and to say this is to note the significant degree to which the culture has turned in the past fifteen or so years.
>
> (*ibid.*)

The reason why sport has often been used politically to articulate nationalist and racist concerns and why the changes Hall identifies have so troubled the far-right, is that sport is perhaps one of the clearest and most public means in demonstrating how Britain has become a multicultural nation. Multiculturalism though is an often misunderstood and problematic term.[2] In one sense the term is profoundly misleading when discussing ethnicity in general and national cultural identity in particular. It needs to be emphasized that *all* cultures – and particularly those associated with the arbitrary regional boundaries largely constructed in the eighteenth and nineteenth centuries which we have come to call 'nation states' – are 'multi-cultural', if by that we mean a cultural space containing more than one cultural presence. And especially so those Western nations – as well as those subject to the subsequent colonial rule – whose economic and cultural development was predicated on imperialist expansion. As Edward Said has pointed out:

> Far from being unitary or monolithic or autonomous things, cultures actually consume more 'foreign' elements, alterities, differences, than they consciously exclude. Who in India or Algeria today can confidently separate out the British or French component of the past from present actualities, and who in Britain or France can draw a clear circle around British London or French Paris that would exclude the impact of India and Algeria upon those two imperial cities?
>
> (Said 1994: 15)

There are no such things as 'mono-cultures' that exist as discrete homogeneous units, disconnected and uninfluenced by those around them: 'all cultures are involved in one another; none is single and pure, all are hybrid, heterogeneous, extraordinarily differentiated, and unmonolithic' (Said 1994: xxix). Cultures are by definition lived social processes that are porous, subject to constant change and are forever being remade, not fixed in some trans-historical moment which can be traced back to some homogeneous, original 'folk', no matter what the mono-culturalists may wish. As Richard Jenkins (1997: 50) reminds us, 'diversity – with respect to ethnicity – is nothing new, it is altogether the "norm"'.

Some commentators have argued that the narrow focus on identities and cultural difference, found in some more uncritical versions of multiculturalism, has actually served to weaken anti-racist struggles. This is because attention moves away from the social conditions that allow for and constitute the parameters of racial oppression, to the cultural arena that ignores power differentials between groups and which instead understands cultural difference as simply a matter of individual, or group, lifestyle choice (see Sivanandan 1990). Indeed the 'celebration of difference' sometimes has worrying parallels with the notions of absolute racial difference – whether cultural or biological – found in nineteenth century racial science and contemporary cultural racism.

It is in such a changing context that questions of cultural identity have assumed heightened *political* significance, in the process giving public cultural practices such as sport an increasingly significant symbolic importance too. The inclusion of Asian and black communities into the lived cultures of contemporary Britain, including Britain's sporting cultures, has decidedly re-shaped questions of local, regional and national identity for *all* Britons. We would argue, therefore, that no account of the changing nature of national and racial identities in Britain today can do so without acknowledging the central importance of sport to these processes.

White Men Can't Jump? Sport science and the preservation of the myth of 'race'

Whether new or old, cultural or biological, what such racisms have in common is their dependency on, and ultimate reduction to, a belief in the biological separation of the human population into visible and discrete groups; that is 'race'. With the widespread belief that it is an open, autonomous and meritocratic arena, sport is influential in informing people's perceptions about the naturalness and obviousness of racial difference. As Hoberman notes: 'The world of sport has thus become an image factory that disseminates and even intensifies our racial preoccupations' (1997: xxii).

Despite more than a half a century of work by anthropologists, biologists and geneticists discrediting the fundamental organizing principle upon which racism exists, namely 'race', the unsubstantiated constant recourse to this flawed concept by many scientists and the lay public remains deeply embedded, and is an indication of how entrenched racism has become in scientific and popular discourses.[3] The belief in the idea of 'race' was used as justification for the exploitation and transportation of up to fifteen million black Africans during slavery and for the domination and colonization by Western powers of millions of peoples throughout Africa, the Caribbean, Asia and South America (Williams, 1964; Walvin 1996). It also supplied the logic for the sterilization of hundreds of thousands of those – unmarried working-class women, homosexuals, Jews, blacks, gypsies, those with physical or mental handicaps, the criminal – deemed to be 'socially degenerate' and therefore a threat to the moral and physical health of the nation, in America, Canada and Europe, especially parts of Scandinavia, as part of the eugenics movement during the beginning of the twentieth century which reached its zenith with the Holocaust in Nazi Germany.[4] However, although the horrors of the Third Reich's 'Final Solution' discredited any public declaration of white racial superiority, Malik argues that 'the assumptions of racial thinking – in particular the idea that humanity can be divided into discrete groups and that these divisions have a social consequence – went unchallenged' (1996: 103–104). Malik continues, '[t]hough the political use of racial science was discredited, its conceptual framework was never destroyed. The discourse of race was reformulated, but the concept never disappeared' (1996: 104). Thus, despite the work of the world's leading geneticists, the stubborn persistence in the belief in 'race' appears as widespread and popular as ever. As Steven Rose points out:

> Modern population genetics makes the concept 'race' in the human context biologically meaningless, although still socially explosive. The definition of race is essentially a social one, as in reference to Blacks or Jews. While there are differences in gene frequencies (that is, differences in the proportions in which particular genetic variants occur) between population groups, these do not map onto the social criteria used to reference race.[5]
>
> (Rose 1998: 37)

'Race' has little value as a biological category, and therefore to apply it to the study of social behaviour, relations and structural inequalities lacks scientific credibility. Despite widespread popular acceptance of the claims made by those scientists committed to forms of biological determinism, the study of DNA has not, as Richard Lewontin clearly states, 'resulted in the discovery of genes for intelligence, aggressiveness, or the ability to play the viola [to which we should add '... or run the 100 metres quickly']. The very aspects of human diversity that fascinate us the most remain outside the domain of genetics' (1995: x).

Fleming (this volume) tackles these debates head on in his critique of the pseudo-science that purports to explain black success in certain sports according to mythical black 'sprinting genes'. Whilst many sport scientists are no doubt good biomechanists or specialist physiologists, most are not geneticists which is why they get into so many conceptual – not to mention methodological – problems when they venture into studying 'race' and sports performance. Indeed even a cursory examination of the sports science literature in this area reveals a pantheon of sometimes barely concealed racist research – especially those reliant upon research originally conducted as part of the eugenics movement from the 1920s and 1930s – that lacks scientific validity on its own terms.[6] It seems that one of the basics of scientific statistical methodology – that all first-year undergraduates know only too well – namely that correlation does not prove causation, is lost on many of those working within university sport science departments. Even Claude Bouchard, who has spent most of his career in search of the elusive sports gene(s) that will one day 'prove' black biological superiority in athletics, and who in contrast to most sport scientists does have some understanding of the complexities of human genetics, has concluded:

> one can observe, based on the evidence ... that racial differences in performance are probably quite limited in comparison to the individual differences seen within each race. The trends currently observed in the world of elite athletes may have more to do with opportunities and socio-economic conditions than with true biological differences between races.
>
> (Bouchard 1988: 103)

The effect that such research has, particularly when disseminated uncritically through the mass media, is to validate popular beliefs about the existence of 'race' and racial difference. It represents the latest chapter in the disreputable history of racial science. To those sports scientists engaged in the promotion of racial science, we would echo the call of the historian Jeffrey Sammons: 'call off the search and get about the business of addressing those things that will make a difference – namely identifying and attacking biases based on *perceived* difference' (1994: 271, emphasis added).[7]

Racism and sport sociology

One of the reasons why there are rarely any informed public discussions about racism and sport is due, in part, to the lack of sustained sociological research into the issues. Until very recently, most of the examples of racism in sport were based on anecdotal evidence, with little comprehensive and theoretical analyses of the problem. It could be argued therefore that the lack of serious academic investigation helped to foster common-sense assumptions that sport did not have a problem. Sociologists have tended to ignore sport's role and position in the social constitution of society, despite the fact that sport is central to many key debates within sociology, such as globalization, national identity, socialization, commercialization and commodification, violence, gender relations and so on. As Tomlinson (1999: vii) has pointed out, 'the place of the study of sport in academic life remains a marginal one, despite sport's profile in the media and everyday popular culture, and a burgeoning volume of research on its political, historical, sociological and cultural dimensions'.

In Britain, the emergence of sport as a sub-discipline of sociology developed in the late 1970s and 1980s. The key debates during the 1980s concerned the role of sport in relation to maintaining and challenging class inequalities and state power (Clarke and Critcher 1985; Gruneau 1983; Hargreaves 1986). More recently, feminist sports scholars have made important inroads into investigating how sport functions as a 'male preserve' within societies, helping to maintain male power; exploring the relationships between gender, sexuality and sport; and the ways in which women can challenge forms of patriarchy and male ideology through their sports participation (Hargreaves 1994; Hall 1996; Clarke and Humberstone 1997).

However, any student interested in exploring sociological research into 'race' and sport would have found precious little material, especially within the UK context. The neglect of sport by mainstream sociology as well as the continuing marginalization of 'race' as a core thematic within the social sciences in Britain – despite the best efforts of critical scholars such as Chetan Bhatt, Avtar Brah, Paul Gilroy, Stuart Hall, Barnor Hesse, Jayne Ifekwunigwe, Heidi Mirza and Lola Young – has meant that any discussion of 'race' *and* sport has been negligible. Put simply, there is not a *critical* school of sociological thought on 'race' and sport within Britain. The seemingly repeated call for 'more work to be done' in the area, stretching back over two decades (Kew 1979, Hargreaves 1986, Wimbush and Talbot 1988; Williams 1994), continually fails to be answered and suggests that many within the discipline of sports sociology at least are not taking such calls seriously.

The work that has been done has tended to come from American sports scholars who have led the way in showing how the operation of 'race' within society impacts into the sports arena. For example, such scholars have shown how 'stacking', the disproportionate placing of blacks into positions that require speed and strength, but little mental skills, due to perceived abilities of blacks based on racial stereotypes, has occurred in many US sports from American football to baseball. Also issues relating to stereotyping within the sports media of black players, discrimination in players' salaries, and their (lack of) ability to attract sponsorship and progress into senior management positions have also been noted. The greater focus on these issues by American scholars is not surprising when we look at how many of the 'great' American sports, such as athletics, baseball, and basketball were often formally segregated along 'race' lines until the 1950s and 1960s.[8]

The American scholarship however has been limited by its often unacknowledged liberal political philosophy – sometimes borrowing theoretical frameworks from the 'race relations' model of sociology – and its unduly narrow empiricist nature. It has largely been concerned with issues of how sports can improve 'race relations' and help 'integrate' new immigrant groups into the host society, or with ending overt forms of discrimination – either in terms of salary, or the opportunity to play. Without wishing to downplay the significance of this body of work, it arguably neglects more important and interesting questions. For example, how do the types of practices, representations and discourses that sport produces in terms of its physically competitive, symbolic and public displays of meritocratic competition, help to sustain (and challenge) our understanding of 'race' and racism in social relations outside sport? How does sport help make 'race' meaningful within society? And what part might sport play in beginning to dismantle the widespread acceptance of racial categories and hierarchies? As Scraton (this volume) points out, 'too often the study of race and sport or black women and sport concentrates on constraints. Although identifying constraints and barriers may be important for a liberal agenda of equal opportunities, this emphasis does little to challenge the ethnocentrism and androcentrism of sport'.

In other words, both sport as a social institution and 'race' as an analytical category are often not explicitly examined within the US work on racism and sport. Further, with some notable exceptions, such as the work of Goldberg (1993) and Omi and Winant (1994), American social scientists in general and American sports scholars in particular, seem at times naively unaware of the conceptual debates raging within British sociology over the ontological and epistemological status of 'race', its problematic relationship to racism (and indeed anti-racism), and how both concepts can be understood within the wider political context of ethnicity, nation, and gender and class relations.[9]

An example of the degree to which racism and sport in Britain has been left off the research agenda can be seen in a recent book by Eric Dunning, arguably Britain's most eminent sport sociologist. In *Sport Matters*, the chapter on 'race', whilst providing many interesting insights, is totally focused on the history of 'race relations' in America. Is this because there are no sociologically relevant issues relating to 'race' and sport in Britain? It is inconceivable that a leading American sports scholar writing on 'race' and sport would write almost exclusively on Britain, saying nothing about her or his own country.[10] We would argue that the theoretical work by numerous black scholars and post-colonial critics – from Fanon, C.L.R. James, and Angela Davis, to bell hooks, Sivanandan and Gilroy – charting the relationships of black peoples to challenging the modernist work/leisure distinction; the role of culture as an active form of resistance to state and imperial power; the place of Empire in the construction of colonial and metropolitan identities and relations; the place of the body as a site of resistance and struggle; localized collective political community participation; the relationship of imperialism and diasporas to discussions of globalization; and the place of 'race' in relation to class and gender exploitation, has much to offer critical scholars of sport.

One of the few academic texts specifically on the topic of 'race' and sport is

Jarvie's (1991) edited collection, *Sport, Racism and Ethnicity*. This text helped to move debates on from examining racism in sport merely in terms of participation patterns to exploring how issues concerning power and ethnicity articulated themselves in and through sports practices. However, of the ten chapters included, less than half actually deal specifically with racism in British sport.

There have been other important texts too, such as Cashmore's (1982) *Black Sportsmen*. This provided important historical material on black athletic history and some fascinating interview material with elite level black sportsmen. It is to be applauded as one of the first serious scholarly attempts to deal with issues of racism and sport within a British context. However the text was, and remains, problematic in that it pathologizes black communities and blackness itself, it conceptualizes racism in a limited way and has a narrow focus in its subject of study.

Whilst acknowledging that there may be certain 'push factors' that lead black youth disproportionately into sports – such as perceptions of innate black physicality held by physical education teachers – Cashmore argues, on the basis of limited empirical evidence, that black families tend to be 'unstable' (Cashmore 1982: 63); that education and career motivation is not a high priority amongst black families (*ibid.*: 63, 107, 200); and that employment discrimination is as much in the minds of blacks themselves, in terms of *perceived* restrictions, as actually existing (*ibid.*: 68–73, 86, 107, 201).[11] Cashmore goes further in suggesting that employment discrimination is actually caused by young black men *themselves* when he states: 'black kids tell each other stories about how difficult it is to get a decent job if you are black and, in a self-fulfilling way, it does becomes [sic] difficult' (*ibid.*: 86). Given this cultural context in which black men supposedly reject society's goals, Cashmore argues it is not surprising that so many black men seek to achieve success in sport, thus giving sport a disproportionate importance in their lives, as this is the one arena where their peers will, apparently, give them 'respect'. In contrast we would argue that Cashmore significantly underplays the continuing importance of racism in structuring the life chances of young blacks in particular, and inadvertently reproduces many of the racial stereotypes concerning the supposed incompatibility and inherent deficiencies of black cultural life found in the arguments of cultural racists.

Conversely, Verma and Darby's (1994) empirical study of participation rates helped to dispel many myths about ethnic minority sports participation, especially the supposed lack of Asian sports involvement at the recreational level, but it lacked a sophisticated theoretical framework to contextualize the data examined. There have also been a number of journalistic accounts of racism and sport (see Bose 1996; Orakwue 1998) which whilst useful in highlighting the continuing problem of racism and sport have similarly lacked a proper theoretical framework to make sense of the information they describe, and to fully link these discussions to wider changes within British society.

More promising work, though again focused on small case studies, can be seen in the work of Fleming (1995) on South Asian sports involvement, which has explored, in both an empirical and theoretically sophisticated way, some of the wider questions concerning sports participation, identity and racism. Unfortunately such studies have tended to be the exception, rather than the norm.[12] Given the continued examples of sports racism, and sport's central position within British social and cultural life, it is time for this situation to change. As we outline below, such a dearth of material also has implications for sports governing bodies, sports policy, and the sports media.[13]

Understanding 'race', racism and sport

This lack of empirically grounded and theoretically astute work has led to space in which polemical but unsubstantiated arguments can be made. Two examples, by senior figures within the field of sports studies, are John Hoberman's (1997) *Darwin's Athletes* and Lincoln Allison's (1998) essay 'Biology, Ideology and Sport'. These texts are particularly apposite, because together they reveal the twin dangers in theorizing black involvement in sport, namely that sport is either an essentially positive experience for black people in particular and 'race-relations' in general, or it is a destructive and subjugating process for black people.[14] Whilst Hoberman's text is based on a comprehensive and systematic overview of the published literature and Allison's is little more than tabloid-style commentary, both positions are nevertheless problematic. First of all they are empirically weak, and secondly, both positions reveal an inadequate understanding of the dialectical relationship between structure and agency. To elaborate further on these criticisms it is necessary to review the two positions.

Hoberman (1997) argues in his book (the subtitle of which is *How Sport Has Damaged Black America and Preserved the Myth of Race*) that sport has damaged the black community (his main focus is on the US, though he does make some cautious comparisons to the situation in Britain) as blacks have become 'fixated' with sport. In this regard, there are striking parallels between the arguments made in Hoberman's *Darwin's Athletes* and Cashmore's *Black Sportsmen*. In a text based largely on anecdotal evidence, Hoberman argues that African-American communities have become fixated on athletes as role models, thus devaluing education as a means for social mobility and betterment. Further, he argues that black communities actively seek to persecute those individual blacks who do not subscribe to this pathological fixation on sport: 'the widespread persecution of academically healthy black children by frustrated and angry black children is a social disaster that few public figures have bothered to address' (1997: xvi). Hoberman is thus especially critical of black male intellectuals for apparently failing to speak out against the damage this has done to black life in America as he believes they too are unable to distance themselves from their own emotional attachment to the central place of sport within black America. The result of this 'clan pride' (p.4) as Hoberman terms it, is that chances for upward mobility are lost as thousands of black male youngsters (Hoberman does not seem to think that black women are as susceptible to the sports-fixation and so largely ignores their position) reproduce their own conditions of subordination: 'African Americans' attachment to sport has been diverting interest away from the mind for most of this century' (p. 4). Hoberman concludes that the African American 'addiction to athleticism' is a 'social pathology' (p. 85).

As with Cashmore's analysis, Hoberman misreads a symptom for a problem *vis-à-vis* racism and sport in America. There is little evidence to show that black working-class families privilege sport any more than white working-class families, and no evidence to suggest that black families do not value the education of their children as highly. The mistake of both Hoberman and Cashmore is to read the lack of black social mobility outside sport as being the result of some cultural 'dysfunction' within the 'abnormal' black family structure, as opposed to there being *real* barriers to progression in other areas such as education and employment. It is a classic way in which those discriminated against are then blamed for their own subordinate position, diverting attention away from structural inequalities, and towards the perceived moral inadequacies of the individuals themselves. Cole and Andrews are correct when they note that *Darwin's Athletes* is 'permeated with images of addiction and disease, which ... code the black community as pathological' (1998: 94).

Hoberman's argument is the catalyst for Allison's essay. Far from being a destructive process, Allison argues that in Britain sports have been a mechanism for social mobility for blacks and have been one of the key ways of improving 'race relations'. Beyond some personal anecdotes from his own 'normally racist English racial environment' (1998: 142) no evidence is provided for these broad claims. He variously subscribes to and endorses the populist beliefs that 'sport is a natural integrator of peoples' (1998: 135); that those who argue against attributing the success of black male athletes to their genes are being politically correct and are offering a 'foolish doctrine' (p. 136);[15] that Clive Lloyd being described by Lancashire cricket fans as a 'Supercoon' is a sign, albeit misplaced, of respect (p. 143); and that sport has helped improve 'race relations' in Britain as white fans in the north of England sang the names of black footballers and cricketers (p. 144). Although it is part of the conservative common-sense orthodoxy to assume that the mere presence of different racial groups demonstrates that racism does not exist, the complex articulation of racism, as examined in later chapters of this volume, clearly demonstrates that such a position lacks sociological credibility,

Allison also implies that racial discrimination exists largely in the minds of black people, and further that if blacks had a different self image of themselves the structural inequalities that they faced would largely disappear. In his attempt to explain away white racism, and to challenge Hoberman's view that one of the ideological effects of sport is to reproduce the notion that black people are defined by their physicality, as opposed to their intelligence, Allison asserts:

> ... the real problem is not that whites classify blacks as 'physical' beings, but that blacks accept this classification. If black people defined themselves as intellectuals, white prejudice would no longer prevent them from achieving the elusively 'normal' levels of social mobility.
>
> (Allison 1998: 146)

That a senior academic can produce such a statement is significant to our case that Britain lacks a critical sociology of 'race' and sport. To argue that it is black people's own failure to see themselves as human agents that is the main cause of racial inequality, is a failure to understand the evidence from other disciplines that racism is actually about socially (and historically) inscribed power relationships, embedded within structural constraints that often lie beyond the scope of the individual to change. In other social areas – crime, education, health – such arguments whilst prevalent two decades ago, are now, rightly, discredited, yet because 'race' and sport has been so poorly theorized up until now, such arguments are still being made in sports studies.

Of course neither of these positions described above, that assert that sport simply improves 'race relations' through inter-racial contact (Allison) or that sport can *only* reproduce racism, in terms of perpetuating biological racial ideologies and inequalities (Hoberman), is accurate.[16] Sport, like many other cultural arenas, is a site for contestation, resistance and struggle, whereby dominant ideologies are both maintained and challenged at particular historical points and in specific social contexts. This applies as much to 'race' and ethnicity as it does to gender, sexuality or class. This point is made by Hartmann (1998: 91) when he states that whilst *Darwin's Athletes* and other such critiques are important in challenging and deconstructing accounts like Allison's, which subscribe to the popular view of 'sport-as-positive-force ideology':

> they do not go any further than this; to put it even stronger, deconstruction is virtually all they do. These critiques make their points only by exchanging one totalization (that sport is a positive force for racial change) for the other (that it is a negative, impending one). In contrast, I would suggest the need for a more complex, multidimensional theory of the relationships between sport and race – one that is critical of the popular ideology of sport as a pure and perfect arena of racial progress, but that tries to grasp its social significance and emancipatory potential for African Americans living in a racist society.
>
> (Hartmann 1998: 91–92)

Such a dialectical view of sport already exists in the earlier writings of black radicals such as C.L.R. James and Harry Edwards. For James this took the form of West Indian anti-colonial politics within the cricket arena (see James 1963, and also Farred 1996). For Edwards, it was linked to an understanding of how sport was deeply implicated in the racial politics of America during the 1960s (see for example Edwards 1969, and also Hartmann 1996). Although writing from different perspectives, it could be argued that both saw sport as a modality of black cultural resistance to racism and a way of exposing the false racial meritocratic ideology of Western liberal capitalist societies. As this book shows, this is a perspective that is equally pertinent to sport in Britain today.

Overview of the book

We believe that *'Race', Sport and British Society* will help to challenge racism in British sport. What, more precisely, do we mean by this? This is essentially a question about the relationship of theoretical works to the policy process and social understanding more generally. In addition to challenging ways of thinking about sport that resort to racial ideologies, we hope that this book will contribute to an emerging policy focus on tackling racial inequality amongst sport governing bodies. Goldberg provides a useful framework for thinking about these two related but operationally distinct levels at which opposition to racism can operate.

> Exposing an expression as racist may sometimes suffice as contestation. The exposure may be enough to make its perpetrators sufficiently self-conscious to limit expressing themselves openly in racist fashion. Yet more will be required: a special ongoing and thoughtful commitment in the face of repeated, insistent, and self-righteous racist expressions.
>
> (Goldberg 1997: 13)

Thus, *'Race', Sport and British Society* challenges racism in sport because it provides a powerful rebuttal of racial ideologies pervasive in the world of sport, and because it equips those engaged in shaping policy agendas and formulating strategies with the necessary understanding of the complex ways in which racism is manifest in sport cultures, institutions and practices. This book is one part of a process in contesting racist expressions *and* their underlying ideologies that help to legitimate not just racist views and beliefs but also the actions and structures of organizations that provide institutional support for such expressions in the first place. In short, by advancing the debate about 'race' and sport within sociology itself to a more self-reflexive critical positioning we hope that this book will provide an important mechanism for those attempting to challenge the complacency evident within the sports world concerning the corrosive effects of racism.

Section One, *'Research into current levels and forms of sports racism'*, offers a number of original and challenging essays documenting the extent of racism within various sports contexts by drawing on recent empirical research, both qualitative and quantitative, based on ethnographic participant observation, survey techniques, in-depth interviews and textual analysis.

Recent discussions concerning the fragmentation of the United Kingdom in the wake of devolution and increased political governance for Scotland, Wales, and, more problematically, Northern Ireland, have been notably silent on the extent to which these nationalist movements have dealt with issues of 'race' and racism. Scotland in particular has often attempted to narrate its sense of self in opposition to a construction of Englishness. In this moment the type of English nationalism that so often predicates itself on xenophobic and racist exclusion has been used as a way to articulate a Scottish identity that is supposedly free from such 'English' cultural traits, even whilst evidence of continuing racial discrimination within Scotland continues (see 'New nation, old bigotry', *The Observer*, 15 August, 1999, p. 17). However as Joyce McMillan has warned:

> this general smugness about Scotland's status as a nice, civic-minded nation seems to have rendered us both complacent and naive about what it means to tackle the bigotries that are closest to our hearts. Already, Scotland has shamed itself in the eyes of the world by electing a twenty-first-century parliament without a single black or Asian member.
>
> ('Scotland's shame', in *The Guardian*, 10 August, 1999, p. 15)

The opening chapter by **Paul Dimeo** and **Gerry Finn** pursues such issues in more depth by using football to trace these discussions within Scottish society. They show how both academic and more popular media discourses have disavowed the problem of racism within Scottish life, and within football in particular, and argue that a clearer analytical distinction needs to be drawn between racism and sectarianism so as not to view anti-Asian and anti-black racism as being a minor appendage to the 'more serious' problems of religious sectarianism. By tracing the often ignored history of black and particularly Asian footballing involvement in Scottish football over the past century, Dimeo and Finn powerfully deconstruct some of the myths concerning Scotland's mono-cultural (footballing) past.

Ben Carrington and **Ian McDonald** draw on two research projects carried out in the late 1990s to argue that racism, though ignored and denied throughout the game, is actually central to understanding the current malaise within both the national and recreational levels of cricket.[17] It is an argument that has been given added urgency following the dismal performance of the English team during the 1999 Cricket World Cup and their run of Test series defeats. The home defeat against New Zealand in 1999 meant that England dropped for a while to the bottom of the unofficial but widely recognized Wisden league of Test playing nations, precipitating an anguished and very public post-mortem amongst the game's administrators and principal commentators. However, amidst the arguments and accusations, there was little recognition of the significance of racism, and the exclusionary culture it perpetuates. Carrington and McDonald conclude that only when the cricketing establishment, including the media, begin to recognize and address the problems of racism can a truly meritocratic and successful game emerge.

Pursuing the themes of 'belonging' and 'identity', **Karl Spracklen** provides a careful exposition of the intersection of 'race', class and gender in exploring how symbolic constructions of the game of rugby league serve to both include and exclude the 'non-white' Other from the imagined community of rugby league. Drawing on recent research material the chapter provides an account of how racism manifests itself within the sporting arena, but also how the activities of Asian and black players may serve to counter such expressions. As with Carrington and McDonald, and also Back *et al.* (this volume), Spracklen begins to explore how 'whiteness' is constructed as a racial identity via the sports arena. Such work is important as the 'anti-essentialist' drive to deconstruct Blackness often leaves its collary Whiteness intact and undisturbed. Whiteness is thus reified, and further stabilized as the central, unmarked norm, against which other racial identities must be judged. In other words, one of the central under-pinnings to the operation of white racism – that is whiteness itself – remains unchallenged (see Bonnett 1997, 2000). By beginning to ask critical questions about the taken-for-granted assumptions about white racial identities we can begin to reveal its configuration and its ability to (re)produce racial ideologies. Spracklen, to this end, shows how many defences of 'traditional rugby league culture' actually concern a defence of a particular historical construction of a version of a white (northern) working-class masculinity.

Finally in the first section **Les Back**, **Tim Crabbe** and **John Solomos** offer a critique, based on ethnographic research material, of previous attempts to con-ceptualize racism within football. They argue that there has been a shift in how racism itself is now expressed from the 'premeditated and crude manifestation seen during the seventies, towards spontaneous, implicit and socially embedded forms of racist expression' (Back *et al.*, this volume). It is vital, they argue, that policy responses reflect these changes and are able to break free from under-standing racism only in terms of the hooligan/racist couplet, which, they argue, actually serves to distort our understanding of the complexity of racism and shifts our attention away from other arenas within sport – say the boardrooms and governing bodies – where processes of exclusion are still at play and perhaps more insidious in terms of their effects. In a similar way to Spracklen, they argue that only by understanding the local cultural and social context of footballing cultures, and the ways in which football gives expression to certain forms of (working-class) identity, can we begin to understand, and therefore have a basis to more effectively challenge, the continuance of racism within the game.

The second section, entitled *'Public controversies over 'race' and sport'* uses a number of high profile public incidents that have expressed some of the anxi-eties over 'race' and sport during the 1990s, particularly in relation to science, the media and the law.

Scott Fleming's chapter takes Sir Roger Bannister's 1995 public pronounce-ments on black athletic ability, when the first four-minute miler speculated that slavery and hot climate conditions had changed the physiological make-up of blacks compared to whites, as his starting point in deconstructing some of the myths surrounding 'race' itself and its alleged relationship to sports performance. Whilst Fleming's powerful and timely rebuttal to such pseudoscientific rhetoric is to be welcomed, we still need to ask why sport scientists themselves have been so slow to publicly challenge the research of some of their colleagues. Even today, sport science text books still suggest, unproblematically, to undergradu-ates that the absence of top black swimmers is due to black people having 'heavier bones' than whites, and that blacks dominate sprint finals due to differ-ences in their power-to-weight ratio and different muscle types compared to whites.

The problem is that such scientific misconceptions about the 'natural' athleticism of black bodies feeds directly into popular and professional misunderstandings about racial difference (see Hayes and Sugden 1999). Notions that 'White Men Can't Jump' as Woody Harrelson and Wesley Snipes' dramatized film version reminds us, is just one example of how racial stereotypes die hard, even in the face, as Fleming argues, of incontrovertible opposing evidence.[18] The fact that for the past decade the white English athlete Jonathan Edwards broke all known records for the men's triple-jump, jumping further than any other human being in recorded history, did not lead sports scientists, even for a moment, to reconsider the category mistakes they have repeatedly made in looking to explain away black athletic achievement. (Nor, of course, did it lead them to start looking for a long-jumping gene amongst white English men.) We in fact need to ask not if blacks (in contrast to whites and Asians) possess special genes for running and jumping, but rather what it is about the centrality of sport to Western countries, and their function as hyper-mediated spectacles and sites of identification, that seems to so trouble and preoccupy the white (male) psyche to speculate on the 'hidden secrets' encased within black (usually male) athletic bodies (see Mercer 1994; Davis 1990).[19] The answer to that question will tell us a lot about the supposed link between 'race' and sports performance.

It is just such media stereotypes and representations that form the basis for **Mike Marqusee's** critical analysis of the cricket media's handling of 'race', nationalism and racism during the 1990s. C.L.R. James once noted, in relation to the racism and prejudice shown towards black members of the early West Indies tour parties to England:

> writers on sport, more particularly writers on cricket, and most particularly English writers on cricket, automatically put what was unpleasant out of sight even if they had to sweep it under the carpet. The impression they created was one of almost perpetual sweetness and light.
>
> (James 1963: 112)

Marqusee's writings over the past decade (see Marqusee 1996, 1998, 1999) have been a powerful corrective to such complacency and complicity concerning racism in sport generally and cricket in particular, and he extends such a critique here. Marqusee is one of a very small band of committed and politically engaged writers who combine, and relate, their love of sport with political activism *and* a sophisticated scholarly approach. In his chapter here, it is his committed involvement in the struggle for racial equality in cricket borne out of his passion for the game and hostility to privilege and injustice that feed his damning analysis of cricket in England.

The last chapter in the second section by **Simon Gardiner** and **Roger Welch** sketches out an original argument concerning the place of the law in regulating racism within the sports context. The authors warn against seeing legal regulation and control as a panacea that will eliminate racism, arguing instead that whilst the law has an important symbolic role to play in signalling societies'

abhorrence to racism, the manifestly social causes of racism have to be challenged and understood more widely as a product of social relations and power
inequalities. Following Goldberg (1997) they argue against the tendency to
reduce racism to the more obvious forms of 'race hate', which the law is more
clearly suited to address, as this has the unintentional consequence of diverting
our attention from more insidious, though less 'public', forms of discrimination
and exclusion based on informal differentials in power relations.

Finally, in Section Three, *'Challenging Discourses/Contesting Identities'*, extends
the analysis and points to new agendas in understanding how 'race', racism and
sport operate within Britain.

Extending the insights offered by Dimeo and Finn, **Sanjiev Johal** provides a
long awaited corrective to those who have argued that 'Asians don't play sport'.
Lack of interest, rather than racial discrimination, was one of the ways in which
the absence of South Asian and black athletes from top-level sport during the
1950s and 60s was explained. For example, Cashmore (1982: 84–85) argued
that: 'the overall picture is of the first generation harbouring little interest in
sport, apart from horse racing! Perhaps they [black people] have no time available nor money to squander on what they consider to be pointless pursuits'. It is
clear from recent work (see Carrington 1998, 1999) and Johal's chapter here,
that such statements are factually incorrect and ignore the existence of South
Asian and black organized sports participation that significantly predates the
'explosion' of black male professional football stars in the late 1970s. As Johal
demonstrates, there has been a long, if neglected, history of South Asian sports
activity that directly challenges contemporary stereotypes about South Asian
non-participation. Johal also argues that by focussing the work on 'race' and
sport on the experiences of African-Caribbean communities, thereby ignoring
the larger South Asian communities, our general understanding about the
subject has been hindered. Countering popular (mis)conceptions, Johal shows
how sport has long been a central component in the emerging British Asian
identities in Britain developed over the past fifty years. Even here, however, the
processes of community and cultural identification through sport remain gender-
specific. That is, it is a discourse of community that is often generated and
sustained by men. As Johal himself concedes, the position of female South
Asian involvement in sport 'is possibly one of the most under-researched areas
of social inquiry' (Johal, this volume).

Developing Johal's concerns about the lack of sustained research into the
lives of Asian and black women, **Sheila Scraton** argues for a new theoretical
approach for contemporary scholarship within sport sociology in general and for
feminist theory in particular. Scraton argues that the radical accounts offered by
Black British feminists provide fertile grounds for advancing our understandings
of the 'intersectionality' of 'race', gender and sport. In many ways, she is developing the concerns raised over a decade ago by Susan Birrell (1989). Birrell's
main charge was that a *critical* sociology of 'race' and sport had failed to develop
with, instead, quantitative and descriptively atheoretical empirical work being
produced that offered little new by way of theoretical insight. The fact that even

today the major sports sociology journals still churn out articles on the extent of stacking, with various statistical analyses to test whether positional segregation has increased or not, is an indication that the field of sports sociology has not taken Birrell's arguments seriously. Where work has advanced, albeit slowly, as Scraton acknowledges, is within feminist and male pro-feminist scholarship on sport (see Hargreaves 1994, 2000; Messner 1992, 1997). As Scraton (this volume) argues, 'we need to interrogate institutional racism and sexism, learn more about sporting cultures and listen to the experiences of women in both competitive and recreational sport'.

The last two essays offer critically reflexive accounts. **Emma Lindsey**, one of the few black sports journalists to have worked on any major national news-paper, offers an account of life 'amongst the men'. Lindsey surveys some of the issues that have affected her as a black female sports writer, and offers her thoughts on the way the media itself deals with the 'race-class-gender' complex within sport. The media continue to occupy a central role in both challenging and reproducing racist discourses. Boyle and Haynes have argued that, as regards racism, the media in Britain needs to become more proactive: 'As a starting point greater scrutiny by the media of areas of discrimination in sporting culture and a willingness to connect this with society at large would be useful' (2000: 126). They continue that the media 'should also expose the reluctance with which some sports governing bodies appear to display in either acknowledging or dealing with any problem [of racism] they may have' (*ibid.*). Emma Lindsey's chapter helps us to better understand these reluctances and the ways in which racism is expressed and dealt with in this field.

Chris Searle's customarily polemical essay concludes the book. The essay, which is inspired by C.L.R. James's own intellectual work and praxis, demonstrates the necessity for academic work to remain engaged with understanding the world as a precondition to changing it, and not, as many social theorists seem to advocate these days, as a way of dissolving themselves from the material world. Searle shows clearly how James's seminal text *Beyond a Boundary* (first published in 1963) still resonates as a powerful example of how sport, and in this instance cricket, is not a cultural oasis, separate from the 'real world', but deeply implicated in societies' own structures and inequalities. As Searle argues, *Beyond a Boundary* is undoubtedly one of the key texts in any discussion of racism and sport and students are well advised to read this text in the full. However, its semi-biographical style, historical and cultural span and theoretical insights mean the book cannot, and should not, simply be contained within a narrow definition of belonging to 'sport studies'.[20] Farred has rightly observed that the outstanding feature of *Beyond a Boundary* and its enduring legacy is that two of James's key interests, Marxism and cricket, as well as his love of literature:

> are integrated to produce a rare socio-political critique that takes sport as its starting point, its metaphorical axis, and as a site of radical cultural opposition. *Beyond A Boundary* is undoubtedly James's definitive work,

singular in its ability to bring together, for the first and only time, all of his passions and ideological commitments in a single text.

(Farred 1996: 174)

Searle adopts James's mode of semi-autobiography to illustrate his own anti-racist and political development in a remarkably honest, reflective and revealing way, through his recollections of his entry into the male cricketing world of white suburban England. Searle himself has, for many years, been one of Britain's leading radical educationalists and rightly deserves his own place alongside figures such as James for his commitment to progressive scholarship and activism (see the profile of Searle in 'Return of a Class Hero', in *The Guardian*, G2, 12 November, 1997). James noted in his monumental study of the 1791 slave revolt *The Black Jacobins: Toussaint L'Ouverture and the San Domingo Revolution* that, 'The blacks will know as friends only those whites who are fighting in the ranks beside them. And whites will be there' (quoted in Fryer 1984: xii). James, no doubt, had people like Searle in mind when he wrote those words.

Notes

1 In 1968 the late Conservative MP Enoch Powell argued that unless immigration from the Commonwealth countries was stopped, and those Asian and black communities that were settled sent home, Britain would have 'race riots' like those gripping America at the time: 'As I look ahead, I am filled with foreboding. Like the Roman I seem to see "the River Tiber foaming with much blood". That tragic and intractable phenomenon which we watch with horror on the other side of the Atlantic but which there is interwoven with the history and existence of the States itself, is coming upon us here by our own volition and our neglect' (quoted in Hall 1998a: 19). Central to Powell's argument was a belief that to be British was to be white, and that the only way to solve the 'race problem' was to 're-emigrate' the 'non-white' immigrant population. For an analysis of Powell's effect on racism in Britain see Hall (1998a). For a critical analysis of Powell's relationship to the new cultural racism see Brown (1999).

2 Useful critical interrogations of the theoretical and political status of the term 'multi-culturalism' can be found in Goldberg 1994; Gutmann 1994; Hesse 1997, 2000; Modood and Werbner 1997; Shohat and Stam 1994; and Werbner and Modood 1997.

3 Students new to the sociology of 'race' will see that many authors, ourselves included, put 'race' in inverted commas to alert the reader that we are referring to the 'idea of race', rather than claiming that the term has any objective biological validity. 'Race' is made meaningful within society via the ways in which we imagine it to exist, and subsequently organize our lives and identities around it. Put another way, if racism did not exist the term 'race' would become meaningless. The speech marks therefore help alert us to the term's problematic ontological status. We have avoided adopting a uniform policy in how 'race', and indeed racism, is used and defined in this volume. It will become apparent, either explicitly or implicitly, how each individual author addresses these issues. What is common, however, is the interrogation of 'race' as a natural process and social relation, and the desire to critique its operations manifest in various racisms.

4 For further material on the promotion of eugenics and programmes of sterilization up until the Second World War, and incredibly for a number of decades afterwards, see

Kelves (1998) review essay 'Grounds for breeding: The amazing persistence of eugenics in Europe and North America', in *The Times Literary Supplement*, January 2, No. 4944, pp. 3–4. It is worth noting that eugenics was not a fringe movement of obscure scientists but often led and supported, in Britain and America, by some of the most prominent public figures of the day, across the political divide, such as Julian Huxley, Aldous Huxley, D. H. Lawrence, John Maynard Keynes and Theodore Roosevelt. Indeed, none other than Winston Churchill, whilst Home Secretary in 1910, made the following observation: 'The unnatural and increasingly rapid growth of the feeble-minded and insane classes, coupled as it is with steady restriction among all the thrifty, energetic and superior stocks constitutes a national and race danger which is impossible to exaggerate. I feel that the source from which the stream of madness is fed should be cut off and sealed before another year has passed' (quoted in Jones, 1994: 9). The return of racial science, Darwinian social-biology and evolutionary psychology to contemporary social debates is a deeply worrying development and a further reminder that the appeal to forms of biological and genetic determinism to explain social inequalities still holds a dominant position within society (see Duster 1990; Lewontin 1993; Montagu 1997; Gould 1997; Rose 1998; Rose and Rose 2000).

5 To quote Steve Jones, 'The theory that races are biologically different has a long and ignoble history which has brought misery and death in its wake … The history of race illustrates, more than anything else, the limitations of biology in understanding human affairs … Modern genetics does in fact show that there are no separate groups within humanity' (1994: 246–247).

6 For those with an interest in reviewing the expansive, sometimes bizarre, but ultimately contradictory and inconclusive literature in this area see, for example: Bouchard, C. (ed.) (1988) 'Special Issue: Racial differences in performance', in *Canadian Journal of Sport Sciences*, 143 (2) June, pp. 103–143; Bosch, A. *et al.* (1990) 'Physiological Differences Between Black and White Runners During a Treadmill Marathon', in *European Journal of Applied Physiology and Occupational Physiology*, 68, pp. 68–72; Cobb, W. (1936) 'Race and Runners', in *Journal of Health and Physical Education*, 7, January, pp. 3–56; Dunn, J. and Lupfer, M. (1974) 'A Comparison of Black and White Boys' Performance in Self-Paced and Reactive Sports Activities', in *Journal of Applied Social Psychology*, 4 (1), pp. 24–35; Hrdlicka, A. (1928) 'The Full-Blooded American Negro', in *American Journal of Physical Anthropology* 7 (1) July–September, pp. 15–33; Jones, J. and Hochner, A. (1973) 'Racial Differences in Sports Activities: A look at the self-paced versus reactive hypothesis', in *Journal of Personality and Social Psychology*, 27 (1), pp. 86–95; Jordan, J. (1969) 'Physiological and Anthropometrical Comparison of Negroes and Whites', in *Journal of Health and Physical Recreation*, November/December, pp. 93–99; Lee, C. and Rotella, R. (1991) 'Special Concerns and Considerations for Sport Psychology Consulting With Black Student Athletes', in *The Sport Psychologist*, 5 (4), December, pp. 365–369; Metheny, E. (1939) 'Some Differences in Bodily Proportions between American Negro and White Male College Students as Related to Athletic Performance', in *Research Quarterly*, 10, pp. 41–53; Ponthieux, N. and Barker, D. (1965) 'Relationship Between Race and Physical Fitness', in *Research Quarterly*, 36, pp. 468–472; Todd, T. and Lindala, A. (1928) 'Dimensions of the Body: Whites and American Negroes of both sexes', in *American Journal of Physical Anthropology* 7 (1) July–September, pp. 35–120; Worthy, M. and Markle, A. (1970) 'Racial Differences in Reactive Versus Self-Paced Sports Activities', in *Journal of Personality and Social Psychology*, 16 (3), pp. 439–443. See also Entine (2000) for an uncritical review of this material, which fails to adequately grasp the complexity of 'race' and its (non-)relationship to sports performance. For a useful corrective to Entine's account, and for a critique which remains attuned to the impact of wider socio-political discourses upon 'objective' scientific research, see Barnes *et al.* (1999).

7 Earlier in the same essay Sammons critiques Wiggins's essay 'Great Speed but Little

Stamina' (first published in 1989, latterly reprinted in Wiggins 1997) which after showing quite clearly how 'race' is a meaningless category for analytical measurement and how science has been abused to find discredited examples of race-linked differences in sports performance ('the weight of evidence indicates that the differences between participation patterns of black and white athletes is primarily due to differences in the history of experiences that individuals and their particular racial group have undergone' (1997: 198)), still ends by calling for more research, in the 'spirit of science' (1997: 199) to be done to 'determine whether the success of black athletes is somehow the consequence of racially distinct chromosomes' (ibid.). Sammons responds: 'What can be argued is that Wiggins' discomforting conclusions would benefit from Jacques Barzun's telling admonition that race thinking is like the Hydra, "although repeatedly killed, it is nevertheless undying." Even more, Wiggins' call alerts us to the danger that the most well-meaning can fall prey to the traps set by misguided, sometimes malicious, intentions of race thinkers' (1994: 205). Sammons' critique would apply just as strongly to Hoberman's (1997) *Darwin's Athletes* (and indeed to Kohn's (1996) review of the research in this area). After spending nearly half the book carefully explicating why 'tabloid science' has been central in maintaining racist stereotypes about black physicality Hoberman concludes by arguing that more research into this area still needs to be done. More worrying is Hoberman's apparent belief that 'race' is meaningful 'at a biological level' (Hoberman 1998: 98), though primarily for 'medical interest' (ibid.). Such a statement from a scholar, who had clearly spent a great deal of time reading the issues surrounding 'race' and sport, demonstrates clearly how powerful raciological thinking can be in influencing academic understanding of what exactly 'race' is and how racism itself can saturate our work and thinking.

8 Jay Coakley's *Sport in Society* (1998) provides an excellent introduction to the work referred to here.

9 Whilst this is not the place to pursue these matters in depth, our general position would be that whilst there is much to be gained by Anthias' (1992) call to situate 'race' categories within a more general framework encompassing belongingness and ethnic collectivity, there is still a specificity to racism that makes the disconnection of 'race' from racism highly problematic both theoretically and politically in terms of effective anti-racism strategies that may still require some strategic embrace of racial categories at particular points in certain struggles. In one sense the precise meaning given to 'race' within our theorization may not be the most important question(s) to ask. It is a mistake to think we can end the theoretical argument over 'race' simply by demonstrating its non-status. In other words we must be mindful of the fact that to theoretically deconstruct 'race' does not mean we have stopped its effectivity in the 'real world'. We need instead to understand how 'race' is used within racist discourses to discursively position people by using particular physical signifiers to make 'race' meaningful in the first place and how 'race' is then used to legitimate social relations between people. For further analysis of these debates see Anthias and Yuval-Davis 1992; Anthias 1995; Banton 1998; Gilroy 1987, 1998, 2000; Mason 1994; Miles 1989, 1993; Rattansi and Westwood 1994; Sayer 1997; Smaje 1997; Solomos and Back 1994.

10 To be clear, we are choosing Dunning as an example precisely because his work serves as an exemplary model for those engaged in seriously studying sport as a way of further developing sociological knowledge about sport's place within society. Our point is that if we can make a case against Dunning, then the rest of sports sociology, at least within Britain, is also likely to be lacking in this regard.

11 Cashmore claims that: 'The [black] family's loss of control over the youth is crucial to his [sic] development in sport, for, if there was a more balanced social management within the West Indian community, it is likely that the vibrancy and energy expended in sport could be directed into more orthodox areas' (1982: 86). Cashmore

continues: 'The overall retardation of black youth is due, in no small measure, to the inadequacy of Caribbean families to cope with the exigencies of education in the modern UK' (1982: 943). In the introduction to *Black Sportsmen*, Cashmore makes the intriguing confession that his earlier work contributed to the popular stereotype of the young black male as a 'dope-smoking, unemployed gang member, structuring his life around reggae music, blues parties and thieving' (1982: 3): 'In the past, I have been guilty of reinforcing this icon; now I am committed either to destroying it or affecting major reconstructions' (1982: 3). Given that Cashmore's text is replete with stereotypes, unsubstantiated generalizations and caricatures of black families, communities and young black men in particular, it could convincingly be argued that the only 'reconstruction' that Cashmore made was to add 'uneducated and sports-fixated' to the list of stereotypes. For a critique of 'white sociology's' (including Cashmore's work) misrepresentation and pathologizing of black communities and young black men, see Lawrence (1982) and Alexander (1996).

12 Summaries of the work on 'race', ethnicity and sport within the British context can be found in Kew (1997), ch. 5; Lashley and Hylton (1997); Polley (1998), ch. 6; Sleap (1998), ch. 7; Cashmore (2000), ch. 6; and Jarvie (2000).

13 In the late 1990s the editors of this collection held meetings with the England and Wales Cricket Board (ECB) to convince them that racism was an issue that needed to be addressed as a matter of urgency by the cricketing authorities. The initial response was that the only evidence of racism was 'anecdotal' and therefore not credible enough for the ECB to take action. A Catch-22 situation whereby the ECB, initially at least, refused to sanction national research into racism in cricket because they had no evidence that racism existed – thus whilst they refused to conduct research they could say that no such research existed. In large part, as we discuss in chapter three, the campaigning work of the anti-racist group 'Hit Racism for Six', and the publication of two important regionally-based studies into racism in cricket (Long *et al.*, 1997, and McDonald and Ugra 1998), finally pressurized the ECB into initiating research and formulating a racial equality policy – see Carrington and McDonald, ch. 3, this volume.

14 It is significant that neither author has much to say about Asian – female or male – sports involvement.

15 Although, on balance, Allison appears to be against the idea he bizarrely asserts that, logically speaking, if we are to believe that 'races' exist in a biological sense and therefore have a deterministic effect on sports performance 'we ought perhaps to introduce racial athletic events, as we have events based on gender in most sports and on size in some, such as boxing and rowing' (1998: 151).

16 We would concur with Hartmann (1998: 90) when he criticizes *Darwin's Athletes* by pointing out that: 'sport, race, and the relationships between them are much more complicated and multi-faceted than this one-dimensional, deterministic critique can capture or comprehend'.

17 A further criticism of the research on racism and sport (and indeed of sport sociology in general) is that it has tended to focus on the 'elite' level of (male) sports, ignoring the participatory level where most people are likely to directly engage with sport. An important exception to this is Long *et al.*'s (2000) analysis of racism within amateur football in the north of England.

18 In February 2000 the BBC Radio 2 presenter Sarah Kennedy gave a new twist to the evolutionary arguments by suggesting, during a live discussion on genetics, that black people made good athletes because they were used to being chased by lions in Africa: 'that's why you black people make such good runners – lions' ('DJ attacked over remarks about black athletes', *Guardian*, March 1, 2000). It is, of course, 'tabloid science' accounts like Entine's (2000), who actually concludes his 'study' of black athletic 'domination' with the cliché 'white men can't jump' (p. 341), that helps provide the legitimation for such nonsensical observations in the first place.

19 For an analysis of the political motivation of accounts such as Entine's (2000) and other similar biological determinist explanations of black sporting achievement see Younge, G. 'White on black', *Guardian* 28 August, 2000.
20 Many of those working within sports sociology will, almost out of a duty to be seen to be referencing 'something on race', make perfunctory remarks about the importance of *Beyond a Boundary*, without ever truly taking on board or engaging with the wider issues of aesthetics, Marxist praxis, cultural resistance, and nationalist politics that the book develops.

References

Alexander, C. (1996) *The Art of Being Black: The creation of black British youth identities*, Oxford: Clarendon Press.
Allison, L. (1998) 'Biology, Ideology and Sport', in Allison, L. (ed.) *Taking Sport Seriously*, Aachen: Meyer and Meyer.
Anthias, F. and Yuval-Davis, N. (1992) *Racialized Boundaries: Race, nation, gender, colour and class and the anti-racist struggle*, London: Routledge.
—— (1992) 'Connecting 'Race' and Ethnic Phenomena', in *Sociology*, 26 (3), August, pp. 421–438.
—— (1995) 'Cultural Racism or Racist Culture? Rethinking racist exclusions', in *Economy and Society*, 24 (2), May, pp. 279–301.
Banton, M. (1998) *Racial Theories*, 2nd ed., Cambridge: Cambridge University Press.
Barker, M. (1981) *The New Racism*, London: Junction Books.
Barnes, B., Zieff, S. and Anderson, D. (1999) 'Racial Difference and Social Meanings: Research of 'Black' and 'White' infants' motor development, c. 1931–1992', in *Quest*, 51 (4), November, pp. 328–345.
Bauman, Z. (1990) *Thinking Sociologically*, Oxford: Blackwell Publishers.
Birrell, S. (1989) 'Racial Relations Theories and Sport: Suggestions for a more critical analysis', in *Sociology of Sport Journal*, 6 (3), September, pp. 212–227.
Bonnett, A. (1997) 'Constructions of Whiteness in European and American Anti-Racism' in Werbner, P. and Modood, T. (eds) *Debating Cultural Hybridity: Multi-cultural identities and the politics of anti-racism*, London: Zed Books.
Bonnett, A. (2000) *White Identities: Historical and international perspectives*, London: Prentice Hall.
Bose, M. (1996) *The Sporting Alien: English sport's lost Camelot*, Edinburgh: Mainstream Publishing.
Bouchard, C. (1988) 'Preface: Racial differences in performance' in *Canadian Journal of Sport Sciences*, 13 (2), June.
Boyle, R. and Haynes, R. (2000) *Power Play: Sport, the media and popular culture*, Harlow: Longman.
Brown, A. R. (1999) ' "The other day I met a constituent of mine": A theory of anecdotal racism' in *Ethnic and Racial Studies*, 22 (1), pp. 23–51.
Carrington, B. (1998) 'Sport, Masculinity and Black Cultural Resistance'. In *Journal of Sport and Social Issues*, 22(3), August, pp. 275–298.
—— (1999) 'Cricket, Culture and Identity: An exploration of the role of sport in the construction of black masculinities'. In Roseneil, S. and Seymour, J. (eds) *Prac-tising Identities: Power and Resistance*, London: Macmillan.
Cashmore, E. (1982) *Black Sportsmen*, London: Routledge and Kegan Paul.
—— (2000) *Making Sense of Sports*, 3rd ed., London: Routledge.
Clarke, G. and Humberstone, B. (eds) (1997) *Researching Women and Sport*, London: Macmillan.
Clarke, J. and Critcher, C. (1985) *The Devil Makes Work: Leisure in Capitalist Britain*, London: Macmillan.

Coakley, J. (1998) *Sport in Society: Issues and controversies*, 6th ed., London: McGraw-Hill.

Cole, C. and Andrews, D. (1998) 'Review Symposium: Darwin's Athletes, Passionate Attachments, and Modern Power' in *International Review for the Sociology of Sport*, 33 (1), March, pp 96–99.

Davis, L. (1990) 'The Articulation of Difference: White preoccupation with the question of racially linked genetic differences among athletes' in *Sociology of Sport Journal*, 7, pp. 179–187.

Dunning, E. (1999) *Sport Matters: Sociological studies of sport, violence and civilization*, London: Routledge.

Duster, T. (1990) *Backdoor to Eugenics*, London: Routledge.

Edwards, H. (1969) *The Revolt of the Black Athlete*, New York: The Free Press.

Entine, J. (2000) *Taboo: Why black athletes dominate sports and why we're afraid to talk about it*, New York: Public Affairs.

Farred, G. (ed.) (1996) *Rethinking C.L.R. James*, Oxford: Blackwell.

Fleming, S. (1995) *'Home and Away': Sport and South Asian male youth*, Aldershot: Avebury.

Fryer, P. (1984) *Staying Power: The history of black people in Britain*, London: Pluto Press.

Gilroy, P. (1987) *There Ain't No Black in the Union Jack: The cultural politics of race and nation*, London: Routledge.

—— (1998) 'Race Ends Here', in *Ethnic and Racial Studies*, 21 (5), September, pp. 838–847.

—— (2000) *Between Camps: Nations, cultures and the allure of race*, London: Allen Lane.

Goldberg, D. (1993) *Racist Culture: Philosophy and the politics of meaning*, Oxford: Blackwell.

—— (ed.) (1994) *Multiculturalism: A critical reader*, Oxford: Blackwell.

—— (1997) *Racial Subjects: Writing on race in America*, London: Routledge.

Gould, S. (1997) *The Mismeasure of Man*, 2nd ed., London: Penguin.

Gruneau, R. (1983) *Class, Sports, and Social Development*, Amherst: University of Massachusetts Press.

Gutmann, A. (ed.) (1994) *Multiculturalism: Examining the politics of recognition*, Princeton: Princeton University Press.

Hall, A. (1996) *Feminism and Sporting Bodies: Essays on theory and practice*, Champaign: Human Kinetics.

Hall, S. (1998a) 'A torpedo aimed at the boiler-room of consensus', in *New Statesman*, 17 April, pp. 14–19.

—— (1998b) 'Aspiration and Attitude ... Reflections on black Britain in the nineties', in *New Formations*, 33, Spring, pp. 38–46.

Hargreaves, Jenny (1994) *Sporting Females: Critical issues in the history and sociology of women's sports*, London: Routledge.

—— (2000) *Heroines of Sport: The politics of difference and diversity*, London: Routledge.

Hargreaves, John (1986) *Sport, Power and Culture*, Cambridge: Polity Press.

Hartmann, D. (1996) 'The Politics of Race and Sport: Resistance and domination in the 1968 African American Olympic protest movement', in *Ethnic and Racial Studies*, 19 (3), July, pp. 548–566.

—— (1998) 'Review Symposium' in *International Review for the Sociology of Sport*, 33 (1), March, pp. 89–92.

Hayes, S. and Sugden, J. (1999) 'Winning Through "Naturally" Still? An analysis of the perceptions held by physical education teachers towards the performance of black pupils in school sport and in the classroom' in *Race, Ethnicity and Education*, 2 (1), pp. 93–107.

Hesse, B. (1997) 'It's Your World: Discrepant M/Multiculturalisms' in *Social Identities*, 3 (3), October, pp. 375–394.

Hesse, B. (ed.) (2000) *Un/Settled Multiculturalisms: Diasporas, entanglements, transruptions*, London: Zed Press.

Hoberman, J. (1997) *Darwin's Athletes: How sport has damaged black America and preserved the myth of race,* Boston: Mariner Books.

—— (1998) 'Review Symposium: Response' in *International Review for the Sociology of Sport,* 33 (1), March, pp. 96–99.

James, C.L.R. (1963[1994]) *Beyond a Boundary,* London: Serpent's Tail.

Jarvie, G. (ed.) (1991) *Sport, Racism and Ethnicity,* London: Falmer Press.

—— (2000) 'Sport, Racism and Ethnicity' in Coakley, J. and Dunning, E. (eds) *Handbook of Sports Studies,* London: Sage.

Jenkins, R. (1997) *Rethinking Ethnicity: Arguments and explorations,* London: Sage.

Jones, S. (1994) *The Language of the Genes: Biology, history and the evolutionary future,* London: Flamingo.

Kew, F. (1997) *Sport: Social problems and issues,* Oxford: Butterworth-Heinemann.

Kew, S. (1979) *Ethnic Groups and Leisure,* London: Sports Council and Social Science Research Council.

Kohn, M. (1996) 'Can White Men Jump?' in *The Race Gallery: The return of racial science,* London: Vintage.

Lashley, H. and Hylton, K. (eds) (1997) 'Special Issue – A Black Perspective', *Leisure Studies,* 16 (4), October.

Lawrence, E. (1982) 'In the abundance of water the fool is thirsty: Sociology and black "pathology"', in *The Empire Strikes Back: Race and racism in 70s Britain,* CCCS, London: Hutchinson.

Lewontin, R. (1993) *The Doctrine of DNA: Biology as ideology,* London: Penguin.

—— (1995) *Human Diversity,* Scientific New York: American Library.

Long, J., Nesti, M. Carrington, B. and Gilson, N. (1997) *Crossing the Boundary: The nature and extent of racism in local league cricket,* Leeds: Leeds Metropolitan University.

Long, J., Hylton, K., Welch, M. and Dart, J. (2000) *Part of the Game? An examination of racism in grassroots football,* Leeds: Leeds Metropolitan University/Kick it Out.

Malik, K. (1996) *The Meaning of Race: Race, history and culture in Western societies,* London: Macmillan.

Marqusee, M. (1996) *War Minus the Shooting: A journey through South Asia during cricket's world cup,* London: William Heinemann.

—— (1998) *Anyone But England: Cricket, race, and class,* London: Two Heads Publishing.

—— (1999) *Redemption Song: Muhammad Ali and the spirit of the sixties,* London: Verso.

Mason, D. (1994) 'On the Dangers of Disconnecting Race and Racism' in *Sociology,* 28 (4), November, pp. 845–858.

McDonald, I. and Ugra, S. (1998) *Anyone for Cricket? Equal opportunities and changing cricket cultures in Essex and East London,* London: University of East London Press.

Mercer, K. (1994) *Welcome to the Jungle: New position in black cultural studies,* London: Routledge.

Messner, M. (1992) *Power at Play: Sport and the problem of masculinity,* Boston: Beacon Press.

—— (1997) *Politics of Masculinities: Men in movements,* London: Sage.

Miles, R. (1989) *Racism,* London: Routledge.

—— (1993) *Racism after 'race relations',* London: Routledge.

Modood, T. and Werbner, P. (eds) (1997) *The Politics of Multiculturalism in the New Europe: Racism, identity and community,* London: Zed Books.

Montagu, A. (1997) *Man's Most Dangerous Myth: The fallacy of race,* 6th ed., London: AltaMira Press.

Omi, M. and Winant, H. (1994) *Racial Formation in the United States,* 2nd ed., London: Routledge.

Orakwue, S. (1998) *Pitch Invaders: The modern black football revolution,* London: Victor Gollancz.

Polley, M. (1998) *Moving the Goalposts: A history of sport and society since 1945,* London: Routledge.

Rattansi, A. and Westwood, S. (eds) (1994) *Racism, Modernity and Identity: On the western front*, Cambridge: Polity Press.

Rose, S. (1998) *Lifelines: Biology, Freedom, Determinism*, London: Penguin.

Rose, S. and Rose, H. (eds) (2000) *Alas Poor Darwin*, London: Jonathan Cape.

Said, E. (1994) *Culture and Imperialism*, London: Vintage.

Sammons, J. (1994) ' "Race" and Sport: A critical, historical examination' in *Journal of Sport History*, 21 (3), Fall, pp. 203–278.

Sayer, A. (1997) 'Essentialism, Social Constructionism, and Beyond' in *The Sociological Review*, 45 (3), pp. 453–487.

Shohat, E. and Stam, R. (1994) *Unthinking Eurocentrism: Multiculturalism and the media*, London: Routledge.

Sivanandan, A. (1990) *Communities of Resistance: Writings on black struggles for socialism*, London: Verso.

Sleap, M. (1998) *Social Issues in Sport*, Basingstoke: Macmillan.

Smaje, C. (1997) 'Not Just a Social Construct: Theorising race and ethnicity' in *Sociology*, 31 (2), May, pp. 307–327.

Solomos, J. and Back, L. (1994) 'Conceptualising Racisms: Social theory, politics and research' in *Sociology*, 28 (1), February, pp. 143–161.

Tomlinson, A. (1999) *The Game's Up: Essays in the cultural analysis of sport, leisure and popular culture*, Aldershot: Arena.

Verma, G. and Darby, D. (1994) *Winners and Losers: Ethnic minorities in sport and recreation*, London: Falmer Press.

Walvin, J. (1996) *Questioning Slavery*, London: Routledge.

Werbner, P. and Modood, T. (eds) (1997) *Debating Cultural Hybridity: Multi-cultural identities and the politics of anti-racism*, London: Zed Books.

Wiggins, D. (1997) *Glory Bound: Black athletes in a white America*, New York: Syracuse University Press.

Williams, E. (1964) *Capitalism and Slavery*, London: Deutsch.

Williams, J. (1994) ' "Rangers is a black club": "Race", identity and local football in England' in Giulianotti, R. and Williams, J. (eds) *Game Without Frontiers: Football, identity and modernity*, Aldershot: Arena.

Wimbush, E. and Talbot, M. (eds) (1988) *Relative Freedoms: Women and leisure*, Milton Keynes: Open University Press.

Part I

Research into current levels and forms of sports racism

Some empirical explorations

2 Racism, national identity and Scottish football

Paul Dimeo and Gerry P.T. Finn

Introduction

The powerful influence of racism on the lives of specific Scottish ethnic minorities continues to receive limited recognition in Scotland. Many of the self-serving devices employed by majority group members to deny racism are common to other societies (van Dijk 1984, 1993), but some local myths on what it means to be Scottish are used to sustain majority self-satisfaction and complacency that racism is absent from Scotland (Finn 1987; Armstrong 1989). Sport has been one of the main means of enacting a sense of Scotland and Scottishness (e.g., Walker and Jarvie 1994), but it has been Scottish football that has, in different ways, become the most prominent, popular representation of Scottishness (Finn and Giulianotti 1998). For that reason, the study of racism in the context of Scottish football offers important insights into racism in Scottish society. This chapter will explore how racism has been evident in Scottish football, but denied, and how this misunderstanding of racism is entangled with the equally misunderstood notion of 'sectarianism'.

Racism? 'No problem here!'

Denial of racism in Scottish football, despite evidence of its presence in banal forms in everyday discourse, is simply one example of this wider societal phenomenon (Dimeo and Finn 1998). There is a truly Scottish version of the common denial that racism is 'no problem here' and a common belief that racism is 'foreign' to Scotland. Murray provides a striking example of this belief: 'however much we may dislike it, anti-Catholicism is part of Scotland's history and can be understood in these terms. Racism is totally odious and foreign to all that Scotland stands for' (1988: 175).

This common fantasy assumes that a Scottish identity contains some inherent resistance to racism (Finn 1999b). Usually this belief is accompanied by an acceptance that 'sectarianism' is common in Scottish life and is partnered by the sibling prejudice that racism is an English characteristic. Xenophobia has mysteriously failed to cross the Anglo-Scottish border, despite Anglo-Scottish union in British imperialism (Cain 1986). Of course, belief in the inferiority of English society, claimed to be evident in easily detectable English racism, is itself evidence of Scottish prejudice.

Contemporary anti-English attitudes of varying importance and intensity are displayed in, and through, Scottish football (e.g., Finn and Giulianotti 1998). However, anti-English sentiments have not been a constant feature of Scottish society and Scottish football, despite uninformed comment to the contrary (e.g., Moorhouse 1984, 1986, 1991). Relations between Scotland, England and other nations within Britain should not be over-simplified. For much of the twentieth century, the Conservative Party has been the mainstream political party that most symbolized some restricted sense of being British. That was demonstrated by Norman Tebbit's infamous cricket test of British loyalty when in 1990 the former MP cited British-Asian and African-Caribbean support for national teams from the sub-continent and the West Indies rather than England as evidence of their unpatriotic outlook. Yet, the Conservative Party was a very powerful political force in Scotland, and has even been the dominant Scottish political party. It remains the only party in twentieth-century Scotland, in 1955, to poll over 50 per cent of the popular vote at a general election.

The Conservatives, styled as Scottish Unionists, welded together a broad cross-class alliance around a form of Protestant, Imperialist, 'One Nation' Toryism. The Unionist label, though applicable to Scotland, had its roots in the dispute over the governance of Ireland, which emphasized further the traditional role of Protestantism in defining being British (Colley 1992). The values of Scottish Unionism identified with the then very strong political current that positioned Scots as Britons. Scottish Unionism was well able to present itself as a formidable political 'tartan army', with a specifically Scottish identity, which represented and fought for Scotland in British Conservative politics in London, but which also represented and fought for British Conservative politics in Scotland (Mitchell 1990).

Scottish Tories successfully differentiated themselves from any sense of being an English body. They presented themselves as Scots, not English, but as Unionists proclaimed the interdependence of Scotland and England. Each nation was claimed to contribute special qualities to the Union that made the whole substantially greater than its parts. Scottish Unionists did not present an anti-English case for the differentiation of Scotland from England: they emphasized the importance of the Scottish contribution to Britain. It was, they claimed, the addition of 'essentially' Scottish characteristics to 'essentially' English characteristics that ensured the global superiority of the combined British nation.

The perplexing and sometimes contradictory relationship of Scotland to England, particularly in terms of Britishness, is illustrated in the ambiguous and ambivalent role of specifically Scottish sport in relation to a Scottish identity, and more obviously to Scottish nationalism (Walker and Jarvie 1994; Finn and Giulianotti 1998). Historically it has been Scottish football that has best served as a symbol of that complex sense of Scotland, and its bemused relationship to England. Football did differentiate Scotland from England, but it could also convey a form of unity, certainly harmony, with the other constituent parts of

Britain (Finn 1994a). Scottish football was a vehicle that expressed a sense of Scotland in partnership, albeit sometimes uneasily, but often enthusiastically, with the other submerged nations that comprise the British state.

England's relationship to Britain is clearly different from Scotland's, but it is a mistake not to recognize that England is itself another example of a submerged, albeit dominant, nation in the British state.[1] Football again has provided a focus for displays of this much more deeply embedded, more contradictory, even more confused, sense of Englishness that exists within the British state. So, it can be no surprise that it is English football that has been the most prominent symbol of Englishness in its myriad – some positive and celebratory, some negative, xenophobic and racist – variants (e.g., Williams, Dunning and Murphy 1984; Redhead 1991; Armstrong 1998; Brown 1998; Carrington 1998).

The historical amalgam of nations that is Britain yielded a State populated by citizens with complex allegiances, and complicated, sometimes misunderstood nationalities. Perhaps, paradoxically, it is this very traditional British confusion that has led so many British politicians to have such difficulty with the notion of a hyphenated nationality. Yet it was this seemingly confused and confusing hotchpotch of levels of nationality and national allegiances, in the peculiarity of a unitary British state with substantially devolved administrative power to minority national members (Patterson 1994), that was especially celebrated in football's 'Home' or British Championships (Finn 1994a). Here Scottish football literally played its role in the iconography of the nationalisms of the British state. National teams competed to win the British 'nation's' football championship.

Administrative arrangements for football in Britain reflected this complexity too. Although all the nations were united in one political entity, each constituent nation had its own national football association. Scottish football's governing body, the Scottish Football Association (SFA), usually symbolized Scotland's traditional relationship with England and acted as a junior partner to England in the 'Home' Football Associations' political efforts in the face of global administrative developments in the world game.

The studied insularity of Britain's national football associations, and the reliance on, and continued assertion of, the importance and significance of the Home Associations, despite developments in the administration and organization of world football, was itself symptomatic of a generalized British xenophobia (Tomlinson 1986; Carrington 1998) in which Scotland played its full part. The persistent promotion and celebration of the British Championship tournament, even to the neglect of the World Cup, was neither an English nor a Scottish characteristic: it reflected an inward-looking, taken-for-granted, and shared belief in the superiority of British values, in sporting fields as in others. And, when the English Arthur Drewery and Sir Stanley Rous directed the Fédération Internationale de Football Association (FIFA) from 1956 until the mid 1970s, similar values informed the Eurocentric, patronizing attitude taken towards football in most of the rest of the world (Sugden and Tomlinson 1997, 1998).

Both Drewery and Rous won support from the SFA; being English, both were seen to be probable allies for Scotland in international football politics. When

England and Scotland no longer saw the British 'Home Championship' to be of either sporting or financial value to them, they dropped it (and Wales and Northern Ireland too), and replaced it with a tournament and trophy in honour of Sir Stanley Rous. Like Scottish society at large, Scottish football has had much in common with England. So it would be a remarkable story if xenophobia had been absent from the history of either Scottish football or Scottish society. Moreover, the presumption of superior Scottish values seems little distant from an earlier shared belief in the superiority of British ones.

Scottish football (and Scottish civil society too) not only shares the same island as England (and the neglected Wales), but has shared in much of the same insularity too. Not only is Scotland not free of xenophobia, but the present tendency to locate various social evils and problems in England, but not Scotland itself, merely provides one illustration of its very existence. These variants of anti-Englishness are simply a special case of a more general Scottish xenophobia in Scottish social thinking; but a xenophobia that often surfaces in complicated forms in the context of football (Finn 1991a,b, 1994a,b,c, 1999b; Giulianotti 1991, 1995; Horne 1995; Dimeo and Finn 1998; Finn and Giulianotti 1998).

Sectarianism and racism: Scotland and England[2]

Scotland's role as England's junior partner in British imperialism made the boasted absence of racism an unlikely claim. Evidence of the extent of racism in Scottish society has clearly disproved this belief (e.g., Armstrong 1989). The Scottish belief in 'no problem here' is simply a Scottish variant of the racist belief that racism is itself a consequence of a numeric black presence (Finn 1987), a belief that still strongly influences views on racism and Scottish football (Finn 1999b).

Dimeo and Finn (1998) showed how this belief was used when a consortium of Asian-Scottish businessmen was associated with a proposal to invest in Glasgow football club, Partick Thistle. When Jim Oliver, the Thistle chairman, publicly rejected the bid, he was quoted in the *Daily Record* as saying that he did not intend to 'give away a company ... at a personal loss to satisfy the wishes of some Indian with a curry shop' (28 August 1995). Oliver's reference was to Charan Gill whose company had a turnover many times greater than that of Thistle.

Gill, who has since been awarded an MBE for services to the food industry, runs a company that controls a range of food-related businesses. It includes a food-processing factory, what is probably Scotland's only Irish–Indian bar and restaurant, as well as a chain of Indian restaurants. Ironically, Gill's Indian restaurant chain had previously been financially involved with Partick Thistle. As a result, the name of his Indian restaurant chain had been emblazoned on the Thistle team shirts. An even greater irony, although not then common knowledge, was that Partick Thistle was already in a very weak financial position. That was known to those considering the bid. However, the seriousness of

Thistle's position only became public knowledge during season 1997–98 when the club narrowly averted bankruptcy and closure.

Oliver's response to the proposed bid, and particularly his use of an ethnic stereotype to caricature Gill, led to accusations of racism from supporters of the bid and a section of the club's own support criticized Oliver for the same reason. In a subsequent interview Oliver was asked whether he believed his comments to be racist. His reported reply, in an attempt at self-defence, was:

> As I understand it he is an Indian, and he owns a curry shop. If he is not an Indian with a curry shop, I'll apologize ... I don't care whether they are Asians, Eskimos or one-eyed black lesbian saxophone players, if they have the money we will talk to them.
>
> (*Herald*, 29 August 1995)

The dominant response to the proposal from the Scottish media was also at odds with the proud boast of a Scotland free from racism. Media reports, taking their lead from Oliver, often presented textbook examples of the belief that racism arises in the majority community because of the actions of the minority group. So Asian-Scots' desire to participate in Scottish football was represented as an unwarranted incursion by a minority community which would inject racism into Scottish football, and even 'denationalize' Partick Thistle. For example, one journalist wrote that the bid demonstrated 'a lack of judgement because whatever Partick Thistle may be they are intrinsically, definitively, and eccentrically Scottish' (*Evening Times*, 29 August 1995).

In a classic demonstration of prejudice, this attempt at participation in Scottish football was greeted as threatening, and an inevitable cause of racism. Yet, paradoxically, the lack of Asian-Scottish participation in Scottish football is used to represent this community as a group apart, and as a sign of a non-Scottish community, with a non-footballing culture. The role of racism in excluding this potential football community is minimized, if recognized at all. Indeed, 'racism' seldom appeared in the discourses studied by Dimeo and Finn (1998). A much more common reference was to the dangers of 'sectarianism', which was deployed to warn of the supposed trouble that would accompany the entry of Asian-Scots onto Scottish football-fields.

Thistle chairman Oliver included this notion in his explanation of his opposition to the proposed Asian-Scottish involvement. As reported in the *Daily Record*, he claimed that 'not everyone views a group of fifty Asian businessmen as non-sectarian' (28 August 1995). Commentators in the media responded in a similar manner. No longer would Thistle be 'a welcome and valued buffer to the prejudices that attach themselves to football and life in the west of Scotland' (*Evening Times*, 29 August 1995). Instead it was the case that: 'After 107 years of religious intolerance between the supporters of Celtic and Rangers, Glasgow has suddenly discovered another theatre of holy war, this time involving the Asian community' (*Scotsman*, 29 August 1995). In this way the belief in Catholic Irish–Scots' responsibility for introducing 'sectarianism' into Scottish football was reinforced, opposition to Asian–Scottish participation in Scottish football was underlined, and the myth of a Scotland free from racism was perpetuated.

Usually it is accepted that something called 'sectarianism' does exist in Scotland. Some commentators have even come close to characterizing 'sectarianism' as a quintessential element of Scottishness (see, for example, Murray, 1988 above). Nonetheless, Moorhouse (1994) argues that there is little evidence for 'sectarianism' in contemporary Scottish society, and indeed he finds none when he looks at a run of one Rangers fanzine. However, Moorhouse then contradicts himself when he adds his endorsement to this fanzine's claims that Celtic Football Club and its fans support Irish republican paramilitary violence, providing clear evidence of the very phenomenon he wishes to argue no longer exists (Finn 1997, 1999b). Then, having failed to recognize evidence of 'sectarianism', he goes on to urge greater clarity in the way in which the term is used: perhaps a strange suggestion if the phenomenon is no longer socially significant, but clearly essential as his own attempt at analysis demonstrates. Moorhouse here adds some sort of support to Finn (1990, 1991a, 1999a,b) and Bradley (1995), both of whom have argued that greater care is required when using this term. 'Sectarianism' is a coy, confusing term that can often obscure much more than it reveals (Finn 1990, 1999a, b). The use of the term:

> avoids any identification of causality, neglects any analysis of social and political power within Scotland and implies equal culpability for prejudice between majority and minority communities and helps retain the myth of Scotland as a democratic and egalitarian society, free from the stain of racism. Much that is claimed to be sectarianism is better described as anti-Irish racism.
>
> (Finn 1990: 5–6)

Now the identification of a racist dimension to 'sectarianism' puzzles some, especially those with racist beliefs in the existence of real 'races'. However, it is racism that constitutes a defined group of people as belonging to another 'race': historically that has played an important part in those activities and events categorized as 'sectarian'. Before that case is elaborated, another myth associated with 'sectarianism' merits examination. Another comparison can be made with more obvious variants of racism: the 'no problem here' constellation of beliefs is embedded in many accounts of 'sectarianism' too. Thus, clubs from the Catholic Irish–Scottish community are blamed for the introduction of ethnicity, politics and religion into Scottish football. So, Murray (1984, 1988) persists in blaming Edinburgh Hibernian and Glasgow Celtic for introducing 'sectarianism' to Scottish football. Murray's research failings, with evidence that contradicts his analyses, have been identified elsewhere (Finn 1991a,b, 1994a,b, 1999b). Instead of undertaking critical research, Murray simply relied upon the traditional Scottish myth of minority culpability: there was 'no problem' in Scottish football until it was introduced by the minority Irish–Scottish community (Finn

1991a, 1997, 1999b). That traditional prejudice was then recycled in a more contemporary racist form to oppose investment by Asian-Scots in Partick Thistle (Dimeo and Finn 1998).

The 'no problem here' constellation is also evident in beliefs that 'sectarianism' is rooted in specific localities, inevitably those in which there is a considerable Irish-Scots ethnic presence. So sometimes 'sectarianism' is seen to be an issue only in Glasgow or the West of Scotland, an account which evidence does not support. Edinburgh was the location for vehement anti-Irish and anti-Catholic campaigns, which led to electoral success for John Cormack's political Protestantism (Gallagher 1987a): the capital city was also the location for one of the earliest anti-Catholic and anti-Irish football clubs, and one which preceded any identifiably Irish-Scottish football presence (Finn 1994b). Nor can the complexity of what is termed 'sectarianism' be restricted to the Scottish central belt or even to Scotland alone. There is a specifically Scottish variant of 'sectarianism', but again the Anglo-Scottish border marked no absolute divide.

Only an English variant of the 'no problem here' approach could deny the British dimension to 'sectarianism'. As Colley (1992) has shown, Protestantism was the glue that held together the British state in a religious communion of differentiated national entities. It was possible to be English, Welsh, Scottish or Irish and be British. Yet to be British was to be Protestant: that is why the Crown, as head of the British State, still promises on oath to safeguard Protestantism. Anti-Catholicism is not peculiarly Scottish, but was, and remains by statute, at the very heart of the British state. Anti-Catholicism was one of the complicating factors in the relationship of Ireland to the British state. Ireland was part partner and part colony: a judgement that varied over time and between the many different parts of the populations of the two islands.

However, the Irish population, particularly the perceived 'native' Catholic majority, was seen by many in Britain, not just Scotland, to constitute a different race (Curtis 1968, 1971; Lebow 1976). Representations of the Irish as a distinct, and inferior, race were common in British social thinking. Adherence to Catholicism was seen to be confirmation of Irish racial inferiority. It is this admixture of religion and racialized discourses that renders 'sectarianism' an often misleading term (Finn 1990, 1991a, 1999a,b).

Racialization of the Irish, the importance of Protestantism, and the successful political mobilization around Irish Unionism, were features of British civic and political discourses. Anti-Irish sentiments were also evident in England. The potency of anti-Irish racism in Liverpool has been recognized (Neal 1988). To assume that these beliefs were concentrated on Liverpool alone would be to succumb to another variant of the 'no problem here' prejudice. Research shows that these beliefs were much more widespread in English society (Curtis 1968, 1971; Lebow 1976), and much more long-lived too (Fielding 1993). Research in the 1980s showed that Irish youth in England can still experience problems (Ullah 1985): anti-Irish racism remains a force throughout Britain (Hickman and Walters 1997). Football supporters of England in Dublin in the last few years have shown that this variant of anti-Irish Britishness can still be publicly displayed. Recent research has shown that this variant of Britishness can still appeal to some England fans and be intertwined with expressions of the more contemporary anti-black racism (Back, Crabbe and Solomos 1998; Bradley 1998).

Racism and religion in Scotland

Nonetheless, anti-Irish racism in Scotland did take different forms from south of the border, often being more virulent, and more easily confused and confounded with religion. Some of this confusion arose from the British belief that Irish retention of the Catholic faith confirmed their racial degeneracy, but confusion in Scotland was deepened by the energetic involvement of leading Scottish Protestant figures in anti-Catholic and anti-Irish campaigns. Anti-Irish racism and anti-Catholic sentiments were probably never so powerful in Scotland as in the inter-war years (Brown 1987; Bruce 1985; Gallagher 1987a,b). The prominent role of the Scottish Presbyterian churches in this overtly racist political campaign pulled the strands of religion and racism into an even tighter knot. Yet these churches took great care to distinguish these dimensions, claiming that their objection to the Irish presence in Scotland was on racial, not religious grounds. Sometimes these Scottish churchmen even claimed inspiration from Nazi Germany's treatment of the Jewish minority (Brown 1991). Other elite Scottish campaigners took a similar line (Findlay 1991). These political currents were very strong in Scotland, and this form of racism gained more electoral support than Mosley was able to garner in Britain (Gallagher 1987a,b, Bruce 1985; Holmes 1989).

Recognition that 'sectarianism' has had a strong anti-Irish racist dimension at its heart contradicts the belief in a Scotland free from racism. Use of the imprecise term 'sectarianism' has long obscured the complexity of the inter-ethnic exchanges between Protestant Scot and Catholic Irish–Scot and hidden the extent to which there was racialization of the minority. Events in the inter-war years dramatically reveal the power of that process. Then there were sustained campaigns to halt the by then neglible Irish immigration to Scotland, calls for the forcible repatriation of categories of the 'Irish', a term that included the Scottish descendants of Irish immigrants, and attacks on the Catholic Church's perceived pervasive influence on Scottish life. Extreme, ultra-right political parties gained electoral success in both Edinburgh and Glasgow. Leading figures in mainstream political parties also advanced the cause of anti-Irish racism.

Genteel advocacy of anti-Irish racism is well illustrated by the comments of the novelist John Buchan, elected Unionist MP for one of the two Scottish university parliamentary seats. He complained in a parliamentary debate that there was a serious threat to Scotland:

> Our population is declining; we are losing some of the best of our race
> stock by migration and their place is being taken by taken by those who,

whatever their merits, are not Scottish. I understand that every fifth child born in Scotland is an Irish Roman Catholic.

(Gallagher 1987b: 145)

For Buchan national identity was genetically determined. These children might be born in Scotland, but that did not make them Scottish. Instead, he argued that they were racially distinct from other Scots-born children: their genetic heritage determined that they were Catholic Irish, not Scottish.

Remarkable advances have occurred in inter-communal and inter-faith relations in Scotland since the 1930s and especially over the last thirty or so years. However, it is foolish to believe that this extensive process of racialization has left no contemporary legacy. Overt discrimination is now much less evident but prejudicial beliefs and accounts influence discourses around certain ethnically marked and disputed areas of Scottish social life. Education and football usually feature in these disputes. In education a similar prejudicial account to that which is supposed to explain 'sectarianism' in football is offered: social division is attributed to the existence of Catholic schools, an account which confounds cause and effect and has to neglect considerable contradictory evidence. In discursive accounts of 'sectarianism' around both football and education, it is the visible Catholic or Irish presence that is assumed in different ways to be the cause of prejudice in Scottish society (Finn 1999a,b). Effectively these accounts are a corollary of the 'no problem here' orientation: the very presence of the minority becomes the explanation of the supposed problem. The majority's negative attitudes are then presented as the result of supposed contact initiated by the minority (Finn 1990, 1994b).

Accounts of 'sectarianism' have so dominated discussion of societal prejudices in Scotland that other variants of racism have been sadly neglected. Indeed, even when the important association between sectarianism and racism has been made, the result has usually been to extend further the misunderstanding of interethnic relationships summarized by the notion of 'sectarianism'. The Thistle case-study mentioned above showed how the use of 'sectarianism' led to a perception of future potential conflict in Scottish football if the minority Asian-Scots community became visibly active in the sport: responsibility for this probable outcome was attributed in advance to the actions of the minority community, even though these actions would have been much better judged as demonstrating the minority's strong desire to join with other Scots in the national game. Consequently, just as 'sectarianism' disguises the reality of anti-Irish racism, the interlocking structure of beliefs associated with its usual meanings obscures the reality of all forms of racism (Finn 1999a,b).

'Sectarianism' in football is typically explained in terms of an understandable majority response to the actions of the visible minority. The general extension of this account to other variants of racism underscores the majority argument that Scotland must have been a nation free of racism. The reality of racism in Scotland is denied and the black – albeit historically limited – presence in Scottish society and Scottish football is made even less visible to the prejudiced majority eye (Finn 1997, 1999b). Tales of the careers of past black footballers elsewhere on the island have been neglected until recently (Jenkins 1990; Vasili 1996, 1998). However, this specifically Scottish myth reinforces this neglect in the history of Scottish football. After all, in a society as free of racism as Murray (1988) has claimed, black footballers' experiences of Scottish football would be indistinguishable from that of their white fellow players. For adherents to this historical amnesia, study of the experience of black footballers in Scotland could teach no lessons on Scottish racism.

Anti-black and anti-Asian racism and Scottish football and society

This prejudicial framework explains why serious examination of the history of racism and the treatment of black and Asian-Scottish players in Scotland has been largely absent until now.[3] In 1898 John Walker moved from playing with local junior team Leith Primrose to Leith Athletic, a senior club, in the Scottish League. His displays for Athletic were so successful that within a few months Heart of Midlothian, then the most prestigious Edinburgh club, paid a substantial transfer fee for him. Walker's background is not certain, but he was believed to have African origins and was frequently identified as 'Darkie' Walker. His experience of Scottish football appears contradictory. There are suggestions of a positive welcome from some opposing fans but, as the term 'darkie' suggests, Walker's presence was also frequently racialized. Contemporary Victorian racism was much more complex than the content of the variants of scientific racism then being proclaimed (see, e.g. Banton 1987). Ryan (1997) has noted that black sportsmen were not treated in the way that the most virulent interpretations of scientific racism would have suggested. Yet that does not lead to Ryan's conclusion that racism was hardly evident in sport at that time. Media commentaries indicate that Walker was viewed as a black man as much as a footballer: his football performances were those of a racialized 'other'.[4]

The 1930s saw the appearance of what is believed to have been the first North African footballers in Scotland. Two Egyptian internationals attended Glasgow's Jordanhill College to train as Physical Education teachers. Mustafa Mansour was goalkeeper with Queen's Park Football Club, the premier amateur club in Britain, and then still playing in the top Scottish league. Mohammed Latif's career with Rangers demonstrated that the club's recruitment policy was anti-Catholic, not Protestant-only (Finn 1999b). Latif mainly played in the reserves, but he did have one match in the senior team for Rangers against Hibernian. Media treatment of both players varied, but some accounts did explicitly represent these players as ethnicized inferiors. However, the treatment of the very brief career of the first Asian player in Scotland, Celtic's Abdul Salim, in 1936, was presented in exotic terms. In part this was because he upheld the Indian sub-continent's custom and played with his feet swathed in bandages. Playing without traditional Scottish leather boots could have been reported as a sign of physical courage, instead some commentators claimed this to be an attempt to seek a merciful advantage from kind Scottish defenders! Salim's place in Scottish football history ought to have had some impact on the belief that Asians have no tradition of playing football. However, when not ignored, Salim's usual role has been to provide some exotic colour.[5]

In 1951–52 Celtic also provided the next known black player in Scottish football. Gilbert Heron is probably now better known as the father of jazz musician Gil Scott-Heron, but he deserves to be remembered for his own talents. Heron not only played for Celtic but also the Jamaican international team. He was an all-round sportsman who ran and boxed and, while in Glasgow, played for leading Scottish cricket clubs too. Heron, a professional photographer, has had two books of poetry published (MacBride *et al.* 1994). He was spotted on the 1951 Celtic tour of America. He impressed the club so much that he was invited back to Glasgow, where he had a brief career, first with Celtic, then with Third Lanark. A firm favourite of the fans of both clubs he, nonetheless, still experienced racism while in Scotland (Cosgrove 1991).

The intricate, often complex, even seemingly contradictory nature of racism becomes especially evident when Celtic's Paul Wilson is discussed. Born in Scotland of an Indian mother and Scottish father, Wilson was signed as a teenager by Celtic in December 1967. Celtic, the European champions in 1967 and runners-up in 1970, was then one of the top teams in the world. Gaining a first team place was no easy matter in a team that included Jimmy Johnstone, Bobby Lennox, Tommy Gemmell, Bobby Murdoch, Bertie Auld and Billy McNeill. Even winning a place in a reserve team packed with star names such as Kenny Dalglish, Lou Macari, Davy Hay, Danny McGrain and George Connolly was an achievement. Young players all had to fight hard to make a sustained run in the first team: that achievement measured genuine football success. Wilson's debut in the first team was in 1970. In season 1973–74 Wilson had an extended run and he contributed to Celtic winning the League championship for the ninth season in a row. He won many other honours with Celtic and in 1975 Wilson was capped for Scotland, coming on as a substitute against Spain. The capping of the Indian–Scot Wilson took place some three years before Anderson became the first black player to be selected by England. Anderson's selection was heralded as a significant step forward for black representation in football: Wilson's selection for Scotland was ignored.

Neither Wilson's international recognition, nor his success with Celtic has been celebrated for the achievement it was. That remains the case. His career is disregarded even when the limited impact of British-Asians in football is being discussed. A player who could be held up as a counter-example to the myths surrounding Asians and football is either neglected or seems to be dismissed for not being sufficiently Asian (Bains with Patel 1996). These latter arguments run the danger of claiming an essentialist conception of Asianness. Wilson's career does not deserve this silence.[6]

The extensive racist abuse faced by Wilson was also met by silence at the time from those who might have opposed it. The duality of his national identities was not explored. Occasional comments by journalists implied that Wilson was the target of some special, but unspeakable, form of abuse. At least one report complained after a match against Rangers that that there was some danger of other prejudices being introduced into Scotland. At a time when 'sectarianism' was not quite tolerated, but seldom directly opposed (Finn 1994b), it can be little surprise that expressions of anti-Asian racism were not identified, let alone challenged. Opposing fans abused Wilson: Rangers fans repeatedly bayed 'Wilson's a Paki' when Celtic played Rangers.[7] There was no silence for Wilson when opposing fans wished to engage in racial abuse of his mixed ethnic background. Wilson overcame frequent racist abuse (Crampsey 1986) and was a very successful player who can be seen to represent both Scotland and India.

Another largely forgotten Asian-Scots football player is Rashid Sarwar, who played twenty-one games for Kilmarnock, then a first division team competing for promotion. He was signed in May 1985 and sustained a lengthy run in the first team during the period in which Kilmarnock topped the division in the 1985–86 season. Unlike Wilson, Sarwar's Asian ancestry was highlighted when he signed for Kilmarnock. His presence in the league was described as 'a little bit of Scottish soccer history' because, it was erroneously explained, he would be 'the first Pakistani to play here at senior level' (*Daily Record*, 10 May 1985). His skin-colour made him the target of racist abuse, being called 'Paki bastard' and told to 'go home',[8] which as he was born in Paisley, near Kilmarnock, was so easily achieved as to be a daily event. Media coverage of Sarwar's career, however, usually failed to comment on, or protest against, the racism to which he was subjected. No support was forthcoming from any institution during his career. As was the case with Wilson, racism met nothing but silence.

One retrospective review of Sarwar's playing days simply added to his marginalization and to the disavowal of the racism he confronted. In what was designed as an anti-racist article, Sarwar was described as having played for 'the spectacularly poor Kilmarnock side of the mid-80s' (*Scotland on Sunday*, 26 November 1997). The implication was that Sarwar's career was a failure. This false categorization of Sarwar as a football failure may explain why he also is not held up as an example to young Asian-Scots of how football's racism can begin to be overcome.[9]

Sarwar played with Kilmarnock until 1987. At the very end of that year the signing of Mark Walters by Rangers offered another opportunity to open up discussion of racism in Scotland. A welcome of sorts was extended to Walters by some supporters of Rangers immediately before his first match against Celtic at Celtic Park. In the last few minutes before Mark Walters made his appearance, a substantial section of the Rangers following could be heard singing 'I'd rather be a darkie than a Tim'. Indeed, this singing was sufficiently powerful to provide the acoustic backdrop to Archie MacPherson's introduction, recorded at the time, to the later television coverage of the match (*BBC Scotland*, 2 January 1988). As was usual, this chanting passed without media comment, then or later. During the game there was some racist barracking of Walters from groups of Celtic fans, mainly, but not exclusively, located in the section of the then covered terraces known as 'the Jungle'. 'The Jungle' ran along one side of the touchlines. When play took Walters to that side of the park, his appearance was the cue for a handful of bananas to be thrown.

Events at Celtic fit some, but not all of the characteristics described by Back *et al.* (1998) in their discussion of racist chants. Historically the ethnic divide between Catholic Irish-Scots, termed 'Tims' in this chant, and Protestant Scot was, as has already been indicated, racialized. Use of the described chant by Rangers supporters was common long before the arrival of Walters. It was used by supporters, sometimes termed 'Billys', of a club whose directors had indeed refused to sign 'Tims' (Finn 1994a), a policy about which there had been traditionally little comment by respectable Scottish society (Murray 1984; Finn 1994b). Indeed, the Rangers fans' chant was an adaptation of the similarly structured chant that directly expressed ethnic preference for 'Billys' over 'Tims' and in which they expressed their relief that they were 'no' so fuckin' silly' as to think otherwise. To which Celtic fans could respond how 'glad' they were to be 'no' a Billy', and express their relief at this outcome in equally emphatic terms. So there is a much more complex and involved interplay between normative belief systems of exclusion and inclusion than in the English examples discussed by Back and his colleagues. The racist version reinforced a social hierarchy that located Catholic Irish-Scots at the bottom. Recognition of that underlying theme may in part explain the historically much more limited reverse use by Celtic fans of a similar chant that expressed preference for 'darkies' over 'Billys'.

However, racist abuse of Walters indicated that the less frequent use of the Celtic variant of this chant did not mean an absence of anti-black racism among Celtic fans. There were, in reality, very mixed views on racist abuse on the Celtic terraces. That mix had even led to disputes among Celtic fans in the past, with racist abuse leading to strong arguments. Forcefully phrased advice was given that racist behaviour was characteristic of Rangers supporters, not Celtic fans; an argument that had some similarities with the simplistic belief in a Scotland free of racism, so easily located in England instead. However, it was that dominant Scottish myth that was again brought into play when media commentators attempted to interpret the racism displayed at Celtic Park. Some media comments adopted a congratulatory tone at this supposed display of a lack of racism! Racist chants were ignored. There was a near-perfect illustration of the use of the 'racist hooligan couplet' (Back *et al.* 1998), in which racism at football games is explained as the actions of a small minority of hooligans. The hooliganism of throwing bananas close to the field of play became the main media focus for most of the few discussions of racism that took place. And, as this action had been the responsibility of only, according to press calculations, somewhere from one to five supporters, then the demonstrated reality of racism in Scotland could simply be disregarded.[10]

A fortnight later, Rangers visited Hearts. There Walters was subjected to a high level of sustained racist abuse. The worst demonstration of this appalling treatment was again when Walters' play brought him close to those areas occupied by Hearts' core fans. That produced a hail of bananas, among other objects, around Walters on a number of occasions. Once, when Walters went to take a corner, he was forced to withdraw by the volley of physical abuse thrown at him. Walters was comforted by other Rangers players. Hearts' player John Colquhoun appealed to the fans to stop. Over the public address system, a club official made pleas for better behaviour. When asked about his experiences of racism, Mark Walters identified that match as his very own worst experience:

> I went to take a corner against Hearts of Midlothian; we were playing Hearts and that was the worst of all, of all the teams we played up there. And, words, even the abuse; I think I can handle the abuse. It was the objects being thrown, like. I was ducking them like that (mimics ducking and dodging with his head). And I went to take the corner and I doffed it right into the ground. 'Cause – it was the least thing on my mind – taking that corner, you know; it was just getting out of that corner safe.[11]

The racist abuse of Walters at Hearts was exceptional. Indeed, it was so extreme as to be a contender for the worst example of overt racism in sport anywhere in Britain, and was without doubt the worst display in Scottish football. Rangers fans had a poor reputation after the abuse of Paul Wilson, as well as that of many visiting black players with non-Scottish teams, so the signing of Walters was greeted by some journalists as courageous. Nor was the poor reputation of the club's fans advanced by the very negative response of some to Walters' signing. Media reports simultaneously complained about Rangers' continuing failure, despite promises to the contrary, to sign a Catholic player. The response to the scenes at this match revealed the extent of the confusion over racism and how deeply embedded racism was in Scottish society. Rangers' own discriminatory practice was used to deflect attention from the anti-black racism so evident during the match. Some argued that 'sectarianism' was more of a problem. Others warned of the need to be vigilant to ensure that racism was not introduced into Scotland from England.

Sheer illogicality lay at the heart of a *Scotsman* leader article that attempted to deal with these cross-currents. While criticizing the racism that Walters experienced, the writer managed to express various racist beliefs, and also illustrated the typical confusion in most Scottish analyses of racism. The editorial was headed 'Alien misbehaviour' and argued that racism was found in England where there were more black players and warned against 'importing a foreign form of misbehaviour'. No programme to tackle racism was suggested. Instead:

> we can perhaps hope that one of Scotland's own much older and traditional forms of racism, a comparatively harmless type, for the most part, will help to drive out the new and much worse variety before it takes root in Scottish football. Scotland and its football have enough prejudices against the English and the Irish without requiring an utterly inexcusable new one against a black, talented and (in the face of taunts) cool football player.
>
> (*Scotsman*, 18 January 1988)

It is unclear whether anti-Irish racism is the unnamed 'traditional' racism that will somehow 'drive out' another variant, though later letter-writers made this assumption, and were unconvinced that it was 'comparatively harmless'.[12] And an article that identifies prejudice against the English, but reiterates the belief that anti-black racism is English in origin, perhaps also proves that this prejudice is not so harmless either.[13] Racism was claimed not to predate Walters' signing. The history of players such as Walker, Heron, Wilson and Sarwar was disregarded, as to recognize their experiences would mean recognizing that Scottish racism had a history. Instead, introduced along with Mark Walters, racism was an import which had no roots in Scottish society before he arrived. It is ironic that this editorial, overtly critical of racism, is based upon the pattern of prejudice common to the accusations made against the founders of Celtic or Hibs, or those Asian-Scots who sought to invest in Partick Thistle.

Conclusion

Minority groups provide targets for prejudice: their presence offers a pretext for the expression of racism. Those who adopt the 'no problem here' perspective persist in blaming minority groups for the prejudices of the majority: it is the minority's presence, and consequent activities, that have 'caused' majority group prejudice. This strategy has worked well in obscuring the reality of 'sectarianism' (Finn 1990, 1991a, 1999a,b), so the interplay between discourses on 'sectarianism' and other variants of racism is especially problematic. 'Sectarianism' can be used to deflect attention from other forms of racism. The oft-cited claim that Scotland does not have racism, but 'sectarianism' instead, denies both anti-Irish and anti-black or anti-Asian racism: the former is disguised by the use of 'sectarianism', the latter forms are supposed to be incapable of existing because either the minority presence is not significantly visible or, as with the *Scotsman*'s improbable explanation, they are somehow driven out by the former. Moreover, if Scottish racism does truly make its presence felt so strongly that its existence cannot be simply dismissed, then the accepted belief structure associated with the notion of 'sectarianism' ensures that it is the actions of the minority community that must first receive serious scrutiny.

The intertwining of these beliefs with various rhetorics of Scottish identity adds to the problem of challenging racism in Scottish society. To be Scottish, it is assumed, is not to be racist, though to be 'sectarian' may very well be! The interplay of these discourses means that the myth of Scottish antipathy to racism cannot be used as an aid to tackle racism (Dimeo and Finn 1998). Instead both variants of racism should be tackled together (Finn 1987, 1999a,b).[14] Examination of beliefs about Scottish identity is also necessary if racism is to be successfully challenged. That examination will lead to the recognition that characteristics seen to be especially Scottish are frequently variants of Britishness, which should stress the need for further analysis of identity myths on both sides of the Anglo-Scottish border.

Notes

1 Since this chapter was written increased attention has been paid to England and Englishness: Marr, A. (2000) *The Day Britain Died*, London: Profile Books; Paxman, J. (1999) *The English. A Portrait of a People*, London: Penguin. The establishment of a devolved Scottish parliament has been one of the catalysts for this rediscovery of England, especially for right-wing political commentators: Heffer, S. (1999) *Nor Shall My Sword. The Reinvention of England*, London: Weidenfeld and Nicolson; Redwood, J. (1999) *The Death of Britain?* Basingstoke: Macmillan.

2 Further analyses and discussion which are particularly relevant to both this and the immediately following section can now be found in Finn, G.P.T. (2000) A Culture of Prejudice: Promoting Pluralism in Education for a Change, in T.M. Devine (ed.) *Scotland's Shame? Bigotry and Sectarianism in Modern Scotland*, Edinburgh: Mainstream.

3 Since this chapter was written there has been some exploration of the history of black players in Scotland: Vasili, P. (2000) *Colouring over the White Line: The History of Black Footballers in Britain*, Edinburgh: Mainstream.

4 A more detailed account and analysis of racism and Walker is in preparation. Further analysis of racism in relation to those players identified below, Latif, Mansour, Salim and Heron, will also be made. The information in this chapter is the result of media-based research which will be reported in future papers and which formed part of Paul Dimeo's PhD thesis.

5 The player's name may actually have been Salim Bachchi-Khan, not Abdul Salim, the name usually used in the Scottish press.

6 A recent overview of Asian-Scottish football from an anti-racist perspective did not mention Wilson's name once in a campaign which ran erratically over a few months (*Scotland on Sunday*, 1996–1997).

7 'Paki' is a racist diminutive of Pakistani resorted to in racist name-calling and other forms of abusive exchange. Wilson's own personal courage was demonstrated by his frequent good play and goal-scoring against Rangers. It should be noted that Wilson did also experience racist abuse elsewhere in Scotland.

8 This information was provided in an interview with Rashid Sarwar by Paul Dimeo in May 1998.

9 Neglect of Wilson and Sarwar is common, even now, when some serious discussion of racism in Scottish football and society is beginning, belatedly, to take place. A radio discussion (*Ghetto Blasting*, BBC Radio Scotland, 11 October 1998) complained of the lack of appropriate role models in football for Asian-Scots, and spoke of the barriers presented by racism. Yet neither Wilson nor Sarwar was mentioned. Nor was there any mention of Jas Jutla, who had been in Rangers reserves, but is now playing with Greenock Morton. Rajiv Pathak, who is reported to have had a spell in the early 1980s with Partick Thistle, as well as with Notts County, was also ignored.

10 This account is based on an analysis of the media response to the racist abuse of Walters. Some newspapers avoided any direct reference to these events. Most reports that did do so, then congratulated the fans on the extent to which the vast majority had behaved! It is revealing that the perceived absence of racism is viewed as praiseworthy. The complexity of the media response to the signing of Walters and his initial experiences in Scotland will be treated much more extensively elsewhere.

11 *All Black: Kicking Out.* BBC TV 1998 In the same programme former Celtic player, Paul Elliot, discussed the extensive racist abuse he had received from opposing fans during his career in Scotland. Elliot said: 'And when I went to Scotland, I had initial problems. Every time I was in possession of the ball there was continued booing, verbal abuse from the terraces. And sometimes socially, there was a problem.' Elliot was repeatedly booked in the early part of his career too. Among Celtic fans, who

almost worshipped Elliot, there was a strong belief that a number of the bookings were dubious and related to the poisonous atmosphere, the result of racist abuse from opposition fans, in which his actions were interpreted. There is an alternative account, based on another widely-shared Scottish belief, which is that it takes newcomers some time to adapt to the pace of the Scottish game. Elliot has given some partial support to this later account by indicating that he was hampered by injuries at the beginning of his Celtic career.

12 See *Scotsman*, 21 January 1988.
13 Scottish prejudice against the English does not merit being called racism without sustained evidence of a process of racialization. Ironically, in a piece in which 'sectarianism' is, unusually, named as racism, the editorial as a whole illustrates just how inadequately racism was understood in Scottish society. Unfortunately, that remains true today.
14 One recent initiative that makes some partial recognition of this interplay is Celtic's Bhoys Against Bigotry campaign. The club has mounted a campaign against bigotry in all its forms. One strand, however, offers support and encouragement to the Asian-Scots community in sporting activities. Parallels have been explicitly drawn between the Irish-Scottish and Asian-Scottish communities in their efforts to participate in Scottish sports. Welcome as this initiative is, the actual value and impact of Celtic's activities remains uncertain. By contrast, the Scottish Football Association is a strong advocate of the 'no problem here' stance and on these grounds refused to participate in the 'Let's Kick Racism' campaign, a refusal that was analysed and criticized by Paul Dimeo in the fanzine *When Saturday Comes* (December, 1995).

References

Armstrong, B. (ed.) (1989) *A People without Prejudice: The Experience of Racism in Scotland*, London: Runnymede Trust.

Armstrong, G. (1998) *Football Hooligans: Knowing the Score*, London: Pavilion.

Back, L., Crabbe, T. and Solomos, J. (1998) 'Racism in Football. Patterns of continuity and change' in A. Brown (ed.) *Fanatics! Power, Identity & Fandom in Football*, London: Routledge.

Bains, J. with Patel, R. (1996) *Asians Can't Play Football*, Solihull: ASDAL.

Banton, M. (1987) *Racial Theories*, Cambridge: Cambridge University Press.

Blain, N., Boyle, R. and O'Donnell, H. (1993) *Sport and National Identity in the European Media*, Leicester: Leicester University Press.

Bradley, J. (1995) *Ethnic and Religious Identity in Modern Scotland*, Aldershot: Avebury.

—— (1998) '"We shall not be moved"! Mere Sport, Mere Songs? A tale of Scottish football' in A. Brown (ed.) *Fanatics! Power, Identity & and Fandom in Football*, London: Routledge.

Brown, A. (1998) 'United We Stand: Some Problems with Fan Democracy' in A. Brown (ed.) *Fanatics! Power, Identity & Fandom in Football*, London: Routledge.

Brown, C. (1987) *The Social History of Religion in Scotland since 1730*, London: Methuen.

Brown, S.J. (1991) 'Outside the Covenant: The Scottish Presbyterian Churches and Irish Immigration, 1922–1938', *Innes Review*, 42, 19–45.

Bruce, S. (1985) *No Pope of Rome: Anti-Catholicism in Modern Scotland*, Edinburgh: Mainstream Press.

Cain, A.M. (1986) *The Cornchest for Scotland*, Edinburgh: National Library of Scotland.

Carrington, B. (1998) '"Football's Coming Home" But Whose Home? And Do We Want It? Nation, football and the politics of exclusion' in A. Brown (ed.) *Fanatics! Power, Identity & Fandom in Football*, London: Routledge.

Colley, L. (1992) *Britons: Forging the Nation 1707–1837*, New Haven: Yale University Press.

Cosgrove, S. (1991) *Hampden Babylon: Sex and Scandal in Scottish Football*, Edinburgh: Canongate.

Crampsey, B. (1986) *Mr Stein: A biography of Jock Stein, CBE 1922–1985*, Edinburgh: Mainstream.

Curtis, L.P. jnr. (1968) *Anglo-Saxons and Celts: A Study of Anti-Irish Prejudice in Victorian England*, Bridgeport, Ct: Conference on British Studies.

—— (1971) *Apes and Angels: The Irishman in Victorian Caricature*, Washington: Smithsonian Institution Press.

Dimeo, P. and Finn, G.P.T. (1998) 'Scottish Racism, Scottish Identities: The case of Patrick Thistle' in A. Brown (ed.) *Fanatics! Power, Identity & Fandom in Football*, London: Routledge.

Fielding, S. (1993) *Class and Ethnicity. Irish Catholics in England, 1890–1939*, Buckingham: Open University Press.

Findlay, R. J. (1991) 'Nationalism, Race, Religion and the Irish Question in Inter-War Scotland', *Innes Review*, 42, 46–67.

Finn, G.P.T. (1987) 'Multicultural Antiracism and Scottish Education', *Scottish Educational Review*, 19, 39–49.

—— (1990) 'Prejudice in the history of Irish Catholics in Scotland', Paper to the 24th History Workshop Conference, Glasgow College of Technology/Glasgow Caledonian University.

—— (1991a) 'Racism, Religion and Social Prejudice: Irish Catholic Clubs, Soccer and Scottish Society – I The Historical Roots of Prejudice', *International Journal of the History of Sport*, 8, 70–93.

—— (1991b) 'Racism, Religion and Social Prejudice: Irish Catholic Clubs, Soccer and Scottish Society – II Social Identities and Conspiracy Theories', *International Journal of the History of Sport*, 8, 70–93.

—— (1994a) 'Sporting Symbols, Sporting Identities: Soccer & Intergroup Conflict in Scotland and Northern Ireland', in I.S. Wood (ed.) *Scotland and Ulster*, Edinburgh: Mercat Press.

—— (1994b) 'Faith, Hope and Bigotry: Case Studies in Anti-Catholic Prejudice in Scottish Soccer and Society' in G. Jarvie and G. Walker (eds) *Scottish Sport in the Making of the Nation: Ninety Minute Patriots?*, Leicester: Leicester University Press.

—— (1994c) 'Football Violence: A Societal Psychological Perspective' in R. Giulianotti, N. Bonney and M. Hepworth (eds) *Football, Violence and Social Identity*, London: Routledge.

—— (1997) *Scotland, Soccer, Society: global perspectives, parochial myopia*. Paper to the North American Society for Sports Sociology Annual Conference: 'Crossing Boundaries', University of Toronto.

—— (1999a) ' "Sectarianism" and Scottish Education', in T.G.K. Bryce & W.M. Humes (eds) *Scottish Education*, Edinburgh: Edinburgh University Press.

—— (1999b) 'Scottish myopia and global prejudices', *Culture, Sport, Society*, 2: 2, 54–99.

Finn, G.P.T. and Giulianotti, R. (1998) 'Scottish Fans, Not English Hooligans! Scots, Scottishness and Scottish Football', in A. Brown (ed.) *Fanatics! Power, Identity and Fandom in Football*, London: Routledge.

Gallagher, T. (1987a) *Edinburgh Divided: John Cormack and No Popery in the 1930s*, Edinburgh: Edinburgh University Press.

—— (1987b) *Glasgow The Uneasy Peace: Religious Tensions in Modern Scotland*, Manchester: Manchester University Press.

Giulianotti, R. (1991) 'Scotland's Tartan Army in Italy: The case for the carnivalesque', *Sociological Review*, 39, 503–27.

—— (1995) 'Football and the politics of carnival: An ethnographic study of Scotland fans at international matches in Romania and Sweden', *International Review for the Sociology of Sport*, 30, 191–224.

Hickman, M. J. and Walters, B. (1997) *Discrimination and the Irish Community in Britain: A report of research undertaken for the Commission for Racial Equality*, London: CRE.

Holmes, C. (1989) 'Alexander Ratcliffe, militant protestant and anti-semite', in Kushner, T. & Lunn, K. (eds) *Traditions of Intolerance: Historical perspectives on Fascism and Race Discourse in Britain*, Manchester: Manchester University Press.

Horne, J. (1995) 'Racism, sectarianism and football in Scotland', *Scottish Affairs*, 12, Summer: 27–51.

Jenkins, R. (1990) 'Survival for the Fittest? A West African Sportsman in Britain in the Age of New Imperialism', *International Journal of the History of Sport*, 7, 23–60.

Lebow, R.N. (1976) *White Britain and Black Ireland: The Influence of Stereotypes in Colonial Policy*, Philadelphia: Institute for the Study of Human Issues.

MacBride, E. and O'Connor, M. with Sheridan, G. (1994) *An Alphabet of the Celts: A Complete Who's Who of Celtic F.C.*, Leicester: ACL Colour Print & Polar Publishing (UK) Ltd.

MacClancey, J. (1994) *Sport, Identity and Ethnicity*, Oxford: Berg.

Mitchell, J. (1990) *Conservatives and the Union: A Study of Conservative Party Attitudes to Scotland*, Edinburgh: Edinburgh University Press.

Moorhouse, H.F. (1984) 'Professional Football and Working Class Culture: English Theories and Scottish Evidence', *Sociological Review*, 32, 285–315.

—— (1986) 'Repressed Nationalism and Professional Football: Scotland versus England' in J.A. Mangan and R.B. Small (eds) *Sport, Culture, Society: International historical and sociological perspectives*, London: E. & F. Spon Ltd.

—— (1991) 'On the Periphery: Scotland, Scottish Football and the New Europe', in Williams, J. and Wagg, S. (eds) *British Football and Social Change: Getting into Europe*, Leicester: Leicester University Press.

—— (1994) 'From Zines like These? Fanzines, Tradition and Identity in Scottish Football' in Jarvie, G. and Walker, G. (eds) *Scottish Sport in the Making of the Nation: Ninety Minute Patriots?* Leicester: Leicester University Press.

Murray, B. (1984) *The Old Firm: Sectarianism, Sport and Society in Scotland*, Edinburgh: Mainstream.

—— (1988) *Glasgow's Giants: 100 Years of the Old Firm*, Edinburgh: John Donald.

Neal, F. (1988) *Sectarian Violence: The Liverpool Experience, 1819–1914*, Manchester: Manchester University Press.

Patterson, L. (1994) *The Autonomy of Modern Scotland*, Edinburgh: Edinburgh University Press.

Redhead, S. (1991) *Football With Attitude*, London: Wordsmith.

Ryan, G. (1997) '"Handsome Physiognomy and Blameless Physique": Indigenous Colonial Sporting Tours and British Racial Consciousness, 1868 and 1888', *International Journal of the History of Sport*, 14, 67–81.

Sugden, J. and Tomlinson, A. (1997) 'Global Power Struggles in World Football: FIFA & UEFA, 1954–74, and their Legacy', *International Journal of the History of Sport*, 14, 1–25.

—— (1998) 'FIFA versus UEFA in the Struggle for the Control of World Football', in A. Brown (ed.) *Fanatics! Power, Identity & Fandom in Football*, London: Routledge.

Tomlinson, A. (1986) 'Going Global: The FIFA Story', in A. Tomlinson and G. Whannel (eds) *Off The Ball: The Football World Cup*, London: Pluto.

Ullah, P. (1985) 'Second-generation Irish Youth: Identity and ethnicity', *New Community*, 12, 310–320.

van Dijk (1984) *Prejudice and Discourse: An Analysis of Ethnic Prejudice in Cognition and Conversation*, Amsterdam: Benjamins.

—— (1993) *Elite Discourse and Racism*, London: Sage.

Vasili, P. (1996) 'Walter Daniel Tull, 1888–1918: Soldier, footballer, black', *Race and Class*, 38, 51–70.

—— (1998) *The First Black Footballer – Arthur Wharton*, London: Frank Cass.

Walker, G. and Jarvie, G. (eds) (1994) *Sport, Leisure and Scottish Culture*, Leicester: Leicester University Press.

Williams, J., Dunning, E. and Murphy, P. (1984) *Hooligans Abroad: The Behaviour and Control of English Fans in Continental Europe*, London: Routledge & Kegan Paul.

3 Whose game is it anyway?

Racism in local league cricket

Ben Carrington and Ian McDonald

> There was racialism in cricket, there is racialism in cricket,
> there will always be racialism in cricket.
> But there ought not to be.
>
> (C.L.R. James, *Beyond a Boundary*)

Introduction

In this chapter we argue that racism is both deeply rooted and pervasive in recreational cricket in England. Our aim is to illustrate the different dimensions and manifestations of this racism. The empirical material used here draws on two separate pieces of research conducted into racism in men's local league cricket: *Crossing the Boundary: A study of the nature and extent of racism in local league cricket* (from here on CB), which was carried out during the 1996 season,[1] with the core of the field-work encompassing Leeds, neighbouring Bradford, and East Yorkshire; and *Anyone for Cricket? Equal Opportunities and changing cricket cultures in Essex and East London* (from here on AFC), which concentrated on clubs from the Ilford region of east London and north and east Essex during the 1997 season.[2] By drawing on these, and a number of secondary reports, we will outline how a discourse of racism resides in the 'narrative structural positions, rhetorical tropes and habits of perception' (Dyer 1997: 12) of the dominant cultural group within cricket.

As with the recreational level of sports in general, scant attention has been paid to the existence and analysis of racism in recreational cricket. Most previous work on the politics of 'race' in cricket has focussed on the elite end of the game. For example, the role of cricket in buttressing British cultural and political imperial authority over colonized people throughout the empire has been extensively documented, (for example see Birley 1979; Holt 1989; Searle 1990; Bradley 1992; and James 1994), while analyses of racism in elite post-war English cricket have recently appeared (Marqusee 1998; Searle 1993). It is perhaps unsurprising that most scholarly work on 'race' and racism has been historical and on the game at the national and international level, for as the cricket journalist Rob Steen remarked, 'No sport relies so heavily on international rivalry as cricket, nor pits white so consistently against black, former master against uppity ex-servant' (1996: 4). Yet, however crucial these analyses have been, our understanding of the nature of 'race' and racism in cricket will remain deficient in the absence of a similar level of critical enquiry at the 'grass roots' of the sport. This is not just a point about comprehensiveness. It is also to do with a coherent analysis of the social configurations of racism in English cricket. The contention made here is that of the three identifiable levels of the game – the international, national (first-class county game) and recreational – it is the first and last levels listed that together constitute the key sites for the articulation of racism. The first-class county game is by no means irrelevant when considering racism, but it is both the international and the recreational spheres that provide the boundaries within which a discourse of racism circulates throughout cricket.

For the purposes of analysis and clarity, we would like to posit three dimensions or levels of racism in cricket. First there are the crude explicit forms of racial abuse. Whilst explicit forms of racist abuse are not commonplace in local leagues, there is a still a significant and unacceptable level of abuse experienced by black and Asian players. Second, there are the more subtle forms of racism that derive from an imperial and colonialist heritage where a discourse replete with cultural essentialisms abounds. (By this we mean the ways in which 'culture' is understood to be an expression of an innate (biological) self – whether identified with an individual or a group – that is often counterpoised to other cultures which are assumed to be mutually incompatible formations.) We examine the ways in which this discourse unfairly discriminates against a large number of black and Asian people. Third, a consequence of this heritage is that it has created a particular culture of 'Englishness' that has produced a form of institutionalized racism in recreational cricket. We show how this culture, in practice, disproportionately disadvantages black and Asian clubs when it comes to accessing opportunities and participating within the same competitive structures as their white counterparts. Our argument is that it is the second and third forms that are the most pervasive and the most difficult to combat.

In a sense, then, many of the debates around cricket centre on the way the game is 'imagined' and its role in people's cultural identities. It could be argued that who 'owns' cricket is the subtext to understanding racism in cricket. This is not simply in terms of who makes decisions about the game's rules, structures and developmental future – though this too is crucial – but of how the game is defined both within the cricketing media, and informally, within cricket leagues up and down the country. What cricket means, how it should be played, and its place within wider society are the crucial questions. The notion that cricket is essentially a white English, middle-class and rural game is being challenged by the very same formerly colonized peoples over whom the game was supposed to act as a form of educative civilizing process. This very act of what we might term cultural resistance means that white, middle-class Englishness is also being redefined. Mirroring the wider discourse of multi-culturalism and the challenge to the hegemonic centre of white English nationalism, many people, groups and communities can now lay claim to cricket as being *their* game too, thus challenging and fragmenting any official notion of there being only one legitimate and authoritative way of playing, watching and consuming cricket. We begin our discussion by addressing what we perceive to be the biggest problem in tackling racism in the game – that is the defensive attitude of the cricket establishment.

Mis-recognition and ignorance of the cricket establishment.[3]

The cricket establishment suffers both from a limited view of what constitutes racism in the game, and from an ignorance of the prevalence and operation of racism at the recreational level. For example, as recently as March 1997, Richard Little, the erstwhile corporate affairs manager at the England and Wales Cricket Board (ECB) argued that 'Racism is not a major issue as far as cricket is concerned. It's always been a multi-racial sport and has worked particularly well in the Commonwealth countries' (East 1997: 4). However, since 1997, significant steps have been taken by the ECB on the issue of racism. Pressured by lobbying group Hit Racism for Six, prompted by Tony Banks in his time as Sports Minister, and pushed by a Sports Council agenda with 'equity' high on their agenda, the ECB (with both eyes firmly fixed on 'getting it right' in time for the 1999 Cricket World Cup) finally accepted that racism was an issue when it released a general Equity Statement containing a clause on 'combating racial disadvantage and discrimination' (ECB 1998).

This statement was followed by a report on racial equality, *Clean Bowl Racism* (1999) which accepted that 'there is a need for positive action as soon as possible and practical against racism that exists in English cricket' (ECB 1999: 8). The report gives a number of recommendations designed to make cricket more racially inclusive, through, for example, introducing measures to encourage more people from the black and Asian communities to attend Test Matches and One Day Internationals, to improving the facilities and opportunities for black and Asian cricket clubs, especially in inner-city areas. The report is without doubt a landmark in the history of English cricket. However, as welcome as this report is, the real test of progress can only be judged on what change it effects. And this in turn depends on its level of recognition and understanding of racism in the game. Unfortunately, there are reasons here to be less sanguine. The level of understanding is revealed in statements contained in the report that English cricket cannot be institutionally racist because only 12 per cent of respondents in their survey of predominantly white cricket players/fans and administrators felt that racism was 'ingrained' in the game. One of the key points of the report (contained in the executive summary) is that black and Asian cricketers use the 'Race Card' to further their case against the cricket establishment (ECB 1999: 8). The ECB accept that there is a widespread *perception* that racism is a problem, but nowhere does it accept that it also exists *in reality*. In carefully maintaining this distinction, the ECB show that they may now accept the issue of 'race', but understand little about the dynamics of racism. One of the most important recommendations commits the ECB to establishing consultative forums involving a range of individuals and organizations to discuss the progress of anti-racism policies and the problems faced by black and Asian cricketers. These forums could well be critical in ensuring that those who do understand racism can exert their influence in developing policies.

When it comes to looking at racism in specific sports, the high profile anti-racism campaign in football is often presented as the model. This can be double-edged. If the point is to show that the governing body, players, supporters and everyone else involved in the sport have a duty to address racism, then it can be positive. However, problems arise if racism, as it has been identified in football, is taken as *the only way* in which racism manifests itself in sport.[4] The focus of attention in football has been racism expressed in explicit ways most often by fans as a product of an insular white working-class culture of aggressive masculinity (Dunning *et al.* 1988). The paradigmatic appropriateness of football depends on the specifics of the particular sport under question. Certainly it would be dangerous to generalize the experience of anti-racism in football to all sports. While the research by Long *et al.* (1995) showed that football offers a useful model for Rugby League, we argue that it does not for analysing and tackling racism in cricket. To do so would lead to the logical conclusion that no significant problem exists because the equivalent of the professional level in cricket, the first-class county game, does not have a large working-class specta-tor base that is prone to shouting racial abuse.

Therefore the starting point has to be the particular ways in which racism is expressed in cricket. We will raise just two important aspects that mark it out as different from football. First, ideologically, most of the racial controversies that have afflicted cricket over the past decade or so have surrounded questions of national identity, which are intimately tied to the chronic decline of England as a premier Test performing side. (For example, the so-called Tebbit Test, and especially Robert Henderson's (1995) call for an all-white team as a remedy for poor performances by England.) These controversies, by definition, tend not to resonate significantly within the first-class county game, though there are of course parallels with the concerns over the number of overseas cricketers playing county cricket.

However, these discourses do have a real impact in recreational cricket, where there is a thriving interest and enthusiasm for the game in the black and Asian communities. Sometimes it can occur in apparently benign ways, such as stereotyping Asian batsman as naturally 'wristy', but often it can be malicious, as with the branding of the West Indian fast bowlers of the 1980s as vengeful and violent (Savidge and McLellan 1995). In the 1990s, the brunt of racist stereo-typing has been aimed at the Asian community. For example, evidence suggests that since 1992 and the infamous ball-tampering series between England and Pakistan, many players in and around the black and Asian diasporas of London, west Yorkshire, Bristol, Birmingham, Manchester and Leicester have been called or heard fellow players called a 'Paki cheat', or 'a black bastard'. Research has to be conducted at the level of these experiences, as this is where the effects of this racialized discourse are felt and reproduced (and challenged). In examining 'race' and racism in recreational cricket, we will have a better picture of the social configurations of 'race', identity and power in the game as a whole. It may also challenge the mis-recognition of racism in the sport, and undermine ignorance of the dynamics of racial exclusion.

Racial abuse and overt racial prejudice

Both the *Crossing the Boundary* (CB: 17–19) and the *Anyone for Cricket* (AFC: 32–34) reports stated that black and Asian players felt that although racism was a common experience, it was less overt and less frequently experienced than in life outside cricket, or in other games, notably football. Some players felt that the 'gentlemanly' nature of cricket protected them against overt abuse. However, instances of verbal racial abuse are not uncommon. In a review of the autobiographies of retired black and Asian cricketers, Fleming (1996) identified three main sources of racist abuse directed at individuals: fellow players, administrators and spectators. Most recreational cricket players do not get the opportunity to record their experiences in autobiographies, so the reality of racism here goes largely unnoticed. However, it is widely accepted that racism is more prevalent in local league cricket than on the county circuit. For example, a survey of club secretaries in the CB report found that they were more likely to think that racism was less extensive in county cricket than in their own surroundings in local league cricket (CB: 14).

In recreational cricket, the absence of crowds means that personal racist abuse tends to come from other players. The abuse of batsmen by fielders is often expressed in racial terms. For example, the captain of an Asian side reported that after one of his batsmen got a thick edge on a ball, he was asked, 'What kind of fucking Paki shot is that?' (AFC: 33). In a different instance a batsman was approached by a white fielder and told to 'get out you black bastard' (CB: 17). One black player, who joined an 'all-white' team from Bradford was even referred to as a 'nigger' by one of his team-mates (CB: 18). A lot of verbal abuse takes place as a form of 'sledging' (the deliberate use of comments designed to distract a player and put them off their game). In a survey of club secretaries in the CB report, a small but significant minority (12 per cent) was prepared to admit that racial abuse of players in sledging was acceptable or sometimes acceptable, as just part of the game (p. 14). Further, 30 per cent of club secretaries conceded that their team and supporters sometimes made racist remarks. These figures are all the more disconcerting when you consider that the methodology used – postal questionnaires – to ascertain the information would have been, if anything, more likely to under-report the amount of racism admitted.

The use of racism in sledging provoked the captain of Billesdon, an Asian team from Leicestershire, to lodge an official complaint after one of its batsmen was racially abused by four members of the Caldy team from the Wirral, during the National Village Cricket Championship quarter-final in 1996. According to the Billesdon captain,

The spectators on the far side of the ground could hear it clearly and a number came round to tell us about it and say how disgusted they were. One or two of their spectators came up to us and said it was shameful on the club.

(*Leicester Mercury*, 1996)

The Cricketer magazine, which organized the competition, reprimanded the Wirral team for 'sledging' but took no action on the racial abuse. This inaction by league and cup competition officials and umpires when presented with allegations of racism is also a common experience for black and Asian sides. For example, the player cited above who was called a 'black bastard' claimed that although he felt the umpire had heard the abuse, he did nothing about it. Such incidents leave an understandable feeling amongst black and Asian cricketers that 'those in authority' do not take racism seriously enough. Indeed the failure of cricketing authorities – leagues, clubs and competition organizers – to discipline clubs and players when found guilty of racist actions and behaviours in effect legitimizes the actions of such people.

When talking about racism in the game, most black and Asian players refer to its subtlety, and feel that it is difficult to prove. However, there is evidence of white clubs discriminating against black and Asian clubs and players because of colour. The *Mail on Sunday* carried a report as far back as 1993 that showed how prejudice was preventing opportunities for black and Asian players. After being refused a trial by county club after county club, Joher Yaqub decided to write again to the same clubs, but this time as Tom Jacob. After telling Yaqub there were no vacancies, Durham asked Jacob for more details so that they could consider his application further. Two weeks after turning Yaqub down, Kent were able to send Jacob an application form and subsequently offer him a trial. As Yaqub concluded, 'I always believed there was racism in the game, now I have the proof. There must be hundreds of young Asian and Afro-Caribbean cricketers out there facing the same prejudice' (Dore 1993: 23).

One club secretary mentioned in the AFC report recounted how he was unable to secure friendly fixtures for his team, Punjab XI, against white teams. However, when he changed the name of the side to Strikers XI he found that fixtures were much easier to arrange. Although, as Strikers XI, the feelings of prejudice against them did not stop, as the same club secretary commented, 'When we would turn up, the face expressions we would get were like "What's happening here?" I don't know whether that is an image of our culture or what.' (AFC: 27). Another fixture secretary also reported how it was difficult to arrange matches with white teams, saying that if, 'there is an accent they're not going to give you a fixture', while a third club secretary was asked by a white club secretary, 'Well, is it a Paki side? We don't really want to play because they don't drink' (AFC: 27). The exclusion of 'teetotal' Asian teams because of the perception of a cultural or religious reluctance to participate in the traditional post-match drink, is often cited as the main reason by white clubs for not playing Asian sides. Indeed, there does appear to be some sort of logical, if misguided, basis for this, as many clubs are dependent on the revenue raised in the clubhouse. However, this rationale would have more validity were it not for the fact that this reluctance to entertain extended to black teams. One black player said his (mainly black) team had lost their ground, because the businessman who owned it said his side did not spend enough money, despite the fact that coach loads of their supporters would drink all evening in the bar. A white team who also rented the ground was treated less harshly, and was not evicted even though its members would usually spend less time and money in the bar. In an attempt to make sense of his club's plight the player could only conclude that the differential treatment was down to racism:

> To me it is just something to get us out. Not only black clubs but Asian clubs, because after we start to establish ourselves on their grounds they get uncomfortable ... Let's get down to the nitty-gritty, they don't even want to mix with us.
>
> (AFC: 28)

Such hostility has sometimes taken more overt and violent forms. For example, the Sheffield Caribbean Club, formed in the 1970s, and one of the oldest black local league clubs in the area, has had to endure much hostility during its existence. For years Sheffield CC was told by league officials that despite its record of success, only by acquiring a decent ground with proper facilities would it be considered for league membership. Eventually, they managed to purchase a ground from a local engineering firm. But as Mike Atkins, the club secretary, explains:

> At that time it didn't suffer any vandalism, but within a week of us getting ownership – which was reported in the newspapers – we had an attack. We had all the glass smashed ... subsequently we had the store-room, the garage and part of the pavilion burnt. Then we had the pavilion burnt down ... which the police claim was the act of someone passing by who put a firework into it. But the ground is way off the road. We subsequently had the pitch being dug up and glass sprinkled across the pitch. We had to get a perimeter fence to exclude that. Ours is fenced off, yet we suffer a great number of attacks.
>
> (Interview in *Hit Racism for Six*, 1996: 6)

Similar incidents have been experienced by Leeds' Caribbean Cricket Club, (the first black cricket club formed in Britain) which during the 1980s and 1990s had its clubhouse vandalized, burgled and burnt down, with racist graffiti left afterwards (Carrington 1998a). Whilst these are undoubtedly extreme examples of racism that fortunately are not commonplace in cricket, that it could happen at all reveals deep rooted prejudice against black and Asian clubs that *is* commonplace.

Ethnic absolutism and racial stereotyping: the men in white coats

Many commentators have noted that critical to the emergence of the political right in Britain during the 1980s was the shift of emphasis in racial discourse. Labelled the 'new racism' or 'cultural racism' it operated within the realm of culture as opposed to biology and asserted the importance of 'cultural difference' as opposed to 'race' (Barker 1981). In this new discourse, identity and ethnicity – and hence racial difference – are 'constructed' in the sphere of culture. It is not that racism based on biologically superiority/inferiority has disappeared, but that racism is more likely to be expressed in other coded forms, hidden in narratives, and concealed by structures that invoke cultural (rather than physical) differences in the first instance. Racism needs to be situated within specific social and economic situations, where its material effects can be identified. For Solomos and Back (1995: 31–41) the key task now facing researchers into this new discourse is to explore the interconnections between race and nationhood, patriotism and nationalism rather than analyse ideas about biological inferiority. It is in the defences of a mythic British/English way of life in the face of attacks from 'enemies within', i.e. black communities and so-called Muslim fundamentalists, that racism is perpetuated. And cricket, as the 'quintessentially English' sport, discursively provides a rich vein of racially inscribed practices.

An Asian player from Essex recalled an instance when his club was banned after an incident in which players from his team and players in the opposing team, who were predominantly white, swore at each other, which led to some jostling:

> What they said afterwards is that we pushed the umpire, he was an old man. We didn't do that. And they called the league meeting and because we were Asians – that's my personal experience – they said no, we pushed the umpire and you are out of the league for one year. They listened to their English captain who said that we had pushed the umpire which wasn't true and we stayed out of the league for one year. They didn't believe us. In the committee they were all English ... there was no sort of Asian person there. So whatever their side said happened, ... they believed them. They didn't believe us.
>
> (AFC: 34)

Apart from the obvious frustration felt by this player about the lack of justice, what is also telling in his account is that for him at least, 'English' is coterminous with 'white'. The incident highlights the way in which racism expressed through cricket can manifest itself in very subtle ways, sometimes with the perpetrators themselves operating unknowingly in discriminatory ways. Put simply such episodes cannot easily be proven (or disproven) either way. It is the actions (and inactions) over a long period of time that are often based on perceptions about racial others that often lead to the explosive situations that occurred in the recreational game. One of the authors of this chapter conducted ethnographic fieldwork which involved participant observation with Leeds Caribbean Cricket Club for over three years during the mid to late 1990s (Carrington 1998a, 1999). It became quite apparent that the 'men in white' held stereotypical views about blacks that undoubtedly, over the seasons, did affect not only the decisions they would give – and in cricket this subjective assessment is most pronounced in the disproportionate amount of lbw decisions given against black and Asian teams – but also in their general manner towards Asian and black teams as opposed to white teams. The point though is that such discriminatory practices due to their very nature cannot be easily seen or labelled. As we discuss in more detail below, this is particularly the case with umpires, who are charged with upholding and enforcing the rules and spirit of the game.

One consequence of the so-called ball-tampering test series between England and Pakistan in 1992, when Waqar Younis and Wasim Akram were accused of cheating, was to popularize a stereotype of 'cheating Pakistanis' in the public imagination. As a result of headlines like 'Pak off the cheats' and 'Paki Cheats' (Searle 1993) a large number of Asian players at all levels of the game, but especially at the recreational level, have had to face accusations and tolerate suspicions. Thus in a cricket discourse replete with racial stereotypes and competitive bowling, enthusiastic appealing by an Asian bowler can very easily be interpreted by umpires and others as 'intimidation' and cheating, typical of 'Pakistani' players. To protest at such treatment merely confirms their 'volatile nature'.

The subjective nature of the lbw law means that the personal beliefs, attitudes and biases of umpires are particularly crucial. Both the CB and the AFC report revealed that umpires in particular display an 'ethnic absolutist' (Gilroy 1993) perspective. Don Oslear's and Jack Bannister's book, *Tampering with Cricket* (1995) exemplifies this. Although it deals with the seamier side of professional cricket – the fixing of games, the smears of bribery, the gambling syndicates, and the impotence of the game's international ruling body – its real target is the issue of ball tampering. Don Oslear was one of the umpires in the aforementioned England–Pakistan Test match, and for him and Bannister (a commentator), it is a given that Pakistani cricketers, as befits a team from a country 'bedevilled by instability' are 'volatile by nature'. The theme of 'volatility' shapes their discussion of the controversy, and 'tampering' is presented as an Asian/ Pakistani trait imported into the English game.

The increasing prevalence in society of what has been termed 'Islamophobia'[5] – that is, religious prejudice towards Muslims who are portrayed in stereotyped ways – is clear from the comments of such accounts, and from the umpires interviewed in the studies: '... the worst by far are the Muslims ... they are very, very aggressive to the umpires' (CB: 27); and the almost laughable – if the issues were not so serious – comment by another umpire, managing to 'inflect' a racist metaphor onto another group, that, 'It's the Muslims. They're the niggers in the woodpile' (CB: 30).

It is worth noting that in the CB report the umpires (in comparison to the players and club secretaries) were more likely – with the exception of the one black umpire interviewed – to subscribe to the view that different racial groups had different abilities; more likely to see overseas players as a threat to local league cricket; less likely to be aware of racist sledging though they claimed they would not tolerate it if they heard it, but acknowledged it as coming from Asian players; and more likely to use racist language themselves when describing Asian and black players. As mentioned, the umpires interviewed also tended to view Asian players and teams as being the most unruly and undisciplined and more likely themselves to engage in abuse – as opposed to being on the receiving end. Though when pressed to give examples the umpires admitted they did not know what was being said as 'they spoke their own language' but could tell it was abusive as, 'it's the way they say it', as one umpire put it (CB: 30). The ability to act in racist ways, unintentionally or otherwise, even whilst claiming to be anti-racist is an example of what Feagin and Vera (1995) term 'sincere fictions'. By this they mean that whites will often develop a self-definition of themselves and society which disavows racism – a sort of colour-blind approach – whilst helping to define their own white identity. Thus even whites who hold stereotyped views about blacks do not acknowledge to themselves, or others, that they are racist:

> Strong sincere fictions often hide everyday realities. One mechanism of sincere denial is distancing oneself from those whites who are considered to be racist, such as Klan members or skinheads, who are viewed as uneducated or psychologically disturbed. Such distancing allows whites to deflect attention from their own role in promoting and implementing anti-black views.
>
> (Feagin and Vera 1995: 161)

Thus, as the CB report concluded, the umpires were adamant that racism was not an issue in the game and sincerely believed that they would 'stamp it out' if it ever did occur. As far as they were concerned racism was certainly not something that they, in any way, contributed to. Indeed they only understood racism, when it did emerge in their view, as coming from black, and particularly Asian, cricketers. As the CB report noted:

> It seems clear that our respondents would have no hesitation in doing their duty and dealing with any racism that they saw at matches. However, on the basis of the terminology they used themselves it is quite likely that they would not always recognize racist behaviours for what they were.
>
> (CB: 32)

There are two related aspects to the operation of cultural racism that are worth, briefly, mentioning here. The first is that its effectiveness is secured through a denial that there is any racism at all, even an embracing of anti-racism. To support this, exceptions to the rule are seized upon as conclusive evidence of claiming anti-racist credibility. So the fact that there are black and

Asian players who have made it to the top 'proves' that whatever problems exist are self-inflicted. The second is that cultural racism does not necessarily operate within a binary structure. According to their ascribed proximity to the normative structure of white collective identity, a hierarchy of racial/cultural groups is constructed. As Solomos and Back note, 'The significance of colour is denied while at the same time an "evolutionary" continuum of cultural forms is imagined' (Solomos and Back 1995: 129). Thus 'lower' cultural forms are those that display an alternative normative structure. It is in this context that we need to place comments made about black and especially Asian cricket. Lack of 'discipline' in Asian clubs, a white umpire said, was due to their ignorance of the rules, 'they don't understand a lot of laws, they don't understand the interpretation' (AFC: 44).

Another umpire said he believed that Asian teams formed leagues because it was, 'a reflection of their culture'. And as if to prove that this culture is incompatible with the dominant culture, he went on to argue that:

> The Asian teams tend to play in their own leagues organized by themselves and I think that's a basis of the way they live here. A lot of them still live like "India within the East End" yeah? And it even goes down till cricket, where they want their own cricket team.
>
> (AFC: 46)

Thus the formation of separate black and Asian leagues is constructed as the preferred option of black and Asian clubs, or as the inevitable outcome of incompatible cultures. And yet, the key point that came out of both reports is that there is an overwhelming desire by black and Asian clubs to be *a part of* official leagues. Indeed, rather than focus on the cultural 'peculiarities' of minority groups, it may well be that the key to understanding the dynamics of racism in cricket can be found in the cultural peculiarities of the majority white cricket culture.

Englishness, whiteness and racial exclusion

According to one renowned BBC Test-match special cricket commentator, 'Cricket is a game which must always be less than its true self if it is taken out of England' (quoted in Roy 1998: 16). And when questioned about the attraction of playing cricket, one of the white players in the AFC report responded, without any sense of irony, with this telling portrait:

> You come down here [to his team's village cricket ground] and you say "That is something which is quintessentially English" ... You come down here at eight o' clock in the morning. It's slightly dewy, a bit of gossamer about and it is glorious, it really is. And to see then the whole game actually starting ... it's absolutely wonderful ... The only problem is that you can always look out over the council dustbins, we should be looking

the other way with the castle behind. That's how cricket should be … it should have a castle … or a church spire in the background and trees.

(AFC: 18)

Neatly contained in this wistful account, is the clear association between village or rather non-urban cricket and Englishness. This construction of Englishness, where traditions are cherished, rituals are enshrined, and hierarchy embraced, is of course profoundly class based. There is also a typically English style of playing, or rather consuming the game. Many of the players interviewed expressed the consensus that 'playing the game' in the right spirit is more important than winning, and that the post-match drink in the bar is an integral part of the match experience. And crucially, as intimated in the complaint about the sight of 'council dustbins' in the previous quotation, it is a culture of cricket that depends on a social exclusivity, as Searle has recognized:

For cricket, this mythical and pastoral game so associated with the continuity and stability of the eternal mainstream of England outside the inner cities, has for over a century been accepted as the emblem of what is pure and uncorrupted in English life, both at home and 'in the colonies'. Indeed anything else simply wasn't and isn't cricket. Yet what had been accepted as symbolic and typical of the English ethos was, and still is, institutionally often fiercely hostile to new contributions and accretions, particularly if they are viewed by its ruling elite as either urban and close to working people, or 'foreign'.

(Searle 1996: 9)

What if these cricket parvenus are not only urban, close to working people *and* 'foreign', but also better? In the case of many white clubs in parts of rural Essex, the answer seems to be to avoid playing them. We have already seen how some white clubs spurn approaches from Asian sides seeking one-off friendlies, often citing the lack of dates available for a game. Regular competition is avoided by the imposition of entrance criteria for leagues that effectively prevent all but a tiny minority of urban-based black and Asian league clubs from access. Traditionally, entrance into official leagues is made by application from a club to a committee, made up of club representatives already in the league who are able to exercise their own discretion when making a judgement. Generally speaking, criteria have related to playing factors, such as the quality and size of the pitch, and changing facilities. But, in keeping with the social nature of recreational cricket, emphasis is also placed on the need to have good social facilities such as a clubhouse and a bar. Very often, the perception amongst black and Asian clubs is that they are not being treated fairly. First of all, because many black and Asian clubs are relatively new, they do not have the private grounds and facilities possessed by many white clubs. So it is always very difficult to meet the criteria. But even when they do meet the criteria, black and Asian clubs have still had their applications rejected:

We wouldn't be able to join the top league in spite of the strength of our club. What they look for is facilities; basically they keep out the clubs they don't want. It's an old boy network.

(AFC: 31)

It is difficult to deny the accuracy of this assessment of leagues acting like an old boys' network. Many black and Asian clubs feel that the discretion held by the leagues is used to prevent their admission. For example after having been told one year that they needed to provide sight-screens, an Asian club in east London was denied admission the following year for not having a proper bar facility. This black player also expresses a sense of injustice felt by many:

From an Afro-Caribbean point of view, we do not have access to the main leagues. We have applied to join [one] league, where we were given several conditions to satisfy, which we think is totally unwarranted. Compared to other clubs in that league, they haven't got the same facilities that we have got and they are in the league.

(AFC: 30)

One of the central findings of the AFC report is that this experience of exclusion, of racism in its various guises, and of a general antipathy to the traditional English cricket ethos, has contributed to the creation of a very different cricket culture. If recreational cricket in the 'white' communities tends to be located in and on private grounds with good facilities in rural/non-urban areas, and played 'in the correct manner', then black and Asian cricket is urban, located on poorly maintained public parks, and played in a spirit of competitiveness often backed by enthusiastic vocal support. It is not merely that the two approaches co-exist, they are symbiotically related – both cultures are informed by a perception of the other. Thus, many black and Asian cricketers assert a competitive attitude as a means of denigrating the importance of etiquette, which they see as a main value in 'English' cricket. Many white cricketers, meanwhile, uphold the tradition of the post-match drink as an indispensable element of recreational English cricket, which is then used as a means of excluding black and Asian clubs in particular who are seen as unable, or unwilling, to engage with this tradition. Given the symbiotic nature of the two cultures, it should not be surprising that playing incidents (such as 'excessive' appealing of Asian fielders to the umpire) and social relations in general are tense and prone to racialization.

However, perhaps the most important finding of the AFC report was the extent to which the culture of 'English' cricket was used as a means of excluding black and Asian clubs from the official leagues. For example, of the 504 clubs known to exist in the area covered by the Essex Cricket Board, 208 were unaffiliated clubs (AFC: 3). Most of these clubs have players who are predominantly black or Asian. So the distinct cultures of cricket that were found to exist in cricket, defined primarily by ethnicity, were reflected in the *de facto* institutionalized segregation of black and Asian cricket from the mainstream.

Such processes of exclusion also powerfully operate around recruitment into county cricket, where traditionally the best league players progress. The CB report showed for example that amongst Asian and black cricketers – and indeed many white players – there was a consensus that Yorkshire County Cricket Club (YCCC) still had a 'racial problem that prevented young Asian and black cricketers from playing for Yorkshire' (p. 21) – Yorkshire CCC has the dubious distinction of being the only first class county in English cricket never to have fielded a British Asian or black cricketer in its first team during the twentieth century despite there being large numbers of Asian and black cricketers in and around Sheffield, Huddersfield, Bradford and Leeds. Most of the black and Asian cricketers in the CB report were able to recount stories of exclusion from YCCC that ranged from the informal process of YCCC being perceived as a 'white space' to more overt forms of discriminatory selection practices. One young cricketer reflected the sense of YCCC being unwelcoming territory when he said:

> I played for Yorkshire when I was 16 and I can see exactly why there's no [Asian or black players] there, 'cause I didn't fit in at all. I felt like a complete outsider. I played for about two seasons and I hated it, I really hated it. It's hard to explain, but you feel like you're on a lower level. I wanted to play cricket at a high level and that put me off completely.
>
> (CB: 21)

Such bitter experiences are clearly damaging for a county that desperately needs to encourage the development of local talent, and more so for the individuals involved. The key point here though is that such cultures of exclusion – which YCCC perhaps more than any other county has actively promoted for many years – which produce a strongly insular, ethnocentric and exclusive sense of identity has wider repercussions for how the game at a local level is then organized and played. As one young Asian player put it:

> I went for their trials, along with three other Asians. Not one of us were selected for the Yorkshire training camp, even though I knew we were good enough. This is the problem in Yorkshire. There are a lot of very talented Asian players out there but they are often passed over for white players. *The formation of the Asian leagues were simply an act of desperation, not an attempt at segregation, because we simply are not getting the opportunity which we deserve.*
>
> (CB: 21, emphasis added)

Given the irrefutable evidence of exclusionary racist practices and cultures at YCCC from the personal anecdotes of local league cricketers, to international Test players such as Viv Richards, to documented reports and studies, the response from many at YCCC has been indicative of the mis-recognition and defensive attitude identified earlier with the ECB. In June of 1999 the former

Pakistani Test captain Imran Khan innocuously asked; 'With Yorkshire, which is flooded with Asian people, how come an Asian just doesn't find a place? It baffles me. There's got to be an element of some prejudice why some players cannot get into the Yorkshire team' (quoted in *Yorkshire Evening Post*, 21 June 1999, page 13). Chris Hassell, Yorkshire's Chief Executive, immediately labelled Khan's comments 'irresponsible and ill-informed' (*Yorkshire Evening Post*, 21 June 1999, page 13), but it was left to former England captain Raymond Illingworth to produce a defence for the indefensible. Illingworth argued:

> I was disappointed that such an old chestnut as Yorkshire's inability to bring through a player from the ethnic minorities was brought up again by former Pakistan international Imran Khan. To allege racism is ridiculous.... Yorkshire have been trying to crack this particular problem for years.... Whatever we did we struggled to tempt them to come and play because they generally seemed more comfortable staying in their own environment. That, to be honest, is the major factor behind the failure of players to come through. While they stay in their own leagues they are not going to progress and it is not for the want of trying that so very few have had a chance of gaining a Yorkshire place.
>
> (Illingworth 1999: 13)

Far from racism being inherent within YCCC, the cause of discrimination is now transposed onto 'those Asians' who keep – for some unexplained reason – setting up their own leagues, thus disbarring *themselves* from progressing to the county level. Lest we forget Illingworth himself was supportive of the 'rebel tours' to South Africa during the 1980s, and was reported to have referred to Devon Malcolm, whilst manager of England during their 1995–96 tour to South Africa, as a 'nig-nog'. Furthermore, the former black English Test bowler 'Syd' Lawrence described Illingworth and playing in Yorkshire thus: 'He seems to love living up to the image of a hard-nosed Yorkshireman. I don't think I've ever played in a game against Yorkshiremen where there hasn't been a touch of racism' (CB: 33). Illingworth was also quoted in *The Sunday Times* in April 1997 as saying:

> A lot of the Asian people are not strong enough to bowl quickly. How many of the Indians have ever bowled quick? Pakistan have had one or two but only in the past few years. They are generally from northern Pakistan where the tribesman are quite tall and strong. It is a fact that a lot of West Indians, because of their physique and their looseness, can usually bowl quicker than white people.

The explicit racist biological stereotyping effused in this account is particularly disturbing as Illingworth himself has held central positions throughout Yorkshire and English cricket – variously player, captain, coach and chairman of selectors – in deciding who gets selected and who does not. For such a high-profile figure to hold such views and still believe himself not be racist is a clear indication of how 'sincere fictions' can operate.[6]

It is clear then that the distinct cultures of cricket do not exist as equals. For many predominantly white clubs, and certainly for most league umpires and officials, the traditional 'English' way of staging cricket is the 'norm' to which black and Asian players should adapt or with which they should integrate. From the white community's perspective, it is simply a case of upholding tradition, rules and procedures that have been in place for some time. In a changing multi-cultural environment, however, these same rules, values and procedures can become, *de facto*, barriers to newcomers. Allegations of separatism are then made against these newcomers, because, after all, the established clubs are merely applying the same rules and values to all – rules and values, moreover, which have 'stood the test of time'. In deconstructing this rationalization, it is useful to refer to the work of Ruth Frankenberg and Richard Dyer, who, in different ways, have explored 'whiteness' as a social construction. They argue that it is important to appreciate that whiteness, like blackness, is more than a description of colour, but carries social and political connotations. Their projects have been to identify the ways in which 'whiteness' refers to a set of un-marked and un-named cultural practices, itself 'part of the condition and power of whiteness' (Dyer 1997, p. xiv) which assist in maintaining its position of structural 'race' privilege. As Frankenberg puts it:

> Whiteness changes over time and space and is in no way a transhistorical essence ... [it] varies spatially and temporally, it is also a relational category, one that is co-constructed with a range of other racial and cultural categories, with class and gender. This co-construction is, however, fundamentally asymmetrical, for the term 'whiteness' signals the production and reproduction of dominance rather than subordination, normativity rather than marginality, and privilege rather than disadvantage.
>
> (Frankenberg 1993: 236–7)

Thus, the constructed traditions, the treasured rituals, and the current procedures for entering leagues are all different aspects of the way in which the 'whiteness' of English cricket ensures the continued subordination, marginalization and disadvantage of black and Asian cricket. It can be argued that our characterization of 'English' cricket presents a false picture of the totality of cricket in England. That, for example, at most levels of the game a strong competitive spirit is the norm, and that the notion of gentle recreational cricket played out on the village greens occupies a minor position in the sport. This misses the point. The culture of Englishness may occupy a minor position within the overall structure of the game, but that position is situated at the point – the lower divisions of the local leagues – at which newer black and Asian clubs are seeking to gain entry. Thus whilst the culture of 'English' cricket, with its dream of church spires and village greens, may not be explicitly racist, it can lead to a culture of racial exclusion. In *Raising the Standard*, the blueprint for modernizing cricket in England and Wales, the chairman of the ECB, Lord MacLaurin states:

> The sheer quantity of 'social cricket' is a great strength of the domestic game which must not be undervalued, but it is at the top end of the recreational game where the structure fails to provide the opportunity for the most talented and ambitious cricketers to fulfil their potential.
>
> (ECB 1997: 8)

Quite how 'social cricket' is a great strength for black and Asian cricketers is not clear, but then MacLaurin is referring to the domestic structure that is overwhelmingly white. It may be correct to say that it is at the top end of the recreational game that talented and ambitious cricketers are being failed by the system, but countless talented and ambitious black and Asian players are prevented and discouraged from even entering the system. In fact, action to remedy the plight and exploit the potential of black and Asian cricket is completely absent, as are any measures to restore cricket's wretched infrastructure in urban areas and the inner cities. 'Like New Labour' notes cricket writer Marqusee, '...the MacLaurin blueprint sought reform and renewal without threatening entrenched privileges' (1998: 327).

Conclusion

In this chapter we have shown how racism is a serious issue in cricket. We have argued that taken together, both the national/international level and the recreational game provide the boundaries within which a discourse of racism operates. In seeking to make sense of this discourse, we have identified three analytically discrete dimensions of racism: overt racist abuse, based on 'race' hatred; racial stereotyping based on cultural racism; and racial exclusion based on a racism derived from a 'white' Englishness. Our argument has been that racism in cricket has drawn more on the second and third dimensions rather than the first.

We have also argued that a serious obstacle to dealing with these forms of racism has been intransigence found in the cricket establishment, especially the ECB. It is vital that the traditionally defensive reactions of the representatives of the cricketing establishment are put behind them and that they actively and publicly seek to develop policies that embrace the cricketing cultures of Asian and black communities. Whilst the ECB senior management team is not alone in the cricket world in its defensiveness, as the governing body it is in a position of power and responsibility. *Clean Bowl Racism* is to be welcomed, but only as the start of the process.

What, practically, can be done then to purge cricket of racism? Clearly, given the historical baggage and current cultural status carried by the game, it is unlikely that significant change will come without a fundamental change in the social relationships of control. The independent lobbying group, Hit Racism for

Six (HR46) formed in the wake of the Henderson article in the July 1995 edition of *Wisden Cricket Monthly*, has made a start. With HR46 having succeeded in challenging the culture of denial prevalent within the game's authorities, the next step is to raise the level of discussion, and to implement action plans to enforce change. HR46 (1999) have argued that the ECB could do much to challenge racism in the recreational game. For example it called on the ECB to convene a black and Asian cricket consultative forum; to produce an anti-racist charter and circulate it throughout the cricket world; and to commission further research into the nature and extent of racism in cricket. It is encouraging therefore that these proposals have been included in *Clean Bowl Racism*. Furthermore, it needs to be made clear to umpires that racist sledging is not 'part of the game' but something that must be met with the severest punishments and further, that umpires have a duty and an obligation to report such incidents to leagues. To quote the CB report:

> Clubs might also be held responsible for any abuse by spectators occurring at their ground. The job of the umpires would probably be made easier if the leagues issued clear guidelines on acceptable behaviour and it was recognised that they would deduct points, impose fines and ultimately bans, for those found guilty of racial abuse before during or after games.
>
> (CB: 35)

Of course it will take more than forums, charters and a rewriting of rules to rid the recreational game of racism. The ECB should also commit itself to a programme of extensive investment into inner-city/urban cricket. This should be part of a strategy based on the three 'R's of cricket development in the black and Asian communities: recognition, respect and resources. Recognition of the existence and plight of black and Asian cricket; respect for the contribution that black and Asian players make to the game; and resources to enable black and Asian clubs, and all of the cricket clubs struggling for survival in the inner-cities, to have access to good quality facilities, coaching and competitions.

Matthew Engel was right when he identified the new 'cricketing apartheid' as being a central barrier in preventing England from once again becoming a successful international Test team and the damage this was doing to the recreational game (see Field 1999). He was wrong however in defining the problem as being one that stems from a self-imposed 'opt out' of mainstream cricket by Asian and black cricketers. As we have demonstrated, this distorts the understandable and logical reaction of a part of the cricketing community whose interests and ambitions have been ignored and frustrated, as being a cause, rather than a symptom, of the developing splits within the game.

We would argue, however, that the desire to construct an integrated multicultural cricket culture is, paradoxically, far more embedded and accepted at the participatory level than it is in the corridors of power within the game. For example, it was a welcome finding from our research that when white players were asked about the arguments put forward by mono-culturalists such as

Tebbit, regarding whether Asians and blacks *had* to support England, or about Henderson's claims that subconsciously Asian and black Test cricketers wanted England to lose, there was near-universal condemnation of such positions (CB: 20–25, AFC: 35). This is important because populist racists often claim to speak on behalf of the 'ordinary man' and the so-called silent majority within England. It appears that despite the evidence of racist attitudes and beliefs amongst some sections of the white cricketing world, there also exists a strong anti-racist and egalitarian strand that needs to be acknowledged and developed. As the CB report concluded:

> There is clearly scope for working with the good intentions that abound. Recognizing the corrosive effect of racism on those in the game opens the way to what one white cricketer called a 'multi-cultural cricket culture that represents the only way forward' – acknowledging, respecting and celebrating diversity.
>
> (CB: 38)

Cricket, due to its central role in the imperial project of the British Empire, now finds itself in a situation where it can boast of a culture that is very much multi-cultural – if currently unequal. Cricket has the potential to be used as a model for a modern, democratic and multi-cultural society rather than being seen as the last cultural vestige of a pre-modern, imperial cultural formation. Of course, if the ECB were to accept the agenda for change outlined here, broader questions relating to power and control of the game would inevitably follow. Fundamentally, it would pose the question of ownership: of whose game is it anyway?

Notes

1 Funded by Leeds City Council, Leeds Metropolitan University and the Yorkshire Cricket Association.
2 Funded by the English Sports Council, the England and Wales Cricket Board, and the Greater London Regional Cricket Forum.
3 'Cricket establishment' in the cricket context generally refers to the authorities at the national, regional and local level, plus the mainstream cricket media.
4 The dominant way in which racism in football has been constructed is also problematic. In their critique of the *Kick It Out* campaign in football, Back, Crabbe and Solomos argue that a failure to understand how racism operates through a denial of 'race' has resulted in a failure by policy makers to make the game genuinely more racially inclusive (see Back, Crabbe and Solomos, this volume).
5 See Modood (1997), Sayyid (1997) and Bhatt (1997) for critical analyses of the ways in which Islam has been distorted and misunderstood in the West by racist and anti-racists alike. For a review of 'Islamophobia' see Halliday (1999).
6 In the same year that the CB report was published Illingworth was awarded an honorary degree in 1997 by Leeds Metropolitan University for 'the major contribution he had made to his profession and the community'. Despite a public protest by staff and students the university management allowed Illingworth to receive his award, although not without his having to change his acceptance speech to deny that he was

racist by listing various 'black friends' he had, and then having to sit and listen whilst acclaimed novelist Caryl Phillips – who also received an honorary award – lambasted those who worked against multiculturalism and who saw Yorkshire's identity in narrow, fixed and essentialist ways: 'The strength of this city [Leeds] is diversity. The more we know or care to know about those who are not ourselves, the more we learn about ourselves' (see 'Illingworth in row over degree award', *Guardian*, May 13 1997, p. 8; and 'On the back foot: The honorary award that landed a Leeds university in trouble', *Guardian 2*, May 27, 1997, p. iv)

Bibliography

Back, L., Crabbe, T., Solomos, J. (1998) 'Racism in football: patterns of continuity and change' in A. Brown (ed.) *Fanatics! Power, identity & fandom*, London: Routledge, pp. 71–87.

Barker, M. (1981) *The New Racism*, London: Junction Books.

Bhatt, C. (1997) *Liberation and Purity: Race, new religious movements and the ethics of post-modernity*, London: UCL Press.

Birley, D. (1979) *The Willow Wand: Some cricket myths explored*, London: Queen Anne Press.

Bradley, J. (1992) 'The MCC, Society and Empire: A Portrait of Cricket's Ruling Body, 1860–1914, in Mangan, J. (ed.) *The Cultural Bond: Sport, empire, society*, London: Frank Cass.

Carrington, B. (1998a) 'Sport, masculinity and black cultural resistance', *Journal of Sport and Social Issues*, Vol.22, No.3, August 1998, pp. 275–98.

—— (1998b) '"Football's coming home" but whose home? And do we want it?: Nation, football and the politics of exclusion', in A. Brown *Fanatics! Power, identity and fandom in football*, London: Routledge, pp.101–23.

—— (1999) 'Cricket, culture and identity: An ethnographic analysis of the significance of sport within black communities', in S. Roseneil and J. Seymour (eds) *Practising Identities: Power and resistance*, London: Macmillan.

Dore, A. (1993) 'Cricketers caught by a change of name', *The Mail on Sunday*, 14 November.

Dunning, E., Murphy, P. and Williams, J. (1988) *The Roots of Football Hooliganism: An historical and sociological study*, London: Routledge.

Dyer, R. (1997) *White*, London: Routledge.

England and Wales Cricket Board (1997) *Raising the Standard: The ECB Management Board blueprint for the future playing structure of cricket*, London: ECB.

—— (1998) *ECB Equal Opportunity and Sports Equity Policy*, 12th November 1998.

—— (1999) *Clean Bowl Racism: 'Going Forward Together'*, A report on racial equality in cricket, London: ECB.

Feagin, J. and Vera, H. (1995) *White Racism: The Basics*, London: Routledge.

Field, D. (1999) 'Wisden cites club "apartheid"', *The Independent*, 1 April.

Fleming, S. (1996) 'You Black ....!' In *Hit Racism for Six*.

Frankenberg, R. (1993) *White Women, Race Matters: The social construction of whiteness*, London: Routledge.

Gilroy, P. (1993) *Small Acts: thoughts on the politics of black cultures*, London: Serpent's Tail.

Halliday, F. (1999) '"Islamophobia" reconsidered', *Ethnic and Racial Studies*, 22, 5, 892–902.

Henderson, R. (1995) 'Is it in the blood?' in *Wisden Cricket Monthly*, July 1995, pp. 9–10.

Hit Racism for Six (1996) *Hit Racism for Six: Race and cricket in England today*, London: Wernham Press.

—— (1999) *Submission to ECB Racism Study Group.* http://www-uk.cricket.org/link_to_database/SOCIETIES/ENG/HR46/ARTICLES/ECB_SUBMISSION.html

Holt, R. (1989) *Sport and the British: A modern history,* Oxford: Oxford University Press.

Illingworth, R. (1999) 'Imran's jibes are way off the mark', in *Yorkshire Sport* (part of *Yorkshire Post*), Monday 21 June 1999, p. 13.

James, C.L.R. ([1963] 1994) *Beyond a Boundary,* London: Serpent's Tail.

Leicester Mercury (1996) 'Race-taunt claim by team', 20 August, p. 33.

Long, J., Tongue, N., Spracklen, K. and Carrington, B. (1995) *What's the difference: A study of the nature and extent of racism in rugby league,* Leeds. RFL/CRE/LCC/LMU

Long, J., Nesti, M., Carrington, B., and Gilson, N. (1997) *Crossing the Boundary: A study of the nature and extent of racism in local league cricket,* Leeds Metropolitan University.

Marqusee, M. (1998) *Anyone but England: Cricket, Race and Class,* London: Two Heads Publishing.

McDonald, I. and Ugra, S. (1998) *Anyone for Cricket? Equal opportunities and changing cricket cultures in Essex and East London,* University of East London.

Modood, T. (1997) ' "Difference", Cultural Racism and Anti-Racism' in Werbner, P. and Modood, T. (eds) *Debating Cultural Hybridity: Multi-cultural identities and the politics of anti-racism,* London: Zed Books, pp. 154–172.

Oslear, D. and Bannister, J. (1995) *Tampering with Cricket,* London: Cassell.

Rice, T. (1995) ' "Blowers" return brings breath of fresh air to box' in *The Daily Telegraph* 30th August.

Roy, A. (1998) 'Beyond the Boundary', in *India Today International,* August 17th, New Delhi: India. pp. 24h–24j.

Savidge, M. and McLellan, A. (1995) *Real Quick: A celebration of the West Indies Pace Quartets,* London: Cassell.

Sayyid, B. (1997) *A Fundamental Fear: Eurocentrism and the emergence of Islam,* London: Zed Books.

Searle, C. (1993) 'Cricket and the Mirror of Racism', in *Race and Class,* Vol. 34, No. 3, London: Institute of Race Relations, pp. 45–53.

—— (1996) 'Reinventing Cricket' in *Hit Racism for Six.*

Solomos, J. and Back, L. (1995) *Race, Politics and Social Change,* London: Routledge.

Steen, R. (1996) 'To shrug is to accept' in *Hit Racism for Six.*

4   'Black Pearl, Black Diamonds'
Exploring racial identities in rugby league

Karl Spracklen

Introduction

Rugby league is proud of its black players: from Lucius Banks, who played on the wing for Hunslet in the 1911–1912 season, through Clive Sullivan, the first black athlete to captain Great Britain in international competition in the 1972 World Cup, to Ellery Hanley, captain of the Wigan side that dominated the late eighties. Hanley – alongside the equally famous black athlete Martin Offiah – represented the finest Great Britain had to offer in its long-standing rivalry on the rugby league pitch with Australia.

Such players belong to rugby league; they have been 'denatured' and are now inside the imaginary community (Cohen 1985), compromised in their self-definition by the symbolic boundaries constructed by the sport (Spracklen 1996). Thus Hanley has entered rugby league folklore as the 'Black Pearl', a nickname that neatly defines both his otherness (his rarity, the fluke nature of the black rugby league player) and the symbolic boundaries that themselves define black identities expressed through rugby league – the nickname is expressive of Hanley's unique abilities and at the same time expressive of the colour of his skin.

This chapter is about the expressions of identity within rugby league and conceptions of 'the game', how they are grounded in discourses about history, 'northernness' and masculinity. In particular, these discourses[1] have produced the cultural norms and symbolic boundaries of an imaginary community – the game – to which rugby league fans, players, journalists and administrators belong (Spracklen 1996). As I will show, the imaginary community defines belonging and exclusion based on conceptions of a northern, male identity that is implicitly white. Asian and black people are then defined as something other than the norm within the imaginary community, and a process of negotiated identity occurs whenever Asian and black people become involved in the game. Who defines the symbolic boundaries then becomes crucial – for example, what the game means, who it is for, its history and its future, the masculine nature of the game (Spracklen 1995) are all contested.

Research on the nature and extent of racism in British professional rugby league concluded that there was a 'small but significant problem' (Long *et al.*

1995). This phrase satisfied commentators in the game who believed the problem was not really there, despite the fact that the number of Asians playing the game professionally can be counted on one hand. As a result of the report, the Rugby Football League, to its credit, launched a campaign to stamp out racial abuse and attract Asian and black children to play the game, a campaign mirrored by development work by the Bradford Bulls in the inner-city of Bradford. Strict rules on racial abuse have led to the first dismissal of a professional player for such a crime[2], though the subsequent disciplinary hearing absolved the player of intent. But racial abuse is clearly still present, both off and on the pitch.[3]

This chapter, then, analyses the imaginary community and identity in rugby league through debates about invented traditions (Hobsbawm and Ranger, 1983), the racialized Other (Gilman 1985), and perceived relationships between the sport, its history, and 'class'. It will explore the exclusivity of the imaginary community, before discussing how far Asian and black people have been 'allowed' into rugby league in England.[4]

The imaginary community

Cohen's (1985) conceptualization of the construction of a symbolic community – the imaginary community – uses the idea of invented traditions (Hobsbawm and Ranger 1983) as one means of defining symbolic boundaries. Who belongs and who does not is dependent on being able to understand these symbols. In rugby league, the symbolic boundaries are created out of shared ideas over what the game means, who should play the game, and myths and invented traditions associated with the game's past. Rugby league invents and reinvents itself as a 'white man's game' because these invented traditions are associated with an idealized past that existed before the changing migration patterns in the second half of the twentieth century.

This idea of 'inventing' or 'imagining' the past has understandably come under criticism from a number of directions. Jarvie (1993) has argued that not all traditions are invented in the present. Rather, they are selected from a range of pre-existing experiences. While this criticism extends the theory, it is clear that this selection is still taking place in the present. Following the work of Wilson and Ashplant (1988), this selection process can be seen to be biased by the interests of the present ideology. And following Baudrillard (1988) it can be argued that the pre-existing experiences and the invented experiences become conflated and impossible to distinguish from one another, that 'history [has become] instantaneous media memory without a past' (Baudrillard 1988: 22): so the real experiences, while they may have happened, are indistinguishable from the invented tradition.[5] In this chapter I shall be concerned with the historical discourses in the present, and how they are used to create boundaries and cultural icons. What Hobsbawm and Cohen are saying is that discourse, symbols, perceived realities, shared understandings, and hegemonic ideologies are far more persuasive in both defining history and identity – what actually happened, who we actually are, become meaningless questions, because we cannot answer them without recourse to these imaginings (see Hall 1992). Secondly, by speaking of imagination, we are not saying these ideas and perceptions are wrong, or false. Rather, for the people doing the imagining, it is the reality they use to shape their everyday life (Cohen 1985).

These concepts are generally applied to a notion of nationhood, of national identity. What these concepts help to delineate is what Cohen calls an imaginary community, a group of people who perceive distinct boundaries and traditions that distinguish them from 'the Other'. This imaginary community – the game of rugby league – is created through invented traditions of northern, white, working-class maleness (Spracklen 1996), using the game's past as a means of explaining the present.

The myth of northern supremacy

For members of the rugby league imaginary community there is a clear historical event that has become a foundation myth (Barthes 1972), a cultural icon: the formation of the Northern Union in 1895. Within 'the game', the formation of the Northern Union – as the Rugby Football League was known until the Australian term 'rugby league' was adopted in 1922 (Gate 1989) – is known universally as the Split (from the Rugby Football Union). This term is commonplace both in the writing of 'insider' historical texts, in the trade papers and fanzines, and in the normal discourse of people within 'the game'. For instance, one fan says that

> 'There's no way people'd let someone control us, or change the game, merge it wi union, it wouldn't happen ... cos the game's all about defiance, toffs who wunt let working lads get brokentime for missing work, y'see that's what the Split was really, defiance of the establishment, sticking it up them down south, them who think they own everything ... Split was about us, rebelling, not doffing our caps ... working class pride.'
> (Spracklen 1996: 212)

The Split, as can be seen, is used to support the invention of a culture defined by what it is not: no southerners, no toffs. The Other becomes a stereotype which is identified and excluded (Opotow 1990). It is also, according to the respondent, about working lads: about men. And by identifying a continuous line from the working class of the Split to the working class of today's community of 'the game', one hundred years of migration patterns in the north of England are glossed over – rugby league, as a historical myth used to ground a northern identity, limits that identity to people who can own and identify with the myth. Hence, the glorification of the men involved in the Split as role models for the men of 'the game'[6] denies access into 'the game' for the large Asian and black populations that live in areas of the north where rugby league is established.

By the very reference to 'The Split' one can see its importance. This event is the critical moment in the history of rugby league as it has been written in hindsight: it is the Bethlehem of rugby league, to go with the singing of Blake's Jerusalem at test matches and cup finals. It conjures up images of working-class resistance, of working-class culture, images that are debated and contested by both the members of 'the game' and outsiders within the academic community (e.g., Dunning and Sheard 1979). It is the moment that is generally agreed upon as the time of rugby league's birth, when twenty-two clubs decided to form their own league structure, administrated separately from the Rugby Football Union.

It is understandable, then, that the debate over the importance of the Split, and what the Split was about, is part of the tension within the imaginary community of rugby league. It is a clear example of history written for the present, to justify and support the ideology of the present (Wilson and Ashplant 1988). The Split is used as a definer for the culture surrounding 'the game', a definer for discourses about masculinity, class and white northern identity.

Popular interpretations of the Split draw upon the imagery of the white, northern worker demanding his right to be paid. The idea that the Split was a clear example of white working-class rebellion is maintained by popular litera-ture and the trade papers. Official history describes rugby league's origin myth as being about 'the working man' demanding his rights, throwing away the shackles of the rugby union mandarins of the middle-class south. It is this image that appeals most to the defenders of rugby league's status quo, who see in this invented tradition a powerful representation of their own class identity, and who fear that in changing 'the game' this relation with a perceived working-class heritage will be lost. In defending this image, of course, they also defend a narrow definition of masculinity and an exclusive white identity asso-ciated with the working-class founders. But the image of the working-class rebel also appeals to expansionists, who see their own aims as being a continuation of this mythical hero: the working-class man (Spracklen 1996). This image does not stand alone – it is inextricably connected to ideas of region, of masculinity, of power, and of exclusion. This sporting hero, described as white, northern, working-class male, is used to justify implicitly the symbolic boundaries of the imaginary community that let in those who resemble the hero, but excludes those who do not.

Northern man

In rugby league, these interpretations of history, the symbolic boundaries they define, the construction of community and male identity, and the relationship between them, create a 'fictive ethnicity' (Balibar and Wallerstein 1988), a belief by people within the imaginary community that their feeling of belonging is commensurable with that of social groups more easily delineated through shared experiences, origins, beliefs and culture. The term 'fictive' does not imply some deceit on the part of these people. Rather, it suggests that the idea of their exclusiveness is created by these symbolically constructed boundaries and invented traditions. Nor does the use of the term imply there are easily defined 'real' ethnicities that can be categorized, marginalized and stereotyped.

The concept also gives the people within the imaginary community a sense of belonging as an insider, an explanation for the boundaries of the community, and a description that is normalized by their interpretation of the history of 'the game'. In 1994, when I travelled to see the 'Kangaroos' in the Second Test at Old Trafford the coach I was travelling in was part of a convoy of coaches on the M62 all displaying local loyalties through scarves and names – Hull, Castleford, Leeds, Batley, Oldham. At the ground there was a carnival of regional pride and identity, displayed by grumbles about the food and sterile stadium, sponsorship by John Smith's Bitter and Regal cigarettes, and Yorkshire-Lancashire rivalry typified by chants of 'Yorkshire sheep shaggers' and 'Lancy-Lancy-Lancy-Lancy-Wankyshire'. In the crowd, this feeling was summed up by a banner that declared 'Great Britain: the pride of the North'. As locality and town loyalties prove to be important in 'the game', rugby league is also associated with a larger place, which gives it another imagined facet: the north of England. An analysis of the distribution of rugby league clubs in this England, both professional and amateur, shows that an overwhelming majority fall into the 'M62 Belt', with another large density of clubs along the West Coast of Cumbria.

Thus, there is a strong sense of 'northernness' among the players, supporters and administrators of rugby league. This perceived natural relationship between rugby league and the north of England is identified by traditionalists who see in the 'northern game' an expression of their distinctive fictive ethnicity and its attendant culture (Moorhouse 1989). For example, one respondent at an amateur rugby league club told me that rugby league 'is a northern game ... [it's] been – the rules, the way all this – [has been shaped] by northerners' (Spracklen 1996: 220). Others spoke of the relationship between this mythical 'northernness' and 'the game' through the way in which 'northernness', northern identity, was expressed in and through 'the game'. Another respondent explained about how 'the game' gave him – as an outsider – a template for the 'northern' form-of-life (Wittgenstein 1968), how it 'showed me a way of living, admitted me into a world where I belonged ... rugby league has this love affair with its people, its geography, you can't separate it from where it is, it is so involved' (Spracklen 1996: 221).

The implication is that 'the game' is inextricably linked to a sense of northern identity that is justified with recourse to the past, and which is expressed through the values seemingly inherent in 'the game' such as working-class honesty, 'pride', distinctiveness, manliness, toughness and physicality, equality of opportunity – 'a chance for any man to play according to his ability', and tension with southerners and the middle class. This sense of northern identity is seen as a source of strength for traditionalists, who see the relationship as natural and unassailable, and an articulation of their own sense of personal and social identity.

Implicit throughout the construction of a northern identity is an understanding that the identity constructed is masculine: it is northern man (Spracklen 1996). Given the way in which the imaginary community produces, maintains, affirms and expresses masculine identity – particularly the hegemonic masculinity of Western society (Messner and Sabo 1990) – it is not too surprising to find his equivalent northerner present in the discourse surrounding 'northerness', particularly in rugby league and the invented traditions of 'the game'. It is this northern man that is the template for the fictive ethnicity of the population of the imaginary community, the cultural icon that defines belonging, that is supported by the invented traditions, and which shapes shared meanings, mutual knowledge (Giddens 1984), and symbolic boundaries. Hence even southerners are excluded from the definitions of proper belonging in 'the game' and women struggle to be accepted on equal terms to men if they take on roles other than the passive supporter or the wife/girlfriend. The tension within the imaginary community between differing expressions of masculinity and traditionalists and expansionists can also be analysed as a struggle over the definition of this cultural icon, and the traditions and symbolic boundaries associated with it.

And, as argued earlier, northern man is, of course, white. He is defined by invented traditions associated with white, working-class communities. He is the exemplar of a beer-drinking, small-town, masculine culture. But his 'whiteness' is also hidden. It is an implicit but implied ethnicity that is invisible except to those Asian and black people who could play and watch rugby league whom it excludes.

Black identity, white pride

As argued earlier, the imaginary community of rugby league as defined in relation to the Other (Opotow 1990) is clear: it is *not* southern, *not* homosexual, *not* feminine, *not* middle class, and *not* for those who do not understand the language and myths of 'the game'. Northern man is a product of historical imagining. He is not a representation of the geographical, contemporary north of England. Northern man is, in the definitions of 'the game',

> 'a picture of someone who is short rather than tall, muffled at the throat with a scarf that's probably white ... or, alternatively ... someone propping up a bar with a pint at his elbow or in his fist. That, according to the mythology, is typical Northern working man; therefore Rugby League'.
>
> (Moorhouse 1989: 45)

In defining belonging as synonymous with northern man and his attendant historical myths, a boundary is created between those who can associate with him, and those who cannot. Northern man belongs to a stage in recent history that is before the post-war movement of Asian and black people to this country. As such, northern man and 'the game' of rugby league take on an implicitly white identity, and Asian and black people in the north of England are not seen as part of the normalized imaginary community.[7]

The first part of this chapter has sketched out the beginnings of a conceptual background to the racialization of notions of rugby league, belonging and identity. It is time now to turn to research which shows how discourses actually materialize in terms of racial discrimination.

Racial discrimination in rugby league

As mentioned earlier, research into the nature and extent of racism in rugby league (Long *et al.* 1995; Long and Spracklen 1996; Long, Carrington and Spracklen 1997) has shown that there is a small but significant problem within 'the game'.[8] The caveat of 'significant' has, however, been largely ignored in favour of the 'small' – problems still persist of racial abuse on the terraces and on the pitch, and the numbers of Asian and black players and spectators remain low (a head count by myself at a first division game three years after the 1995 report showed that although there were three black players on the pitch, out of thirty-four, there was only one black face in the crowd, out of approximately two thousand).

A survey of fans' attitudes in the 1995 report was even more telling. Of those sampled, 13 per cent of rugby league supporters who were willing to admit it[9] believed it was acceptable to abuse a player just because the player happened to be black. The Rugby Football League's 'small but significant' is a strange compromise: 13 per cent is totally significant to the Asian and black players at all levels who are at the receiving end of the abuse.

The report found that Asian and black participation in rugby league at an administrative and spectator level was negligible – out of over thirty-one thousand fans, the report counted only twenty-four Asian and black spectators (Long *et al.* 1995). In terms of numbers on the playing field, there was an almost complete absence of Asian players. Though black players were not under-represented (Long *et al.* 1995), there was clear evidence of 'stacking' (which I will discuss later).

Given the size of the Asian and black populations in the towns along the 'M62 Belt'[10], one would have expected to see Asians and blacks at all levels of 'the game'. However this is not the case. Long *et al.* (1995) explore a number of reasons for this, and although racist abuse is a factor, more telling are the stereotypes and assumptions made by white people within 'the game', particularly those in positions of power such as coaches and chairs[11], and the image of 'the game' described earlier. As one white player explained, in trying to work out why Asians were not involved more in rugby league, 'A lot might think it's a northerner's kind of sport, pits and all that, all white men, aggressive, hard … they just don't want abuse' (Long *et al.* 1995: 36).

Asians were seen as being culturally bound, preferring cricket or avoiding mud and contact because of 'religion'. As one chairman (for they were all men) of a professional club put it, in trying to explain the under-representation of professional Asian players, 'Asians cannot wear turbans in the scrum' (Long et al. 1995: 27). Biological explanations were also offered in trying to account for the lack of Asian participation, some even suggesting that Asians were not built for the game. Finally, it was suggested that Asians just were not interested in rugby league. While this may be true for some individuals (especially given the white imagery and identity implicit in 'the game'), according to two of the players interviewed (Long et al. 1995: 40–41) there are enough Asians who want to play rugby league.

An explanation can be provided by understanding the tacit racism that exists in rugby league's imaginary community. The imaginary community of rugby league is bounded by 'northernness', by a 'white' identity. Asian people are simply not welcome, as white people try and protect 'their game's' heritage – and the white northern male identity created by that heritage. Asian and black people are denied access to the symbolic boundaries because people in the game fear that their own identities will be compromised if the power to change those boundaries is shared.

Black players entering 'the game' also find it hard to overcome stereotypes. Unlike their white counterparts, black players do not have the same familial and social access to 'the game', they start out as outsiders already objectified as the Other (Opotow 1990). They have to prove themselves, while at the same time receiving abuse because of the colour of their skin (Holland 1995). They are being stereotyped according to racist beliefs about biological attributes (Long, Carrington and Spracklen 1997) which leads to some playing positions being available to them such as the wing and second row, and others being denied: what Phillips (1976) calls 'stacking'.[12] It is clear that 'the game' – being culturally associated with these invented traditions that imply a certain white, northern, working-class male hero – is unattractive to some Asian and black sports fans and athletes. And at the same time, those who do wish to be involved in 'the game' find racism and prejudice built into the boundaries of the imaginary community in the form of shared history and meanings which they do not share, and stereotypes and assumptions (Gilman 1985).

The idea that black players do not grow up in 'the game' is given credence from research into the creation of identity in English rugby league (Spracklen 1996). At one amateur club a black player who joined for a season only did so, according to one white respondent, because he was spotted by another player in a nightclub. His size, the white player felt, made him suitable for rugby league, and the black player was encouraged to join at a time when the club was short of big players. Another black player, Neville Livingstone, has continued in the amateur game after a career as a professional player which included spells as a coach. Livingstone was born in the West Indies, but moved to England as a youngster. At school in West Yorkshire he was the only black boy in a class of white boys, who all supported the local team – to fit in, he began to play for the school team, though his parents disapproved of his playing what they felt was 'a rough game for beer-bellied white men'

(Spracklen 1996: 228). Livingstone used rugby league as a means to (im)prove himself 'as a man' and gain acceptance into predominantly white social circles. However, even though he worked hard and became a moderately successful professional, he found all the problems described by Long *et al.* (1995):

> 'It [racism] ... it's still in t'game, but not now as prevalent ... as a professional you have to ignore it, don't let it get to you ... some players do it ... but you can't give away a penalty. [You] just have to smile, to diffuse the situation.'
>
> (Spracklen 1996: 228)

Although he did not explicitly say why, his brief tenure as a coach at a professional club in West Yorkshire was fraught with problems of discipline and differing opinions between himself and some of the players and directors, and it may be that racism was a factor. However, this speculation must be compared to this professional club's record of black involvement, which has produced a number of quality juniors, and which has had for the last twenty years a higher than average proportion of black players in its ranks.

The report by Long *et al.* (1995) focused on the professional game. Anecdotal evidence at the time of the report suggested that the levels of racism were higher in the amateur game.[13] At amateur level, Livingstone suggested that racism, especially overt abuse, was worse than in the professional game, and this tallies with some of the comments in Long *et al.* (1995). As a player-coach of a team he set up in an area where a large number of Asian and black people dwell, Livingstone is proud of the fact his team is not an all white pub team (when I interviewed him he had four black players and one Asian player in his squad – later another Asian player joined, who according to Livingstone was good enough to play professionally). However, the league they play in is a regional league, with many teams operating out of small villages with few 'non-white' families, where Livingstone's team suffers regular abuse from the players and spectators. This occurred frequently at another amateur club (see Spracklen 1996) when they had a black player on their team, though their own fans themselves made racist comments when the team played a club like Livingstone's from the inner city (Spracklen 1996: 229).

Another black respondent, a player at a professional club, felt that rugby league was potentially a sport that welcomed everyone, and he suggested that the other black players in the team were part of 'the rugby league family'. However, he was not enjoying his time at this professional club as he was on the fringes of the first team and felt he was being deliberately ignored. He did not blame the club or coach for being racist, but he still felt that:

> 'you feel it, you start to think – is it cos of my colour? Is it cos I'm a black man? ... you can't win, when you're playing good everyone loves you, but you get dropped and you just disappear, so people think 'he's just after the money' ... I mean, money's important, that's why I play, that's why anyone

plays, really, but you wonder maybe white players aren't seen as mercenaries'.

(Spracklen 1996: 229)

For the black men in the white man's game, there is an extra burden to deal with – they are constantly judged with their colour in mind (Holland 1995). The belief that this particular respondent was only in the game for the money is something that is often said about the 'outsiders' who make the grade, whether they be southerners, foreigners, blacks or union converts. Whilst conducting field research (Spracklen 1996) I was told that certain black players like Ellery Hanley and Martin Offiah 'couldn't give a shit about rugby league, they're not bothered about tradition, they just want our cash'. The use of the possessive 'our' is significant – even though both players mentioned have boosted rugby league's national profile, and have helped teams like Widnes, Wigan and Leeds to success (as well as the national side), they were still seen as 'not ours', and as such dismissed as uncaring mercenaries (when in fact both players have expressed pride in rugby league as 'their' game).

It seems that playing for money, as a living, is seen as morally inferior to playing rugby league for the love of 'the game', an attitude that paradoxically resonates with the sound of outraged defenders of rugby's amateurism in the 1890s. Yet there is a clear case of double standards – white players, those who come from 'the game', are seen as role models when they sign big contracts, unlike the black players. This corroborates the picture developed in this section, of 'the game' as inherently biased towards the attitudes and values of white men. But it also suggests that players are white working-class heroes. As one successful white player said, 'I'm always aware that I'm a figurehead for my class, a boy done good' (Spracklen 1996: 230).

Conclusion: redefining the game

Rugby league is not a game for white northern men only. Women play the game and challenge dominant male ideas of both masculinity and femininity. Amateur clubs in the south of England and the London Broncos have destroyed the myth perpetuated in the media that rugby league is, in essence, a northern English game. Around the world, rugby league is played in places as diverse as Morocco and the Cook Islands, and in New Zealand the game serves a means of defending and maintaining Polynesian cultural identities against a white establishment. Like all sports, rugby league is open to be used to define and shape identities.

But for rugby league to be a powerful tool in developing Asian and black cultural identities in England, there has to be a significant shift of power to give Asian and black people control over the symbolic boundaries. The game is seen as a white man's game, but this is only so because it is defined by white men. Things can and do change. Yet to enjoy rugby league in England, Asian and black people not only have to face tacit and overt racism and assumptions about the game that are themselves based on definitions of white masculinity, they also have to make compromises over their own identity. As yet it seems that very few Asian and black people have been willing to face the 'whiteness' in the imaginary community and subvert the masculine discourse to reinvent and recreate their own identities.

However, things can change. One of the findings from both Long *et al.* (1995) and Spracklen (1996) is that many within the game of rugby league believe it to be a genuinely family-oriented, community sport. In 1997, the Rugby Football League launched a thirteen-point action plan to tackle racism and encourage the development of rugby league in Asian and black communities. In 1999, a team from the south of England, London Broncos, reached the Challenge Cup Final at Wembley Stadium, challenging conceptions of 'northernness' in the imaginary community. If the game itself can begin to address the problems it faces then the future need not be constrained by the imagery of pit-heads, pies and pints which has been so detrimental to Asian and black involvement in the game. If this is so, then there may be a whole new generation of Martin Offiahs and Ikram Butts, who are able to embrace (and be embraced by) rugby league without their racial identities being questioned in the process. If rugby league can lose the black diamonds of coal, it may be able to lose nicknames like the Black Pearl.

Notes

1 By discourses I mean the discussions, commentaries, representations and taken-for-granted assumptions that help to inform our understandings about a particular phenomenon.

2 The incident occurred in the 1998 season, when a Bramley player was dismissed from the field for racially abusing an opposition player in a match against York.

3 Incidents of racist comments in the crowd are recorded frequently in the rugby league press. In the fanzine *The Greatest Game* (32: pp. 3–4) Michael O'Hare has suggested such comments are on the increase. Racist abuse from players and spectators has also led to the resignation of one team from the Leeds and District Sunday League (*Open Rugby*, 209: p. 49).

4 In 1999, Ikram Butt became a rugby league development officer for Bradford Council, with a specific brief to encourage the game in areas of the city with large communities of people of Kashmiri descent.

5 For example, the England victory in football's 1966 World Cup and the invented tradition that this victory secured the election of Harold Wilson and the Labour Party.

6 Women are only allowed to access the imagery through the male identifications, and even then they are given a subservient role as wife or mother (Spracklen, 1996).

7 While agreeing with Miles (1993) that 'race' as a concept emerges out of the explicitly racist nineteenth-century pseudo-scientific discourses developed from the biological and social Darwinian beliefs in biological distinct 'races', I follow the position of Anthias and Yuval-Davis (1993) that 'race' needs to be maintained as an analytical concept as it alerts us to the ways in which it is operationalized in everyday life as a discriminatory tool. Thus, whilst being aware of the dangers in reifying 'race', it is still sociologically productive to use the term ourselves in an attempt to show the complexity and contradictions inherent in racial dialogue. In other words, 'race' is still an important sociological concept, despite its lack of biological validity. Further, while acknowledging that the use of the nomenclature 'Asian' (and indeed 'black', by which I mean people of sub-Saharan African descent) as a way of marking a

homogeneous cultural group within England is erroneous – see Johal in this volume, it is used here as it was the simplified category used in the work in rugby league by Long et al. (1995).

8 The report examined the extent of racism through a three-fold methodology. Fans at six grounds were given the chance to fill in survey forms and place them in collection points anonymously; twelve white, Asian and black players were interviewed in a semi-structured manner; and club officials were sent questionnaires to fill in and return anonymously to the researchers.

9 The report did not take into account people who may hold racist views but are unwilling to divulge them, albeit in a confidential and anonymous manner.

10 Towns and cities such as Salford, Rochdale, Oldham, Huddersfield, Halifax, Bradford, Dewsbury and Leeds, all of which have professional rugby league clubs.

11 Ikram Butt, a retired professional rugby league player of Asian descent, has claimed that throughout his career only one coach ever made allowances for his Muslim faith (*Total Rugby League*, 23 April 1999).

12 Research has shown that 'stacking' occurs in certain sports whereby black players are 'stacked' in disproportionate numbers in certain playing positions (due to the perceived natural abilities of blacks) which are usually those which are related to greater athleticism – for example, in American football blacks occupy the positions of running-back and wide-receiver disproportionately. Linked to stacking is the concept of 'centrality' which sees certain positions as being more central to a team's chances of winning. These central positions are thus accorded greater cognitive responsibility and it is these 'central' positions that white players tend to dominate. For example, Maguire (1991) identifies stacking in football and rugby union.

13 Amateur rugby league is played throughout the country, but most amateur clubs are based in the old counties of Yorkshire, Lancashire and Cumberland.

References

Anthias, F. and Yuval-Davis, N. (1993) *Racialised Boundaries: Race, Nation, Gender, Colour and Class and the Anti-Racist Struggle*, London: Routledge.

Balibar, E. and Wallerstein, I. (1988) *Race, Nation, Class: Ambiguous Identities*, London: Verso.

Barthes, R. (1972) *Mythologies*, London: Cape.

Baudrillard, J. (1988) *America*, London: Verso.

Cohen, A. P. (1985) *The Symbolic Construction of Community*, London: Tavistock.

Dunning, E. and Sheard, K., (1979) *Barbarians, Gentlemen and Players*, Oxford: Martin Robertson.

Gate, R. (1989) *The Illustrated History of Rugby League*, London: Arthur Baker.

Giddens, A. (1984) *The Constitution of Society*, Cambridge: Polity.

Gilman, S. (1985) *Difference and Pathology: Stereotypes of Sexuality, Race and Madness*, London: Cornell.

Hall, S. (1992) 'The question of cultural identity', in S. Hall (ed.) *Modernity and its Futures*, Cambridge: Polity, pp 273–325.

Hobsbawm, E. and Ranger, T. (eds) *The Invention of Tradition*, Cambridge: Cambridge University Press.

Holland, B. (1995) 'Kicking racism out of football: An assessment of racial harassment in and around football grounds', *New Community*, 21: 567–586.

Jarvie, G. (1993) 'Sport, nationalism and cultural identity', in L. Allison (ed.) *The Changing Politics of Sport*, Manchester: Manchester University Press.

Long, J., Tongue, N., Spracklen, K., and Carrington, B. (1995) *What's the Difference?*, Leeds: Leeds Metropolitan University/The Rugby Football League/Leeds City Council.

Long, J., and Spracklen, K. (1996) 'Positional Play: Racial stereotyping in rugby league', *Bulletin of Physical Education*, 32, 1: 18–23.

Long, J., Carrington, B., and Spracklen, K. (1997) ' "Asians cannot wear turbans in the scrum": Explorations of racist discourse within professional rugby league', *Leisure Studies*, 16, 4: 249–260.

Maguire, J. (1991) 'England's elite male Afro-Caribbean soccer and rugby union players', in G. Jarvie (ed.) *Sport, Racism and Ethnicity*, London: Falmer, pp 94–123.

Messner, M. and Sabo, D. (eds) (1990) *Sport, Men and the Gender Order*, Champaign: Human Kinetics.

Miles, R. (1993) *Racism After 'Race Relations'*, London: Routledge.

Moorhouse, G. (1989) *At the George*, Sevenoaks: Hodder and Stoughton.

Opotow, S. (1990) 'Moral exclusion and injustice: An introduction', *Journal of Social Sciences* 46, 1: 1–20.

Phillips, J. (1976) 'Towards an explanation of racial variations in top level sports participation', *International Review of Sport Sociology*, 11, 3: 39–53.

Spracklen, K. (1995) 'Playing the ball, or the uses of league: Class, masculinity and rugby', in G. McFee *et al.* (eds) *Leisure Cultures: Values, Genders, Lifestyles*, Eastbourne: Leisure Studies Association, pp105–120.

Spracklen, K. (1996) *Playing the Ball: Constructing Community and Masculine Identity in Rugby*, unpublished PhD thesis, Leeds Metropolitan University.

Wilson, A. and Ashplant, T. (1988) 'Present-centred history and the problem of knowledge', *The Historical Journal*, 31, 2: 253–274.

Wittgenstein, L. (1968) *Philosophical Investigations*, Oxford: Blackwell.

5 'Lions and black skins'

Race, nation and local patriotism in football

Les Back, Tim Crabbe and John Solomos

Introduction

What distinguishes football as a form of popular culture is that it can provide one of the key vehicles for the ritual articulation of identity, be it through the expression of regional pride, local patriotism or national belonging. Equally, football makes available a means for expressing the boundaries of inclusion, exclusiveness, xenophobia and racism. Evidence of racism in football first became a subject of widespread concern in the late seventies and eighties, a time when there was increasing racist behaviour related to football and attempts by extreme right-wing movements to use football as a basis for recruitment (Clarke 1973, 1978). Groups such as the National Front were regularly seen selling their newspapers and magazines outside football grounds. But interest in the issue was also partly related to the increasing presence of black players amongst the ranks of professional footballers during the period since the 1970s. With the emergence of black players at all levels of football, phenomena such as racist chanting and abuse directed at them became a common occurrence at many football grounds. What was striking about the fan racism of this period was the premeditated quality it possessed. Fans would prepare to perform their racism by taking bananas to throw at black players or writing hate mail letters. Cyrille Regis played alongside two other black players – Laurie Cunningham and Brendon Batson – for West Bromwich Albion in the early eighties. He remembered:

> 'We used to get letters all the time, you know ... When I was called up for England for the first time there was a letter, an anonymous letter saying 'If you go to Wembley and put on an England shirt you'll get one of these through your knees'. There was a bullet in the envelope.'[1]

The earliest discussions of racism in football tended to see the phenomenon as an extension of the problem of football hooliganism, often connected closely with support for the national team (Williams, Dunning and Murphy 1989). The portrait of racism offered in most studies is limited to the behaviour of young white working-class men, in which racism and hooliganism are coupled as mutually reinforcing social phenomena. What we want to argue is that the relationship between racism and football culture is more complex than is often assumed.

The 1990s has seen an overall decline of overt racist chanting in football crowds and the emergence of fan-led campaigns and new multi-agency anti-racist campaigns (Kick It Out 1999). In 1995 The Advisory Group Against Racism and Intimidation (AGARI) was set up to bring all the major footballing authorities together as a forum to discuss strategies for countering racism. The group initially involved the Commission for Racial Equality, the Football Asso-ciation, the Professional Footballers' Association, the FA Premier League, the Football Trust, the League Managers' Association, the Football Supporters' Association and the National Federation of Football Supporters' Clubs. The group was expanded to include representatives from the Football League and a wider variety of other football agencies. The nineties have also seen the arrival of sizeable numbers of continental European players and this has in turn led to new responses among football supporters. We want to suggest that the forms of racist practice in football are shifting from the premeditated and crude manifes-tation seen during the seventies, towards spontaneous, implicit and socially embedded forms of racist expression.

What we want to do in this chapter is to make a case for trying to situate the discussion of racism within the local ecology of social relations that give football meaning for its devoted fans. In this respect we are arguing for a sensitive appre-ciation of both the enduring ways in which racism is given voice by white football fans without recourse to the all too familiar archetype of the thumb-head white working-class thug. It should be made plain at the outset that we are in no way attempting to explain away, justify or defend the popular racism still evident amongst football fans. Rather, the ethical position we want to occupy is both critical of the racist fan vernaculars, while remaining suspicious of the tendency to caricature 'the racist' as a degenerate working-class folk devil (Back, Crabbe and Solomos 1996). As we have argued elsewhere, focusing on working-class racism in this way makes invisible the racisms that reside in the board-rooms, football institutions and training grounds (Back, Crabbe and Solomos 2001). At this point we want to shift back in time and journey into one of the most misrepresented and reviled corners of English football culture, namely the ex-dockland districts of south-east London where Millwall FC's ground is located. The ethnographic interlocutor for the Millwall research is Les Back – a white researcher with a longstanding connection with this part of south London and the politics of race found there – while Tim Crabbe conducted the ethno-graphy of England fans discussed later in the chapter. This said, the concerns and ideas generated throughout this argument are very much the result of a three-way collaboration.[2]

Love and hate in south-east London – 2 May 1998, the new den

The sun is shining on south London's industrial wasteland as Millwall Football Club prepares for its last home game of the season. It's been a bad season, the club is verging on bankruptcy and has languished in the bottom half of the English Nationwide League Division Two. Millwall, although never really a successful club on the pitch, has occupied a central and iconic place in English football. The lack of on-field success has been more than made up for by its tradition of passion, sometimes violently expressed, and pride. The club's symbol is the rampant blue Lion and its stadium is referred to ominously as 'The New Den'. Located in the former dockland areas of London, in the seventies and eighties the club and its supporters became branded the quintessential manifestation of football hooliganism, xenophobia and racism. Everyone in football, it is said, from the highest-ranking Football Association official to the lowliest opposition fan, loves to hate Millwall.

For fans particularly, the lure of Millwall is part of why it is loathed. The visitor's aversion to straying into this corner of south-east London is more than compensated for by the cache of bar-room folklore engendered by those male adventurers who made the journey into this metropolitan heart of darkness and lived to tell the tale. The grudging respect offered to Millwall fans is garnered because they have proved so resistant to the wider changes in English football, including the move to all-seater stadiums, the growing numbers of middle-class fans and the decline in football-related violence. For many – friend and foe alike – Millwall is one of the last vestiges of unfettered white working-class male culture. Having said this, the Millwall fan community is not only a male bastion. Throughout the club are numerous working-class women of all ages who share the men's passion for Millwall and all it stands for. On Coldblow Lane where the famous old Den stood, fans gather around a burger bar for a pre-match cup of tea. Amid the smell of fried onions and the traffic of burgers and hot dogs over the counter, a silver-haired woman called Dorothy offers predictions and insightful commentary on the state of the Millwall team. The spectacular male rituals of football violence and disorder have often eclipsed the presence of women like Dorothy and their contribution to football culture.

Approaching the walkway to the entrance of the South Stand a T-shirt seller is displaying his wares on the wall of a warehouse. One shirt sponsors a Lion backed by the Red Cross of St George and the Millwall supporter's anthem 'No-one Likes Us We Don't Care' is emblazoned across the top. Another shirt shows the American cartoon characters Beavis and Butthead in Millwall strip, their shorts dropped and their hairy behinds are 'mooning'. 'West Ham can kiss my Arse!' reads the shirt's caption directed at their hated East London rival West Ham United. This all stands in stark contrast to the spectacle of the World Cup France '98 and its international festival of corporate multiculturalism, at this point just a month away.

Today's game in the south London sunshine marks something more than just the end of the season: it is Tony Witter's last game for Millwall. In his five-year tenure at the club, Tony Witter, a little-known black centre-half and a journeyman footballer in every sense, has become something of a cult figure amongst Millwall's fans. He started his professional career relatively late in life, he first qualified as an electrical engineer before spending short periods at Crystal Palace and Queen's Park Rangers and then finally signing for Millwall. What he lacked in skill he made up for in passion, commitment and speed. In recent times Tony Witter had fallen foul of successive managers and lost his regular first team place. As I run up the stairs of the South Stand and step out into the brilliant May sun, I see the fans are on their feet giving a spontaneous ovation. Tony Witter stands in the centre circle and receives an award for making 100 appearances for the club. The crowd strike up with Witter's own personalized song, an honour only bestowed on the most revered of players. Witter's theme tune was coined during a particularly bleak winter in 1995 and it is sung, bizarrely, to the lyrics of Bing Crosby's 'Winter Wonderland': 'There's only one Tony Witter, one Tony Witter. Walking along, singing a song, walking in a Witter wonderland.' The chant is repeated over and over again. The voices of 6,000 mainly white fans swirl around the stadium in tribute to the passing of their black hero. Witter's apparent complete acceptance now and perhaps forever in this alleged den of intolerance, complicates the image of racial prejudice associated with Millwall and its status as the exemplary face of English bigotry.

What we want to argue is that the acceptance of black players like Tony Witter is actually very conditional. As Kobena Mercer has pointed out such conditional acceptance is not necessarily an indication of less racism:

> Turn to the back pages, the sports pages, and the black man's body is heroized and lionized; any hint of antagonism is contained by the paternalistic infantilization of Frank Bruno and Daley Thompson to the status of national mascots and adopted pets – they're not Other, they're OK because they're 'our boys'.
>
> (Mercer 1994: 178–9)

Further we want to suggest that these processes of accommodation may have particular local, gendered and class-inflected qualities. In order to understand how the boundaries of acceptance, and for that matter vilification, work, it is necessary to develop an appreciation of how the rules of entitlement and belonging operate within particular football fan cultures.

What follows is an exploration of the complex ways in which black players and fans both gain entry to English football culture. Sport is a ritual activity in which the relationship between race, nation and inclusion is repeatedly stated and defined, through representations of the 'us' that is manifest between the team and its devoted supporters. Here, 'race' and 'nation' function not as given entities but social forms that are staged through 'big games' and repeated sporting dramas. Their form and quality are defined through the performance itself and continuities are established through repetition. So, here 'race'[3] is not a given but the process in which 'racial difference' is invoked and connected with issues of identity, entitlement and belonging. Through focusing on the repeated or cyclical nature of this process in sport, it is possible to identify moments in which ruptures occur that may challenge the tenets of racial exclusion.

'Wearing the shirt': racism, locality and masculinity

Tony Witter was not the first black player to wear the Millwall shirt. The first player of colour to appear for Millwall was Hussein Hegazi. He was born in Cairo, Egypt on 14 September 1891. We don't know how he came to London but he made two appearances for Millwall and posed in the 1912–13 team photograph. He also played for Fulham and Dulwich Hamlet and went on to attend Cambridge University. He gained a 'blue' for football through representing Cambridge in a 2–1 victory over their rivals Oxford University in 1914. It was another fifty years until another minority player represented Millwall. On 21 December 1968 Frank Peterson made his debut as centre forward in a match at Fratton Park versus Portsmouth in front of 21,868 spectators. It wasn't a winning debut, the Lions going down 0–3. In fact, Frank never appeared on a winning Millwall side (Chapman 1998).

While Peterson never really made an impact, two black players who followed him did, namely Phil Walker and Trevor Lee. Walker and Lee made their debut on 4th December 1975 and throughout the late seventies – when the association between Millwall and hooliganism and right-wing politics were at their height – they were very popular players. Walker was a midfielder with speed, skill and application. More than anything Millwall fans admired his unflinching commitment and passion echoing the wider uncompromising male cultures of working-class dockland. During this time the archetypal representation of this was Harry Cripps, a blond-haired Londoner who came to personify the values of Millwall. Walker and Cripps, while 'racial opposites', were galvanized from the same footballing mould and loved with passion by the Millwall faithful.

So the scenes of adulation on this May afternoon are not without precedent. But the significance of the moment was not lost on Tony himself. Three weeks after the game he recounted:

> 'The preconceived idea of Millwall is of a quote 'racist club' or 'racist fans.' So it just doesn't seem to fit that such an accolade should be given to a black player. It was touching for me and it was nice to be remembered in that way.'[1]

What is telling is that the adulation of figures like Tony Witter, Phil Walker and the other black players who have played for Millwall can co-exist with overt racism, particularly when directed at opposition black players. It is often said within football that the general decline in racism in English football is due to the growing numbers of black players within the game. Current black professionals make up between fifteen and twenty per cent of all professional footballers playing in England. However, platitudes like this mask a more complex reality.

When asked about his worst moment playing for Millwall Tony Witter recounted an incident that took place during an FA cup fixture against Arsenal in January 1995. During this game Tony was matched against the England

Figure 1 Tony Witter
(Published with permission of Millwall Football Club)

Figure 2 Harry Cripps and Phil Walker – Millwall players 1976
(*Published with permission of Millwall Football Club*)

Figure 3 Tony Witter puts pressure on the Arsenal defence from a free kick
(*Published with permission of Millwall Football Club*)

international, and one of the most prominent black English players, Ian Wright. Wright himself was born and bred in south London, he had played with Witter at Crystal Palace and even had a trial at Millwall at the very beginning of his career. Wright was no stranger to the intense atmosphere at the New Den where he had watched Millwall play as a boy.[5] Here two black players – both Londoners – were pitted against each other: one loved and venerated, the other loathed and vilified. Tony recalls an incident that laid bare these tensions:

> Nigel Winterburn played a ball down the line and Ian Wright was just over the half way line tried to turn against me and I tackled him and put the ball out of play. He's gone to get the ball, it's just rolling on the track and he's gone to pick it up. The amount of racist abuse that came from the Millwall fans in the lower stand was incredible: 'black this, black that,' monkey chants and the rest. Basically, I am standing not more than five feet away from Ian. I sort of looked at them, looked at Ian and Ian shrugged his shoulders. Then I hear this voice from the crowd – 'Not you Tone, you're all right – it's Wrighty.' I think they just see a blue shirt when they look at me. But with Ian Wright they see a red shirt, then they see a black face. But do they not see my colour? Do I wear this shirt over my head?[6]

In his blue shirt Tony's racial difference was somehow dissolved, or seen to be irrelevant. The notion of 'wearing the shirt' summons in football vernacular the deepest levels of symbolic identity and commitment. It captures the embodied meanings associated with the football club as an emblem of locality and identity. This is ultimately manifest in the expected style that players perform within the game. Waiting for a coach to take a group of fans to a Millwall away fixture earlier in the season, some disquiet was registered by an older white man about a new signing who was black. His son immediately checked him: 'I don't care what colour he is as long as he wears that shirt.'[7] Tony Witter always played for Millwall with pride, passion and authority. This was his 'passport to inclusion' within the Millwall pantheon. What is telling, however, is that such an incorporation need not unsettle the wider culture of racism within these specifically working-class and often male cultural settings.

   Tony commented on the discussion he had with Ian Wright in the bar after the game that ended in a 0–0 draw.

> After the game Ian says to me: 'Witts, man, how can you play here, man?' I said to him: 'Ian, they're as good as gold *to me*.' That's the whole thing, I am playing *for them* [with emphasis].[8]

The inclusion of players like Tony Witter is engendered through the embodiment of highly localized working-class values and cultural capital.[9] The shared experiences of class and masculinity offer a terrain in which contingent forms of inclusiveness can be established across the line of colour.

This is reflected in the stadium as well as on the pitch. A small but significant number of black men have always followed Millwall largely from the district of Brockley in South London. In fact, some of the most prestigious figures in the 'hooligan firms' are black. Indeed one of the most interesting paradoxes on football is that the hooligan networks are often much more multicultural than the 'respectable fans'. This is certainly true at Millwall where the people involved in football violence, acutely aware of the fact that they are being surveyed, remain quiet and laconic inside the ground during the game. Those most commonly indulging in racist name-calling and abuse are shockingly respectable.

The position of black Millwall fans needs to be carefully evaluated. Like their white counterparts some black Millwall fans are equally vituperative in their abuse of opposition players, some of whom also happen to be black. Trevor Little, a well-known black Millwall fan, wrote in the aftermath of the replay victory against Arsenal in February 1995:

> As a black Millwall fan, what can I say? arsenal[10] 0 Millwall 2. ian wright can f**k off – there's only one Tony Witter. ian wright claims Millwall fans are racist. Just ask Tony Witter what he thinks. ian wright is a tosser. It was the most exciting night of my life, and I was glad to see the many black Millwall fans that were there. The team played 100 per cent out of their skins. I had Millwall fans hugging me, shaking my hand, jumping up and down with delight – on this great night of glory. Tell me, does colour really matter? We are called the Millwall Blackskins – Congratulations Millwall.
>
> (*The Lion Roars*, Issue 62, 1995: 30)

Accounts like these ought not to be dismissed too quickly as some ethnic equivalent to false consciousness. The sense of inclusion and involvement articulated here by Trevor Little as a black fan is deeply felt. Perhaps, this is best understood through appreciating the common points of reference he shares with his peers. In this respect the conditions of belonging are related to his participation in a working-class male cultural matrix. In this sense the inclusion of black fans is determined by their competence with embodied forms of masculine culture that operate through implicit class-coded means.

Another issue here is the status of the 'race talk' that is expressed in the footballing context. Within the ritual arena of the football ground verbal abuse can take on an altered meaning (see Bateson 1978). In this process comments, practices and actions which are invested with non-play meanings are subverted and inverted by collective agreement. Through playing, singing or shouting a negotiated alteration of meaning takes place which modifies a particular practice from what it 'stands for' in wider usage. In the footballing context this doesn't exactly dislocate the efficacy of racist language but it certainly changes its status, such that, on occasion, black fans have themselves engaged in explicitly racialized chanting. Equally, a white Lions fan remembers an incident in which this 'altered quality' was betrayed:

> There was an 80s match at The Den (can't remember who we was playing) with a group of thumbheads [skinheads] at the front of the terracing shouting out some racist stuff while about eight rows back, three youngish black guys were rolling their eyes in mock terror and pissing themselves laughing. [This incident] always comes to mind when I hear shit in the news about the 'fascists' at Millwall – yeah it's always there but it's a bit of a bad joke.
>
> (*The Lion Roars*, Issue 51, 1994: 29)

The mistake that is all too often made is that such 'race talk' is either read as 'meaningless play' or taken as 'consequential race hate' and the expression of deep felt racial animus. Rather, its true significance is found in the ambivalence between these two positions, i.e. within a mode of expression that oscillates between the ludic and the literal. In order to be able to read and ridicule racism as described in the above quotation, it is necessary to be able to explicate these taunts in their context. Such acts of subversion involve participation and proficiency in this highly class-coded and gendered oral culture. A black person who did not share these experiences or anyone else not familiar with this highly specific milieu would not see a 'bad joke' but a grotesque performance of racial zealotry.

This raises important questions about the contingent forms of inclusion that black fans and players experience within football. In many respects the boundaries of this incorporation are circumscribed by the degree of fit or compatibility with the hegemonic white working-class masculinities that form the normative centre of football culture. In keeping with the kinds of negotiations that take place between black and white young people within football culture it becomes possible for 'black cockneys' or 'blackskins' to be included as *contingent insiders* (Back 1996). These fraught inclusions mirror the same processes that operate with regard to black players. In both cases racism stands on the 'side-lines' as a potential resource to be used strategically to exclude or undermine the belonging and legitimacy of black fans and players. 'Blackskins' can be assimilated within the Millwall fan collective, but depending on circumstances and context they can be transformed into vilified 'black bastards'.

From the perspective of Millwall's white fans, high-profile black figures became almost totally assimilated, gaining notoriety and unquestioned respect. They became majestic figures within the symbolic dominion of the white fan collective and when they attended games this respect would be embodied through highly ritualized patterns of acknowledgement in the form of verbal and non-verbal greetings. This, however, does not preclude the same figures being targeted by opposing fans in a racialized fashion. Equally, white peers and even friends can indulge in the mirror-opposite forms of racialization when directed towards black fans that support Millwall's rivals. While other groups, most strikingly Britain's South Asian communities, are completely excluded and reviled through a whole range of anti-Asian songs (Back, Crabbe and Solomos 1998).

What is established is a racialized hierarchy. In order to understand this process it is important to cross the analysis of racialized identities with an understanding of how these intersect with gender relations and masculinity. Commensurable class-inflected ideals about black and white masculinity provide a common ground within black–white peer groups. Where young white men are forming alliances and friendships with black peers it is important to question the constructions of blackness they may be finding attractive. For young white men this may be located around racialized definitions of masculinity. In this sense the image of black masculinity as invulnerable, 'hard' and 'terrace tough' is alarmingly similar to racist notions of dangerous/violent 'black muggers'. At the moment when racist ideas are most vulnerable, in situations where there is intimate contact between black and white men, stereotypical ideas can be reproduced as positive characteristics to be emulated. Equally, this can operate in the sphere of sexuality revealed here in a story of inter-racial fraternity offered by a white Millwall fan. This incident took place in the aftermath of a game at Chelsea in the 1980s:

> Coming out of that game some black bloke fainted in the crush getting through the poxy stupid gate. Immediately a group of other (white) Millwall supporters shouted for order while they tried to lift the unconscious geezer to his feet. He could have literally been trampled to death in half a minute. Even so it was hard to get him upright, he seemed to weigh more than Ken Bates' head [the Chelsea Chairman]. Then I heard one of the other lifters offer an explanation – 'it's his bloody knob [penis] innit?'
> (*The Lion Roars*, Issue 51, 1994: 29)

This example of terrace humour shows that racialized constructions around black men's sexuality may underpin the affiliations established between black and white fans. The point here is that these stereotypical ideas like black men have 'big dicks' and a 'penchant for violence', may be undisturbed while black peers are integrated within the fan culture. These formulations may even be reinforced through inter-racial banter and friendship. The parameters of black inclusion in this class-defined cultural milieu are relatively narrow. It excludes black women or black men who adopt other versions of black masculinity more centrally placed within the rituals of London's black alternative public sphere.

The important point to reiterate here is that particular 'passports to inclusion' within this version of local patriotism are issued through shared participation in class-inflected and masculine notions of local identity. While this admits black male fans, it does so on quite specific and racially scripted terms. We want to argue two things: firstly, it is important not to over-politicize these involvements beyond a kind of prosaic coming to terms around localized forms of legitimate entitlement and belonging; secondly, that the nature of these ambiguous dialogues have been ignored within the wider attempts to address racism in football, precisely because they are not easily rendered comprehensible within the established frameworks for anti-racist campaigning that viewed racism as a component part of a broader definition of unwanted anti-social behaviour. It is telling that the emphasis of the Kick Racism Out of Football Campaign was shifted in large part because of the insistence of the Football League who wanted a focus on intimidatory behaviour in the broadest sense. This contributed to the decision of the Advisory Group Against Racism and Intimidation – the campaign's steering group – to adopt the twin themes of 'Let's Kick Racism' and 'Respect All Fans' during the 1995–6 football season.

The notion of local identity articulated through football fandom does not correspond to any ethologically coherent 'urban community.' This version of the 'local' is embodied around the repeated or routine rituals of football fandom. Here, community is sustained through repetition, and acts of collective definition or what we want to call iterative processes. In the Millwall case, it keeps alive the memory and history of local community that in many respects is no longer evident in the immediate surroundings of the ground. One of the striking features of this culture is how the language of south London local patriotism can endure even in circumstances where patterns of urban 'white flight' mean that many fans no longer live in the south London area, but in the suburban hinterlands of Kent and beyond. Our argument, put simply, is that the complex and ambiguous nature of black entry into class-based football cultures needs to be taken seriously, particularly in the context of 'local' footballing rituals. Here we want to examine how these relationships compare and connect with articulations of race and nation around the England national team.

'Ain't no black in the Union Jack': England and the politics of race and nation

As mentioned earlier, the English national side has been the context in which the most extreme form of racially exclusive nationalism has been harnessed to football culture. During the seventies and eighties England fans would regularly sing 'There ain't no black in the Union Jack, send the bastards back!' This was also combined with Unionism and opposition to Irish Republicanism, where England fans would sing 'No Surrender to the I.R.A.' with equal venom. More recently this was brought into focus during a match between the Republic of Ireland and England in Dublin in February 1995, which led to the eventual abandonment of the game, in the midst of scenes of violence on the terraces. The events in Dublin focused attention on the supposed influence of organized racist groups, such as C18,[11] over sections of football supporters, particularly those that follow the national team. While the impact of C18 is debatable, the prevalence of racist rhetoric within the subculture of England support is without question. As one of the England supporters interviewed after the Dublin events showed:

> You've got to show pride in your team. It's fucking pride. It's Eng-erland we follow. I mean, I know two blokes who are in Combat 18 because they believe in the English, no black in the Union Jack and all that. I mean I'm really there for the football, but I do agree with them.
>
> (*The Guardian*, 17th February 1995)

There is little doubt that a small proportion of fans with ultra right-wing political leanings attempt to attach themselves to football culture. In the ethnographic work conducted with England fans for this research, a minority of fans showed a clear interconnection in their accounts between English nationalism, Ulster Unionism and popular racism. Here the racism was defined through overt political content and ideological affiliations with Ulster Unionism and white patriotism, as compared against the local forms of neighbourhood nationalism evident amongst clubs like Millwall.

During the European Championships held in England (Euro '96) there was a concerted attempt to whip up jingoism by the tabloid press, particularly in the run up to the semi-final match between England and Germany.[12] The Euro '96 tournament was significant in other ways. It marked a real attempt to assert a benign patriotism. Ben Carrington (1998) has argued persuasively that this project brought with it a more coded form of racially exclusive Englishness, that combined the new laddism enshrined in Frank Skinner and David Baddiel's 'Football's Coming Home' lyrics with a new form of cultural racism. This version of patriotism appealed to a 1966 nostalgia that whitened and purged the national character of racial difference. One of the more notable spectacles of Euro '96 was the thousands of English fans with their faces painted with the Red Cross of St George. Carrington suggests in his analysis of this conjuncture that implicit within the coverage of the event is the way Englishness is coded as white.

While journalists and television presenters deployed this notion of racial nationalism through implicit and normative means, the significance of this was not lost on the racist right in Britain. John Tyndall, then leader of the neofascist British National Party, wrote in the aftermath of the tournament: 'What was noticeable in the demonstrations of crowd patriotism ... was the overwhelming whiteness of those taking part' (Tyndall 1996: 7). Tyndall goes on to lament reports that during the dramatic semi-final against Germany, which ultimately resulted in England's defeat by a penalty 'shoot-out,' more than half of a poll of Afro-Caribbean football enthusiasts were cheering for Germany. Tyndall's article is written from the perspective of a racial nationalist wagging his finger at liberal multiculturalism. However, there were signs during Euro '96 of shifts that Tyndall would be less comfortable with.

Vince, a black England fan, recounted a series of incidents he experienced during the tournament, which suggested that small-scale renegotiations were occurring around issues of race, nation and belonging (see Back et al. 1998). He described an incident that took place in the toilet at Wembley Stadium during the half-time interval. Vince is a well-known fan – he has appeared on a TV football fan programme – so in addition to being one of the few black English fans he is also conspicuous because of his involvement in the media:

> I'm in the toilet – right – and I've gone in the cubicle and I've locked the door. Then these two white Villa fans come in behind me and they obviously don't know I'm in the cubicle. They go: 'Did you see that fucking

cunt from [the TV] upstairs, he's a cunt.' Then they just started singing: 'English, white and proud of it, English, white and proud of it.' Then I come out the toilet – right. And they looked and they just looked at me and sort of like stared. It went totally silent 'cause there were loads of people in there, and then I answered them: 'English, black and proud of it, English, black and proud of it'. And they all just laughed ahhhhhh![13]

This incident could have quite easily had a very different outcome. Vince could have been attacked but he was not. In that micro-political moment the racial circumscriptions around Englishness were opened so that Vince could legitimately be 'English, black and proud of it'. In these lived interactions the meanings of race and nation are prised open, revealed and momentarily transcended. Such forms of acknowledgement and racial inclusion are perhaps more temporary and contingent than those described in the local context. It is entirely plausible that the inclusion of black fans like Vince can occur simultaneously with complexly articulated forms of racist culture.

England away: black England fans abroad

It is important to look at the admittedly small numbers of black and Asian fans who follow the England team, because their experience reveals the articulation between race and nation and the limitations of a more inclusive notion of national identity. At least seven black fans were encountered by Tim Crabbe during the course of his trip to Poland in 1997 and, from a much larger sample, almost thirty at the England World Cup matches in Marseilles and Toulouse. What was interesting about a significant number of these fans, though, was their proximity to some of the violent disturbances, which took place in these locations which are typically characterized as the product of an essentially 'white' English subculture. In one incident in Katowice, after a minor confrontation with the Polish police had been headed off through a retreat into a bar at the bottom of the main street, several fans attempted to encourage a movement back outside in order to 'save face'. The most prominent of these supporters was a tall black fan, probably in his mid to late twenties who was pushing his way to the front shouting 'Well come on let's go back outside ... what are we doing hiding in here? We are England? Let's get out, let's get at 'em. Why do we stand around? Why do we hide in the pub?' About thirty or forty fans followed his lead and regrouped outside the pub before the main body of England fans reappeared and an elaborate game of 'cat and mouse' took place between Polish and English supporters and the police. Later on in the day, another black supporter who was with the predominantly white West Ham fans was centrally involved in the confrontation with the rival 'firm' of Aston Villa supporters and the running battles with Polish supporters outside the stadium.

Other black fans on the trip were not involved in any of the observed incidents but all of the black supporters seen in Poland and the majority of those in France for the World Cup were located within broader groups of white supporters. What these multi-racial alliances seem to indicate, in the context of support for the England team is the significance of the cultural forms associated with England supporters rather than the racial appearance of those involved. As we have already seen in our discussion of 'local' fan cultures the boundaries circumscribing black fans' inclusion within such arenas can be dependent upon their conformity with the 'white' working-class masculine normative structures associated with certain aspects of football culture. It may well be that black fans have to prove their credentials in these contexts by taking leading roles in order to have their inclusion recognized.

Vince argued the case for black English football fans to support the England national team and commented on the greater numbers of black fans following England in France. In doing so it is interesting that he made specific reference to these fans' accommodation with the codes of self-presentation typically associated with England's 'hooligan' supporters:

> There were a lot more black England fans in France. It was still pathetic given that we are supposed to be a multi racial country, but there was a lot more black faces than I've ever seen before. I saw maybe twenty or thirty black fans and they were all boys ['hooligans'], man. They were all boys. They were all labelled up. All in their Stone Island and all up for it. I couldn't believe it. I even saw Asian fans. That's the first time I've seen Asian fans supporting England away from Wembley and they were all boys, they all wanted some, I'm telling you.[14]

The reference here to 'even Asian ...' is significant. In one sense it is a response to the perceived lack of Asian football fans more generally, although the depth of commitment to football support is often vastly underestimated (see Johal, this volume). But, equally it also points to the ways in which such acceptance is based largely on a conventional notion of masculinity which Asian men are supposed to lack. So the 'even' here is as much about the surprise in their display of aggressive masculinity as to their 'race.'

Beyond this embracement of and conformity with the working-class masculine values associated with sections of England's support there is some evidence that these forms of behaviour may even intersect with the broader use of racialized and xenophobic language by black fans themselves. This was most dramatically illustrated in Marseilles when a group of England fans in the age range twenty eight to thirty five, which included two black members, became involved in a violent confrontation with local youths. Following the match against Tunisia a group of around a dozen Huddersfield fans, including two black members, one dressed in designer casual clothes and one in an England shirt, were in a side street with a similar sized group of Leeds fans. In the domestic context these supporters have a long history of confrontation and would normally be fierce rivals. However, in this instance they had just been involved in a violent confrontation with a gang of local youths and were now faced by three groups of Tunisian supporters and local youths, mostly of North African appearance.

The England fans who were by now receiving some element of police protection whilst being assaulted with bricks and bottles, were essentially cornered but
were operating as a united unit, punching any rivals who ventured through the
police line and 'fronting' their opponents with performative gestures and insults.
The fact that their adversaries appeared to be of North African backgrounds led
to their uniform description as Arabs and the racialization of insults within that
framework. The black Huddersfield fans, and one fan particularly, were centrally
involved in the confrontation and fully embraced by the broader group of
England fans. After up to an hour of this stand-off, which had been characterized by a cool, streetwise demeanour amongst the England fans, a bus was
brought in to evacuate them. However, once on the bus the release of tension
appeared to give these supporters a context in which they could perform a
whole series of overtly nationalistic and racialized chants at the crowd outside
which were largely constructed around references to the second world war, Nazi
concentration camps and Arabs.[15] In this context, the colour of individual
England fans' skin appeared to be dissolved into the England shirts and Stone
Island clothing that they wore, despite the overtly racialized insults that were
being directed at their commonly recognized 'Arab' opponents. They reveal the
temporary and contingent nature of these forms of acknowledgement and racial
inclusion.

The shifting meanings of race and nation are also being profoundly registered
within the England team itself. In a pre-World Cup 'warm-up' game against
Morocco in Casablanca, England fielded four black players. With the teams
lined up on the pitch the stadium manager lost the tape with the recording of
the English national anthem. A moment of silent chaos ensued. Quickly, the
players led by Ian Wright and captain Paul Ince sang 'God Save the Queen' at
the top of their voices and the travelling England fans – almost all of whom
were white – joined in. The following day *The Sun* newspaper showed a picture
of three black players – Ince, Wright and Campbell and Paul Gascoigne as
national heroes singing their hearts out (*The Sun*, 28 May 1998: 1). The
presence of black players in the England side has been an enduring feature of
the national game since 1978 when Viv Anderson made his debut against Cze-
choslovakia (Woolnough 1983). However, what has been striking recently is the
degree and variety of black internationals playing the game at the highest level,
though as yet few players of South Asian origin have broken through into the
professional game. Also, despite the presence of considerable numbers of black
players in the England team it is still the case that comparatively few black supporters actively support the national team.

This brings into focus the complex iterative relationship between race, nation
and inclusion. Clearly, there are different things at stake when black and white
people lay claim to icons of Englishness, or add their voice to the song of
national stirring in sport. Paul Gilroy, perhaps more than anyone else, has
pointed to the difference made when black people identify with Englishness
and/or Britishness and in so doing establish new possible vectors of contingent
racial inclusion (Gilroy 1993). This is a phenomenon of European states with

colonial histories that brought citizens from the colonial margin to the metropolitan centre through pre-established imperial networks and routeways. The sentiment embodied in the English fan's football song – 'There ain't no black in the
Union Jack – send the bastards back' is a stark reminder of the intense articulation of race and nation. This is the context in which struggles over the possibility of 'black' and 'English/British' being repositioned in a relationship of
inclusive mutuality takes on a political resonance. The situation in the United
States is very different because these struggles over national belonging took
on a very different form, where white supremacy has endured in a situation
where people of colour are awarded the status of being 'American' without
ambiguity.[16]

Equally, black identifications with Englishness are not necessarily viewed as
transformative. This is where the elision between notions of Englishness and
Britishness is most acutely significant because these two ideas can be coded differently in terms of racial exclusion, citizenship and belonging. During the game
between England and Argentina which resulted in England's exit from the 1998
tournament by the inevitable penalty shoot-out, Ian Wright, who missed the
finals because of injury, was pictured on UK television wrapped in a St George
Cross flag. Lez Henry – a black fan – commented in the aftermath of the game:

> I looked at him [Wright] on the screen and I thought 'What the fuck is he
> doing – has he lost his mind completely!' I mean the St George Cross!
> That's the worst thing for a black person because according to them people
> you can't be black and English. Maybe Britishness would be something else
> because you can be 'black British' but English? Never.[17]

The notion 'British' is widely held to be less racially or culturally exclusive and
such identification can be sustained alongside associations with the Caribbean
and the African diaspora (Back 1996: 148–152). The relationship between
these identity registers was brought into sharp focus through the Jamaican
national team's debut at the World Cup finals in France '98 (see Back et al.
1999). It is almost certainly the case that more black fans went to see the
World Cup in France as Jamaican supporters, than black fans supporting or
fighting for England. It is important here to stress that the kinds of negotiations
discussed in this chapter between black fans and white working-class cultures –
at least in terms of engaging in violence – are not in the majority. The reason
for the discussion here is precisely to bring into focus the persistence of racism
despite the existence of contingent forms of dialogue across the line of colour.

A moment of equal significance to the incident with Ian Wright was the
appearance of John Barnes, a player who, it has to be said, was never fully
accepted by England's 'hardcore' fans throughout his international career, on
national TV waving a Jamaican flag during their fixture with Croatia. Ron
Atkinson said in his commentary during the lead up to the game: 'We travelled
in on the mini bus with John Barnes and the Jamaican fans were greeting him
like royalty. They've been a real credit ... Well over half of Birmingham are

here tonight. I've seen them on the way in.'[18] After some discussion with Atkinson, Clive Tilsley commented:

> '[The Jamaicans] are an unconventional team with an unconventional set up which goes from the training pitch to the fans. But what we've seen here is miles away from the disturbing stories we've been hearing coming out of Marseilles.'[19]

What was fascinating in the moment was how John Barnes was re-figured as a Jamaican icon and the black fan presence in football, most of which hailed from English cities, was coded a 'law-abiding carnival' to be placed in contrast to English football hooliganism. This was a stark contrast to the ways in which districts like Handsworth in Birmingham – name-checked by Atkinson – had been represented previously as a haven of black criminality (Hall *et al.* 1978). We do not have the time to discuss the nature of these diasporic processes in detail, but it is important to stress that the defining centre of Jamaican fan culture radically re-configured the levels of black participation in football support. This opened the possibility of black fans going to football regardless of their age and gender (Lindsey 1999).

Conclusion

Throughout this chapter we have looked at the ways in which the defining centre of football culture both at a local and national level defines the terms of legitimate inclusion for black football fans. One of the things we argue is that it is important to understand these processes because they show how the intersection of class and gender produce complex combinations of racial dialogue and exclusion. In this sense, we are arguing that the conflation within the policy arena of racism with other sorts of violence and intimidation misses the nuances that we have tried to explicate. More than this, some of the strictures of moral anti-racism that haunted the 'Let's Kick Racism Out of Football Campaign' in its early stages make it impossible to understand the complex forms of contingent inclusion won by black fans. The result is that these histories are made at once both incomprehensible and invisible. This is not to say that the passports to inclusion offered here are unambiguously progressive in terms of some latent class romanticism that has elsewhere dogged the debate about football violence.[20] The point we want to make emphatically here is that these dialogues are profoundly partial and limited.

We have explored the intersections between gender, nation and class that police the boundaries of acceptance in football culture. Football provides a key context in which racial exclusions and negotiations are manifest both within the local and the national body politic. These issues have been explored through looking at the presence and growth in black participation within the English game. We have developed an argument about the scope of black inclusion in football fan culture and its limitations, be it by the defining centre of English

football fandom or the variegations of local patriotism and its normative structure. The nationalisms of the neighbourhood and the circumscriptions of Englishness we outlined here offer black fans passports to entry that are always
issued with specific terms and conditions. These circumstances are largely
restricted to black males who perform and participate in class-inflected forms of
hegemonic masculinity, which may at the same time exclude gay black men, or
women, and Asian fans both male and female. Perhaps, the significance of
football as a form of popular culture is that it allows the politics of these identifications and definitions to be laid bare. It is important to look at these encounters for they show how the micro-politics of race and nation is lived.

Notes

1 Interview, 4 December 1996.
2 The research discussed here is part of a wider project entitled The Cultures of Racism
in Football which was funded by the Economic and Social Research Council (project
number R 000 23 5639). We would like to thank the ESRC for their support.
3 Following Robert Miles (1989).
4 Interview, 21 May 1998.
5 He writes in his autobiography: 'The only sniff I ever had [from professional clubs]
was with Millwall. I was 14 at the time and they were the local team to me and the
side I used to worship. A mate and I would bunk in at the old Den at the Coldblow
Lane End to watch the Lions, so it was a dream come true when they invited me to
the Crofton Leisure Centre for a six-week trial. I know I showed enough in skill and
ability in that time to warrant something from it; instead I got nothing, and that
began a love-hate affair with Millwall that lasts even to this day.' Ian Wright (1996:
41).
6 Interview, 21 May 1998.
7 Les Back, Fieldnote book 1996–98.
8 Interview, 21 May 1998.
9 Here we are thinking of Pierre Bourdieu's notion of embodiment. This is developed
fully in relation to football in the work of Garry Robson (2000).
10 In this fanzine, *The Lion Roars*, it is customary not to give despised enemies the
dignity of proper noun capitalization. We would like to thank Gary Robson for
pointing out these passages from the Millwall fanzine.
11 C18 stands for C = Combat; 1 = A (i.e. first letter of the alphabet); 8 = H (i.e.
eighth letter of the alphabet): Combat Adolf Hitler. It is a violent neo-Nazi group
established in the 1980s to defend organized neo-fascist political interest. Recently,
C18 has been racked by implosive division with the imprisonment of its leader
Charlie Sargent for his part in the murder of another neo-Nazi, Chris Castle.
12 This was particularly evident in the *Daily Mirror* (see 25 and 26 June 1996),
although this was largely out of step with the mood of English fans and the nation as
a whole.
13 Interview, 30 October 1996.
14 Interview, 22 July 1998.
15 We would like to thank Pat Slaughter for these observations.
16 Thanks to Roger Hewitt for this point. See also John Hoberman (1997).
17 Discussion with Les Back, 10 July 1998.
18 Independent Television coverage of Croatia versus Jamaica, 13 June 1998.
19 Ibid.

20 See discussions of this debate in Armstrong (1998); Giulianotti Bonney and Hepworth (1994); Murphy, Williams and Dunning (1990).

References

Armstrong, G. (1998) *Football Hooligans: Knowing the Score*, Oxford: Berg.

Back, L. (1996) *New Ethnicities and Urban Culture*, London: UCL Press.

Back, L., Crabbe, T. and Solomos, J. (1996) *Alive and Still Kicking*, London: Advisory Group Against Racism and Intimidation & the Commission for Racial Equality.

—— (1998) 'Racism in Football: Patterns of Continuity and Change', in Adam Brown. (ed.) *Fanatics! Power, identity & fandom in football*, London: Routledge.

—— (1999) 'Gringos, Reggae Gyals and "Le Français de la Souche Recente": nation, diaspora and identity in football', *Soundings*, Issue 11, 1999 pp. 78–96.

—— *The Changing Face of Football*, Oxford: Berg.

Bateson, G. (1978) 'A Theory of Play and Fantasy', in Gregory Bateson, *Steps to an Ecology of Mind*, London: Paladin Books.

Carrington, B. (1998) ' "Football's coming home" But whose home? And do we want it: nation, football and the politics of exclusion', in Adam Brown (ed.) *Fanatics! Power, identity & fandom in football*, London: Routledge.

Chapman, K. (1998) 'Black and Blue: A History of Black Millwall Players', *Millwall Official Match Magazine*, 21 February 1998, Millwall Football Club.

Clarke, J. (1973) *Football and the Skinheads*, Occasional Paper, Centre for Contemporary Cultural Studies, University of Birmingham.

—— (1978) 'Football and Working Class Fans: Tradition and Change' in Roger Ingham (ed.) *Football Hooliganism: The Wider Context*, London: Inter-Action.

Gilroy, P. (1993) *Small Acts: thoughts on the politics of black cultures*, London: Serpent's Tail.

Giulianotti, R., Bonney, N. and Hepworth, M. (1994) *Football violence and social identity*, London: Routledge.

Hall, S., Critcher, C., Jefferson, T. and Roberts, B. (1978) *Policing the Crisis: Mugging, the State and Law and Order*, London: Macmillan.

Hoberman, J. (1997) *Darwin's Athletes: how sport has damaged black America and preserved the myth of race*, Boston & New York: Houghton Mifflin Company.

Kick It Out (1999) *Annual Report 1997/98*, London: Kick It Out.

Lindsey, E. (1999) 'di' France ting', in Marcela Mora Y Araujo and Simon Kuper (eds) *Perfect Pitch: 4. Dirt*, London: Headline.

Mercer, K. (1994) *Welcome to the Jungle: New Positions in Black Cultural Studies*, New York & London: Routledge.

Miles, R. (1989) *Racism*, London: Routledge.

Murphy, P., Williams, J. and Dunning, E. (1990) *Football on Trial: Spectator Violence and Development in the Football World*, London: Routledge.

Robson, G. (2000) *No One Likes Us, We Don't Care: The myth and reality of Millwall fandom*, Oxford: Berg.

Tyndall, J. (1996) 'Euro '96: faces of nationalism', *Spearhead*, No. 330, p. 7.

Williams, J., Dunning, E. and Murphy, P. (1989) *Hooligans Abroad: The Behaviour and Control of England Fans in Continental Europe*, London: Routledge.

Woolnough, B. (1983) *Black magic: England's black footballers*, London: Pelham Books.

Wright, I. (1996) *Mr Wright*, London: Collins Willow.

Part II
Public controversies over 'race' and sport

Science, media and the law

6 Racial science and South Asian and black physicality

Scott Fleming

Introduction

The possible links between sport and 'race' continue to be the subject of heated public discussion and debate. Media images of a disproportionate number of elite black athletes are prevalent and it does not seem unreasonable to question why this should be (cf. Gladwell 1997; Price 1997). Yet this area of research is far from straightforward and, as I argue in this chapter, often characterized by superficiality and over-simplification. At their worst the arguments concerning biology, 'race' and sports performance are often illogical and unscientific. What is unmistakable, however, is the popular impact that such discussions have on sports folklore in Britain.

Partly as a result of the high media profile that men's soccer and cricket enjoy, comments that have been made by certain prominent figures from elite professional clubs have attracted a considerable amount of interest and scrutiny. For instance, speaking of black footballers, different managers and club 'chairmen' have variously observed: 'I think you're a coward. All you people are' (cited in Cashmore 1982: 193); 'I don't think too many can read the game ... You get an awful lot, great pace, great athletes, love to play with the ball in front of them ... when it's behind them it's chaos' (cited in Hill 1991: *viii*); 'When you're getting into midwinter in England you need ... the hard white man to carry the artistic black players through' (cited in Wilson 1991: 41); 'The reason the agents chose you black kids is because you are all naive ... Where was your agent when we dragged you black kids off the streets?' (cited in Silver 1995: 59).

Of South Asian cricketers, First Class County officials are reported to have remarked: 'Typical Paki (*sic*), never get their heads down'[1] (cited in White 1990: 29); 'If [they] had less children like the whites then they would be able to afford cricket equipment and lessons' (cited on Yorkshire Television 1990).

Some of these attracted disapproval at the time of their publication or broadcast; and that, in itself, is a cause for some optimism. In a climate in which concerns have been expressed that so-called 'political correctness' may have gone too far[2], discussions about 'race' are of particular sensitivity. John Hoberman (1992) has suggested that in predominantly mono-cultural societies, there is a greater willingness to discuss these matters openly. Yet even in a multi-cultural society like Britain the opportunity for constructive and interesting debate can exist.[3] The citations listed above from significant individuals in the administration, management and coaching of sport also demonstrate the willingness of some to 'put their heads above the parapet' and risk reproach.[4] Yet these attitudes also betray a particular set of views (almost all are negative) about the groups to which they refer. Importantly, they reflect assumptions about the limited cognitive and psychological capacity of these 'racial' groups whilst at the same time – in the case of black soccer players – acknowledging physical prowess and athleticism.

These are crude stereotypes, and in that sense there is no need to distinguish between those that are positive (or benign) and those that are negative; but there are clearly some implied mixed messages about sports performance and 'race'. In order to conceptualize this stereotyping, an important point of departure is provided by Abercrombie *et al.* (1994) in their assertion that the evidence of a set of attitudes and beliefs about the characteristics of so-called 'racial' groups constitutes a form of racism. The 'case for the defence' provided by those accused of being racist is often, at best, spurious and unconvincing. Just as the response 'I'm not a racist, one of my friends is black' is a flimsy *non sequitur*; the reported response from the New Zealand men's rugby union media liaison officer to the allegation that captain Sean Fitzpatrick directed verbal racist abuse at England player Victor Ubogu simply does not follow logically and/or necessarily. He remarked: 'It is inconceivable Sean would employ such abuse, especially as his prop and good friend is Olo Brown, who is Western Samoan. Fitzpatrick is captain of the most multi-racial sides in the world' (cited in *The Guardian* 29/11/1993: 17).

More weighty than this particular brand of flawed logic however, is the manner in which science has been manipulated and misused to create the facade of a robust theorized explanation for some of the observed phenomena with regard to 'race' and sport. In this chapter the basis for some of the current popular discourse is interrogated in relation to the pseudo-scientific (even anti-scientific) explanations that have been advanced. The chapter is organized around three key themes: conceptual and operational difficulties associated with 'race'; a contextualization for the contemporary (mis)understanding of the sport-'race' relation; and a deconstruction of some of the major concerns with recourse to the principles of natural science.

'Race': conceptual and operational difficulties

The first recorded use of the word 'race' was 1508 in a poem by William Dunbar (Husband 1987), but it was some time before the concept was appropriated by natural scientists. Since then the term has become embedded in scientific (and more often pseudo-scientific) discussions, and herein lies the greatest difficulty associated with the 'race' and sport discourse. The application of the concept of 'race' to human beings is a direct consequence of the attempt to apply a taxonomic classification of organisms (Tobias 1972). That is to say, attempts are made to group organisms if they show shared characteristics that are considered to be derived from common ancestors (Baker 1974). Hence, in terms of the taxonomy, 'phyla' (e.g., *Chordata*) are divided into 'classes' (e.g., *Mammalia*), then into 'orders' (e.g., *Primates*), then 'families' (e.g., *Hominidae*), then 'genera' (e.g., *Homo*), and then 'species' (e.g., *Homo Sapiens*). It is at the level of species that humankind can be considered, for, as Baker (1974: 4) puts it (and risking considerable over-simplification), '[species] must be regarded provisionally as a group of animals that interbreed with one another'.

Hence it is the next level of the taxonomic hierarchy, sub-species, that 'races' might be encountered. Yet in spite of the apparent systematic clarity of the taxonomic process, it is fraught with ambiguities and complexities that make the operational utility of the concept of 'race' troublesome – to say the very least. The first of these is the conceptual leap from the commonality that characterizes the species to the difference that distinguishes between 'races'; and there is a perplexing inexactitude in the treatment of this issue by some natural scientists. For example, it has been estimated, according to Peter Farb (1978: 276) that when 'an individual from one geographical population (such as an African, an Asiatic, or a European)' is contrasted with an individual from a different geographical population, there is a difference of about 35 to 40 per cent of the genes. Yet he adds that the difference between individuals from within the same geographical population may be 'close to 30 per cent'. Given this evidence, he concludes, quite properly, that 'the genetic difference *between* two geographical populations is very much the same as the difference *within* a single population' (*op. cit.* [original emphasis]). The vagueness that haunts Farb's description is uncharacteristic of the precision with which molecular chemists and geneticists undertake their work. The ambiguity is increased when the work of Tobias (1972: 23) is considered. He asserts that the characteristics common to all human beings occupy 90–95 per cent of the genes that constitute the genotype. A mere 5–10 per cent of the human genes account for the differences between 'races'. Human beings would seem therefore to be much more alike than they are different. The obscurity is still evident, but additionally there is a significant discrepancy around the factual accuracy of what is being quantified.

The second point is highlighted in the lack of precision over the quantitative analysis of genes, and concerns the difficulty in defining 'races' with any absolute criteria. As the UNESCO (1972: 68) proposals on the biological aspects of 'race' – first published in 1964 – make explicit, 'Pure races – in the sense of genetically homogeneous populations – do not exist in the human species.' This being the case, the analytical description of 'races' is blurred and indistinct. The following quotation from Baker (1974) illustrates the point by highlighting the cloudy and equivocal nature of the taxonomic distinctions that are at the heart of 'racialized' scientific discourse:

> One may argue that a population 'A' is distinguishable from a population 'B' if x per cent of the individuals constituting population 'A' can be recognized as not belonging to population 'B'. It will be understood that the correct

value to be assigned to x cannot be discovered by objective means; never-theless, if a high figure (perhaps 75) is agreed upon by taxonomists, one can scarcely doubt that there is a distinction worthy of recognition as subspecific or 'racial'. Very commonly, however, the differences observed are so evident, and x is clearly so high, that no statistical investigation is necessary to convince other taxonomists that races should be distinguished.

(Baker 1974: 99)

Leaving aside the failure to articulate statistical confidence limits satisfactorily, this arbitrary description for asserting difference does not look like the rigorous and robust basis for valid and reliable scientific enquiry. Indeed, given the absence of clear 'racial' boundaries and attributes, it would seem to be almost impossible to categorize every individual according to 'race' (Howells 1974).

The third area of conceptual uncertainty is related to the descriptions (as opposed to definitions) of 'racial groups'. Classifications of 'races' and even 'sub-races' have occupied the attentions of various scholars since the late eighteenth century (cf. Baker 1974; Bouchard 1988), yet the failure to come to any sort of consensus over these inevitably undermines the status of the work. On a broad level there does seem to be some agreement that there are (at least) three major groups: 'Caucasoid', 'Negroid' and 'Mongoloid' (Tobias 1972). Yet this broad typification is inadequate as it fails to accommodate certain other groups, for instance the indigenous Aborigine population of Australia. Hence, as Miles (1989) explains, when confronted by empirical evidence and logical inconsis-tency, new classifications have been advanced. In this case the typology was therefore extended by some commentators (cf. Bouchard 1988) to include Aus-traloids. The difficulties do not, however, end there. Within the Caucasoid group there are further distinctions: Nordic, Alpine, Mediterranean, Armenoid, and East Baltic. Nordics are described by Tobias (1972: 21) as: 'robust, hairy, tall and fair, long-headed and long-faced'; whilst Alpines are described as: 'squat, medium in stature and dark in hair colour, short-headed and short-faced'. Inevitably these attempts to classify within the 'Caucasoid' have been discredited, not least, Farb (1978) confirms, because even in the heart of 'Nor-dicdom' only 10.1 per cent of the draftees in one study bore the characteristics of the Nordic sub-species. The argument that analyses of 'race' need to deal with 'typical' representatives of a 'race', and therefore manifest the greatest var-iation from 'typical' representatives of another 'race', are ontologically suspect, theoretically unconvincing, and empirically tendentious.

The fourth area of concern is related directly to the empirical difficulties (even impossibilities) associated with the descriptions of 'racial groups'. For if it is difficult to distinguish between 'races', and perhaps more difficult to accom-modate the differences within a 'race', the implications for the kind of empirical research that is conducted are serious. So serious that they might be confound-ing variables of such magnitude as to render the findings of research invalid – regardless of the experimental rigour and the sophistication of the measurement protocols involved. In short, if it is not possible to empirically demonstrate the differences between 'races', any attempt to categorize an individual into a particular 'racial' group must be based on the subjective judgement of the researcher. Given the obvious lack of clarity over taxonomic distinctions (outlined above), this is – at best – an insecure basis from which to proceed.

A brief background to 'race' and sports science

In spite of all the ambiguity, there is some general consensus that the concept of 'race' emerged in an apparently meaningful and recognizable way during the period of Enlightenment, towards the end of the eighteenth century.[5] At a time when there was increasing freedom of expression and criticism of religion, natural science was seen to embody the 'Age of Reason'. A biological interpretation of the differentiation between 'races' predominated, and with it came attempts to quantify the characteristics of each of the 'races' as well as to develop a hierarchical order amongst them (Miles 1989). These characteristics were not confined to descriptions of phenotype, they also included reference to behaviour and even personality. Quoting from a translation of *Systema Naturae* by eighteenth century Swedish biologist Carolus Linnaeus, Farb (1978) illustrates the value-laden classification of Homo Sapiens:

> Africans, for example, could be recognized by their dark skin colour, frizzled hair, and flat noses. In addition, declared Linnaeus, they were 'crafty, indolent, negligent ... governed by caprice.' As for the fair-skinned Europeans, Linnaeus found them 'gentle, acute, inventive ... governed by laws'.
>
> Farb (1978: 272)

With scientific legitimacy attached to these views the 'classical racist ideology' (Callinicos 1993: 17) was cultivated, and the most virulent form of scientific racism took root: the spurious 'race'–intelligence link. It is not a huge leap of the imagination to see how the comments about the 'inventive' and law-abiding white person became established and consolidated in populist conceptions of the intelligent white 'race'. Indeed so much so that this assumed causal relationship was subsequently investigated by leading academics and scholars during the first half of the twentieth century. The inadequacies of this biological determinism are laid bare by Lewontin (1993) in his penetrative analysis of natural science as a social institution.[6] His underlying theoretical position is a commitment to fundamental principles of developmental genetics, and he concludes that there is: 'no reason *a priori* to think that there would be any differentiation between racial groups in characteristics such as behaviour, temperament, and intelligence' (p. 37).

The similarity of the parallel explanation for biological determinism and the links between 'race' and sports performance is striking, though no less fallacious. John Hoberman (1992: 37) cites the work written in 1800 by J. M. Dégerando entitled *The Observation of Savage Peoples*, and quotes, 'We shall be given more positive information of the physical strength of the individual savage.' The list of human performance variables that Dégerando then describes might easily be interpreted as running (sprinting and endurance), swimming, jumping (long), and climbing. The notion that there was a hierarchy of 'racial' groups in connection with physical activity had begun to emerge very explicitly, and with it came the suggestion that black people had a physique that was better suited to physical activity. The symmetry of the argument about scientific racism being attached to intelligence also led to convergence around the 'brain/brawn' theme (Hoberman 1997). The 'law of compensation' which assumes an inverse relationship between intelligence and physicality (and makes some particularly vile connections to the 'man/beast' distinction) was being supported in what was being perceived as the apparent physical superiority and intellectual inferiority of the black 'race'.[7]

To illustrate how this racist ideology has become commonplace in popular conceptions of sport, a cartoon in Coakley (1994: 245) is illuminating. In it a white alpine skier reaches the finish line of a competition and one observer remarks to the other: 'That's another downhill medal won by the Swiss. Those white people from Switzerland must have a skiing gene, or they must have natural abilities to twist their bodies around slalom gates.' The point of the cartoon, as Coakley goes on to emphasize, is that the success or failure of black athletes is treated in a very different way from the success or failure of other groups of athletes. For whilst black sporting success is often explained with reference to a genetic predisposition associated with being black, similar analyses are seldom (if ever) advanced for white athletes.[8] This is an important point because associations are advanced that purport to connect two independent variables. The first is that sports performance *is* very demonstrably related to genotype, and genotype is a clear limiting factor on sports performance. (Or to put it another way, with a somatotype of a meso-ectomorph and a height of 1.90 metres, it was always unlikely that I would become an Olympic gymnast.) The second variable is that phenotype *is* very clearly linked to genotype. (Skin pigmentation is directly related to genetic make-up.) What does *not* follow from this, however, is that skin pigmentation is linked to sports performance. The inadequacy of such a proposition is clear from a similarly flawed argument:

- An individual's hair colour is influenced by genetic variables;
- An individual's shoe-size is determined genetically;
- Hair colour is logically and necessarily linked to the size of an individual's feet.

The humour of Coakley's cartoon rests on the way in which the sports performance of different so-called 'racial' groups is analysed and (mis)understood by sports scientists, and the unequal treatment of these groups by investigators.[9]

More fundamental than the issue of inequity however, is the scientific racism that is implicit within many studies. For it is evident that not only have certain studies sought to establish and consolidate the artificially constructed 'racial' classifications, but have resorted to a hierarchy of 'races' to explain sports performance (e.g., Hutinger 1959; Messerli *et al.* 1979; Bouchard 1988; Himes 1988; Malina 1988; Samson and Yerles 1988; Berry *et al.* 1993). *In short, investigations about sport from within the natural sciences have been under-pinned by a commitment to a classification of 'races' and hence the ideology of racism.* The point of principle relates to notions of objectivity. For though sports scientists examine observable phenomena, they purport to do so through *objective* empirical methods (Martens 1987). The paradox is that whilst sports science research is often characterized by rigorous and robust data collection, as well as objective and theorized interpretation and analysis, it is also undermined by bias and prejudice in the generation of hypotheses (Davis 1990).

It is now three decades since Martin Kane's (1971) article 'An assessment of black is best' was published in *Sports Illustrated*. In it Kane synthesized studies from a variety of academic disciplines[10], as well as coaches and athletes, and included the following summary remarks from Professors and Assistant Professors: 'Evidently the Negroes (*sic*) have longer limbs and narrower hips than whites' (p. 74); 'In total arm circumference Negroes (*sic*) are just significantly greater than whites' (p. 75); 'The Negro (*sic*) has more tendon and less muscle than the white' (p. 75); and the Black athlete has 'hyper-extensibility – or what the layman (*sic*) might call being double-jointed' (p. 75).

The paper was rebutted by angry responses, especially by Harry Edwards (1972, 1973) who challenged the methodological basis of the assertions that were being made. This critique has been developed by Ellis Cashmore (1982, 1996) who made specific mention of the unquestioning acceptance of the theoretical concept of 'race', of its homespun Darwinism, and of the overwhelming empirical falsification to the proposed causal links (a theme to which the discussion will return). Indeed in an attempt to accommodate this final point, Kane engages in a particular brand of anti-scientific mental gymnastics:

- I think power is the key to the black athlete's success ... The black athlete is more adapted to speed. (p. 80)
- In the 1968 Games, Ethiopia's Mamo Wolde won the marathon, the three Kenyans – Kipchoge Keino, Naftali Temu and Amos Biwott – took gold medals in the 1,500 metres, the 10,000 metres and steeplechase respectively. (p. 74)
- The black Africans on the east coast – the Ethiopians, Kenyans and others – have a genetic mix. Keino is a man with black skin and many white features. (p. 76)

Yet in spite of the clear inadequacies of Kane's article it seems to have made a huge impact and lasting impression on the discourse that surrounds the issue of 'race' and sport; and has even spawned other (equally contentious) forays by natural scientists into this area of enquiry.[11] One notable example was by Sir Roger Bannister. In his well-publicized comments to the Association for the

Advancement of Science in 1995, he remarked on the propensity of the black athlete for elite sports performance:

> It may be that their heel bone is a little longer or maybe it is because of their adaptation to a warm climate. Or it may be their lower subcutaneous fat which means their power-weight ratio is better. Maybe they have an elasticity or a capacity innately of their muscle fibres to contract quickly which is some adaptation to a warmer environment because this would increase the speed of chemical reactions.
>
> (Connor 1995: 3)

Bannister was widely condemned in the print media, but as is often the case the contestation of his remarks did not receive the same glare of publicity as the original comments. The set of circumstances surrounding the episode has a much greater significance than merely opening up an old and festering wound – though that would have been worthy of condemnation; and there are (at least) two important points to make. The first is concerned with Bannister's own biography as a consultant neurologist, track and field athlete and former world mile record holder: a scientist with *gravitas* and an athlete of renown. The second is about the audience to which his comments were addressed: a credible academic forum for scientific enquiry. As a result, Bannister's observations have the veneer of rigour and robustness and bring apparent legitimacy to some of these ideas, but are actually little more than speculative atheoretical rhetoric.

The damage caused by Bannister, Kane and others is especially profound, for pseudo-scientific and anti-scientific explanations of the relation between sport and 'race' have become embedded in many of the stereotypes that exist. When they, in turn, permeate the consciousness of coaches, teachers and even athletes themselves, the impact of scientific racism is very severe. Some of these have found expression in the discourse surrounding physical education. For example Bayliss (1983: 6–7) cites the following:

- Blacks will never make good swimmers because their bones are heavier. They cannot float easily and they have weak ankles;
- Blacks run faster because they have wider nostrils and can breathe in more oxygen;
- Blacks have an extra muscle at the top of their legs which helps them run faster;
- Blacks possess a muscular structure suited to power/explosive events;
- There is a relative precociousness in the psychomotor development of black children compared to their white peers;
- Blacks are good at boxing because they absorb a heavier beating.

This synthesis presents a set of flawed perceptions that were prevalent in the early 1980s. What is especially worrying is that there is little evidence to suppose that the sophistication of the 'race' and sport understanding has advanced significantly since then. Indeed recent research evidence suggests that many contemporary physical education teachers continue to subscribe to the view that blacks (and young black males in particular) have a 'natural' ability to excel in sports and should therefore be pushed to pursue success in these areas (Hayes and Sugden 1999).[12]

Sport, 'race', stereotypes and the principles of science

The process of stereotyping provides a valuable theoretical underpinning for a further consideration of the scientific racism that undermines many of the attempts to engage in serious analysis of the relation between sport and 'race'. To paraphrase Nugent and King (1979), the logic often works along the following lines:

- the identification of a category – such as black people;
- the attribution of characteristics to the category – black people run fast:
- the application of the traits to anyone belonging to the category – all black people can run fast.

Additionally, when flawed natural science is factored into the analysis the argument can appear to be even more compelling and emphatic. For example, there is the evidence that in 1996 all the finalists of the Olympic men's 100m and 200m track events were black; then the argument by example that 'they do because they can'; and the bogus explanation that black people are anatomically and physiologically suited to power sporting activities soon follows.

Parry's (1986) lucid insight into some of the rudimentary principles of science provides further illustration of the inadequacy of the scientific racism that is often applied to sports performance. The traditional view of the scientific method is that it demonstrates two components: first, the use of sensory perception to make observations of empirical facts; and second, the inductive reasoning that moves from particular observations into general laws (Sankey 1993). These have been assumed to demonstrate objectivity. Yet since 'observations are theory-dependent' (Parry 1986: 210), they are also subject to previous experience – including bias and prejudice. In order to make observations researchers need to know what to observe, and this must inevitably reflect some preconceived idea that the research question being posed is worth answering. Why, for instance, did Ponthieux and Barker (1965) decide to investigate the relationship between 'race' and physical fitness if not as a consequence of their previous experience and understanding of 'race' and sports performance? Sport scientists' engagements with 'race' and sport are not therefore impartial, and thus their work is evidence of an implicit commitment to a fundamentally racist ideology.

Having established that observations are affected by subjectivity, the way that induction moves from the particular to the general in natural science is also problematic. Parry (1986: 210) makes the nature of the concern unambiguous: 'The crucial question is: how do we legitimately infer law-like generalizations from singular instances of observation (no matter how numerous)? The short answer is: we can't.' Indeed to move from the specific instance to the general law in natural science can be construed as the kind of false universalism and stereotyping that has blighted much of the discourse in this area (cf. Fleming 1994). For example, consider the example of the general acceptance of the perception about the physical stature of South Asians based on some particular observations:

> South Asian girls are 'usually small and quite frail' (Lewis 1979: 132); South Asian boys and girls are 'generally of small stature and of a slight physique' (Wills 1980: 42); South Asian boys were characterized by being of 'generally smaller stature and slighter physique (Wills 1980)' (Leaman 1984: 214); 'The Asian pupil is typically seen as physically frail, lacking in stamina and likely to underachieve in physical education' (Williams 1989b: 167); 'Asians are too frail for contact sports' (cited in Bayliss 1989: 20); 'The Asian build is not that of a footballer ... It may well be that Asian ingredients in food, or their nutrition that they take, [is] not ideal for building up a physical frame' – Dave Bassett [former manager of Sheffield United Football Club] (BBC TV 1995).

Leaving aside the methodological issues associated with the observations themselves, there is a sense in which these particular observations have become the basis for a generalization. In those citations where the 'usually' and 'generally' disclaimers have been invoked it is clear that the observations should *not* be interpreted as having law-like qualities; and Leaman (1984) actually acknowledges the hazard of dangerous *over*-generalization. To illusrate, the distinction between the 'general law' of natural science and a generalization is clearly illustrated through the contrast between an example from inorganic chemistry and this suggestion of South Asian frailty. In the former, the properties of *bromine* have been catalogued, verified, and subjected to repeated trials. It is assumed that they are known (at least until they are refuted – to which the discussion will return shortly), and this constitutes a law of natural science. So when an unknown reddish-brown element in liquid form under normal conditions is shown to have a melting point of $-7.3°C$ and a boiling point of $59°C$, it is concluded that it is bromine. In the latter, South Asians have been observed to be small and slight, these observations have been replicated elsewhere. This is only a *generalization* though for if it was a law of natural science it would be possible to apply the same deductive reasoning to any particular South Asian person. Moreover, it assumes an unacknowledged (white) group who are considered to be the 'norm' against which South Asians should be evaluated. The false syllogism emphasizes the point: All South Asians are frail; 'X' is South Asian; *ergo,* 'X' is frail.

Yet, of course, there are many South Asians who are not physically frail. Suvra Bannerjee and Susheela Sundaram have enjoyed superstar status in India because of their level of performance in *Kabaddi*, a traditional sport of the

Indian sub-continent which has been described as a mixture of 'rugby, wrestling, karate and "tag"' (Channel 4 Television 1991). Furthermore, the Pakistan men's Test cricketer Shoaib Akhtar simply could not bowl a cricket ball in excess of 94 miles per hour (150 kmh) if he was 'frail and puny'. The inescapable conclusion is either that Shoaib Akhtar is not South Asian (which for reasons already described would be virtually impossible to demonstrate empirically), or that the assertion about the frailty of South Asians is not a law of natural science at all. The latter, to put it mildly, seems more probable. There is also a third alternative to which Parry (1986: 211) draws attention: 'to deny that the traditional view is an adequate account of science'.

An alternative approach to the philosophy of science is provided by Popperian falsificationism (cf. Popper 1963). Parry (1986: 212) again provides a succinct description of the logical point: 'countless confirming instances can never conclusively verify a general proposition, but a single counter example can conclusively falsify it'. That is to say, if there is a general understanding, for example that South Asians are excitable; and there is a single piece of evidence to the contrary, for example that cricketer Inzamam-ul-Haq is anything but excitable (however that might be measured); then the general understanding ceases to apply as a *necessary* condition. It is no longer true that in *all cases* South Asians are excitable. Other examples from a variety of sports are included in Table 1. In each of these the stereotype is based on an observation of negative characteristic; this is then linked to a flawed explanation and supported by bogus or spurious evidence; the single case that demonstrates that the general law of natural science does not apply provides the empirical falsification.

In short, general laws of natural science do not accommodate 'exceptions that prove the rule'. If exceptions exist then the assertion being made can be no more than a generalization. The implications for scientific racism are especially far reaching, for if 'race' is being linked to mere generalizations, the theoretical basis for causality is unsustainable.[13]

Concluding comments

The arguments presented in this chapter can be summarized as follows: the theoretical concept of 'race' is fundamentally flawed; the operational application of 'racial' definitions is fraught with insurmountable difficulties; the objectivity of natural science is contentious, especially in these avenues of enquiry; the principles of science (based on either verification or falsification) undermine scientific racism; and hence, conclusions about the links that are asserted between 'race' and sports performance are invalid and unreliable.

Notwithstanding the philosophical, theoretical and operational shortcomings of the ideology, the impact of contemporary scientific racism is profound (Hoberman 1997). The benign stereotype of the 'natural ability' argument has been internalized by many people, not least the subjects of the argument themselves. To acknowledge this fact, however, is not to excuse those who continue to promote such views, but rather to demonstrate how pervasive racial

Table 1 The falsification of stereotypes about 'racial' groups.

Proposition	'Blacks are not good at swimming'	'South Asians are not good at contact sports'	'Whites can't jump'
Observation	Few black swimmers have achieved success at international swimming	Few South Asians have achieved success at rugby (league or union)	Basketball, a game that rewards the capacity of its participants to jump effectively, is dominated disproportionately by blacks
Flawed explanation	Blacks are disadvantaged physiologically and anatomically in swimming performance at elite levels of competition	South Asians are not robust enough physically for vigorous, collision contact sports	Compared to their black peers, whites are not equipped physiologically and anatomically for jumping
Bogus evidence	'Blacks have "heavy bones", "weak ankles", and can't float'	'Asians dislike contact sport' 'Asians haven't got the character and haven't got the build'	'Whites don't have the natural athleticism and power of blacks'
Empirical falsification	Anthony Nesty, Olympic gold medal winner for the Men's 100m butterfly in 1988	Ikram Butt was capped by the senior England international men's rugby league team in 1995	Jonathan Edwards, Olympic gold medal winner for the men's triple jump in 2000

stereotypes are in informing our understandings about ourselves. For example, the former Indian tennis player (turned Hollywood star) Vijay Amritraj has stated: 'As a race, we are also handsomely endowed with hand-to-eye co-ordination, which is why so many of our youngsters excel naturally at ball sports like cricket, squash and tennis' (Amritraj and Evans 1990: 116). Even apparent inability in other sports is rationalized with recourse to more confused theorizing about genetics and heredity: '[it is an] hereditary problem that may take a generation or two to overcome' (*ibid.* 117).

The factual accuracy of these analyses is, in one sense, largely immaterial. If something is believed to be true, whether it is or not, it will often become real in its consequences. The catalogue of uninformed stereotypes presented throughout this chapter is the evidence of that. The key point is that natural science provides legitimacy, and people in general are seduced by the power of natural science. With regard to 'race' and sports performance specifically, it is pseudo-science (and even anti-science) that provides the unsatisfactory explanations for the stereotypes that exist. These are seldom challenged effectively, and hardly ever with the assumed authority over popular consciousness that natural science carries. Once they take root they permeate every layer of society (Godrej 1994). This chapter has attempted to challenge such ascribed authority and to reveal the ideological and political implications of the work that sport scientists, often naively, claim to be 'value-free'. The final provocative word rests with Lewontin (1993: 37), who has argued that the 'vulgar error that confuses heritability and fixity has been, over the years, the most powerful single weapon that biological ideologues have had in legitimating a society of inequality'.

Acknowledgement

I am grateful to various colleagues and students – too numerous to mention by name – with whom I have shared the ideas contained in this chapter, and for their willingness to share their ideas with me. I am especially indebted to Mark Burley, Ben Carrington, Jim Fleming, David Howe, Megan Llewellyn, and Mike McNamee for bringing valuable source material to my attention, and to David James for constructive suggestions for developing this important area of work.

Notes

1 An observation about an alleged lack of discipline and responsibility amongst Pakistani cricket batters.
2 See, for example, tabloid headlines such as 'Now you can't even ask for a black coffee – It's racist, say council loonies' (*The Sun*, 11 February 1994: 19).
3 The joint session entitled 'Is the sporting success of racial groups culturally or genetically determined?' presented by Eric Dunning and Bengt Saltin at the Third Annual Congress of the European College of Sport Science in Manchester during the Summer of 1998 was a clear example of a good intention to bring together differing perspectives on 'race' and sport.
4 S.L. Price (1997) has even argued that many researchers are reluctant to investigate the subject of 'race' and sports performance because of their fear that their work (and intentions) will be misunderstood and/or misconstrued. This theme is developed in Hoberman's (1997) chapter 'The fear of racial biology' (pp. 221–242).
5 For a further discussion of the historical derivation of the terms 'race' and 'racism', see Banton (1985) Mason (1995), Miles (1989), and Solomos and Back (1996).
6 See especially the chapter entitled 'All in the Genes' (pp. 17–37).
7 The theme of black intellectual inferiority was brought into sharp focus by the black tennis player Zina Garrison-Jackson. She accused Pam Shriver of racism explaining: ' ... she called me stupid, and I take that as being racial'. ('Racist slur leads to red faces', *The Guardian*, 14 June 1993: 17.)
8 The nearest to this is the misapprehension that white people are anatomically and physiologically predisposed to elite-level swimming performance. However this is

typically couched not as white people having an advantage, but rather as black people being *disadvantaged*. (See, for example, Johnson 1967.)

9 The work of Bengt Saltin and colleagues is commended by Hoberman (1997: 206) as 'the first and only credible research on the physiology of elite athletes involving racial comparisons'. Somewhat unusually, it has also received attention from the national print media (e.g., Gladwell 1997). Yet even this work does not address the central ontological point of the nature and operational definition of 'races'.

10 Of the published sources referred to however, J.M. Tanner's book *The Physique of the Olympic Athlete* (London: George Allen & Unwin) is the only one for which some bibliographic detail is presented – no date of publication is provided.

11 Some of these are cited by Hoberman (1992), though few are in English.

12 There is also anecdotal and undergraduate research evidence from students (including Initial Teacher Training students) at a number of higher education institutions in Britain that perceptions of black people being unable to swim but having 'natural ability' at dance and power athletic events are as prevalent at the start of the twenty-first century as they were in the preceding century.

13 In an article provocatively entitled 'Too frightened to ask' in the *Evening Standard* newspaper (28 September 1988, p.61), Peter McKay emphasizes the point unwittingly. In arguing that blacks have 'greater synchronization of mind and body', he suggests that this is acknowledged in dance. Needless to say he does not cite the glaring exceptions to this suggestion: Nureyev, Fonteyn, Astaire, Sleep, Flatley, Bussell etc. What he does note, however, are 'a few anomalies which confuse the issue. Why don't blacks shine at swimming? The qualities that triumph in the 50 metres swimming sprint are not so different to those in the 100 metres [on the track]'. These confounding anomalies refute the very essence of the causal link that he has sought to establish.

References

Abercrombie, N., Hill, S., and Turner, B.S. (1994) *The Penguin Dictionary of Sociology*, 3rd Edition, Harmondsworth: Penguin.

Amritraj, V. and Evans, R. (1990) *Vijay!*, London: Libri Mundi.

Baker, J.R. (1974) *Race*, London: Oxford University Press.

Banton, M. (1985) *Promoting Racial Harmony*, Cambridge: Cambridge University Press.

Bayliss, T. (1989) 'PE and racism: making changes', *Multicultural Teaching*, 7 (5), 18–22.

BBC Television (1995) *East – out of the game*, BBC 2.

Berry, M.J., Zehnder, T.J., Berry, C.B., Davis, S.E., and Anderson, S.K. (1993) 'Cardiovascular responses in black and white males during exercise, *Journal of Applied Physiology* 74, 2, 755–760.

Bouchard, C. (1988) 'Genetic basis of racial differences', *Canadian Journal of Sports Science* 13, 2, 104–108.

Callinicos, A. (1993) *Race and Class*, London: Bookmarks.

Cashmore, E. (1982) *Black Sportsmen*, London: Routledge & Kegan Paul.

—— (1996) *Making Sense of Sports*, 2nd edition, London: Routledge.

Channel 4 Television (1991) *Kabaddi*, London: Endboard production.

Coakley, J.J. (1994) *Sport in Society – Issues and Controversies*, 5th edition, Missouri: Times Mirror/Mosby.

Connor, S. (1995) 'Bannister says blacks were born to run', *The Independent*, 14 September, 3.

Davis, L.R. (1990) 'The articulation of difference: white preoccupation with the question of racially linked genetic differences among athletes', *Sociology of Sport Journal*, 7, 179–187.

Edwards, H. (1972) 'The myth of the racially superior athlete', *Intellectual Digest*, 2, 58–60.

—— (1973) 'The black athletes: twentieth century gladiators for white America', *Psychology Today*, 7, 58–60.

Farb, P. (1978) *Humankind – A History of the Development of Man*, London: Jonathan Cape.

Fleming, S. (1994) 'Sport and South Asian youth: the perils of false universalism and stereotyping', *Leisure Studies*, 13, 159–177.

Gladwell, M. (1997) 'Why are blacks so good at sport?', *The Sunday Telegraph Review*, July 20, 1–2.

Godrej, D. (1994) 'Race – unlocking prejudice', *New Internationalist* October: 4–7.

Hayes, S. and Sugden, J. (1999) 'Winning through 'naturally' still? An analysis of the perceptions held by physical education teachers towards the performance of black pupils in school sport and in the classroom', *Race, Ethnicity and Education*, 2 (1), 93–107.

Hill, D. (1991), 'The race game', *The Guardian Guide*, 31 August, viii–ix.

Himes, J.H. (1988) 'Racial variation in physique and body composition', *Canadian Journal of Sports Science* 13, 2, 117–126.

Hoberman, J. (1992) *Mortal Engines – The Science of Performance and the Dehumanization of Sport*, New York: The Free Press.

—— (1997) *Darwin's Athletes – How Sport Has Damaged Black America and Preserved the Myth of Race*, New York: Houghton Mifflin.

Howells, W.W. (1974) 'The meaning of race', *New Community*, III, 1–2, 26–30.

Husband, C. (1987) 'Introduction: "Race", the continuity of a concept', in C. Husband (ed.) *'Race' in Britain – Continuity and Change*, 2nd edition, London: Hutchinson Education.

Hutinger, P.W. (1959) 'Differences in speed between American negro and white children in performance of the 35-yard dash', *The Research Quarterly* 30, 3, 366–368.

Johnson, R.L. (1967) 'Why aren't there more good negro swimmers?', *Swimming Technique* 4, 2, 25–27.

Kane, M. (1971) 'An assessment of black is best', *Sports Illustrated*, 34, 3, 78–83.

Leaman, O. (1984) 'Physical education, dance and outdoor pursuits', in A. Craft and G. Bardell (eds) *Curriculum Opportunities in a Multicultural Society*, London: Harper and Row, pp. 210–222.

Lewis, T. (1979), 'Ethnic influences on girls' PE', *British Journal of Physical Education*, 10, 132.

Lewontin, R.C. (1993) *The Doctrine of DNA – Biology as Ideology*, London: Penguin.

Malina, R.M. (1988) 'Racial/ethnic variation in the motor development and performance of American children', *Canadian Journal of Sports Science* 13, 2, 136–143.

Martens, R. (1987) 'Science, knowledge and sport psychology', *The Sport Psychologist* 1, 29–55.

Mason, D. (1995) *Race and Ethnicity in Modern Britain*, Oxford: Oxford University Press.

Messerli, F.H., DeCarvalho, J.G.R., Christie, B. and Frohlich, E.D. (1979) 'Essential hypertension in black and white subjects. Hemodynamic findings and fluid volume state', *American Journal of Medicine*, 67, 27–31.

Miles, R. (1989) *Racism*, London: Routledge.

Nugent, N. and King, R. (1979) 'Ethnic minorities, scapegoating and the extreme right' in R. Miles and A. Phizacklea (eds) *Racism and Political Action in Britain*, London: Routledge & Kegan Paul, pp. 28–49.

Parry, S.J. (1986) 'Philosophy and sport science', *Annali*, V, 1, 203–220.

Ponthieux, N.A. and Barker, D.G. (1965) 'Relationships between race and physical fitness', *Research Quarterly*, 36, 4, 468–472.

Popper, K.R. (1963) *Conjectures and Refutations*, London: Routledge & Kegan Paul.

Price, S.L. (1997) 'Is it in the genes?', *Sports Illustrated*, 87, 23, 53–55.

Samson, J. and Yerles, M. (1988) 'Racial differences in sports performance', *Canadian Journal of Sports Science*, 13, 2, 109–116.

Sankey, H. (1993) 'Kuhn's model of scientific theory change', *Cogito*, Spring, 18–24.

Silver, N. (1995) 'Soccer boss in race storm', *Sunday Mirror*, 29 January, pp. 59 & 68.

Solomos, J. and Back, L. (1996) *Racism and Society*, London: Macmillan.

Tobias, P.V. (1972 [first published in 1961]) 'The meaning of race', in P. Baxter and B. Sansom (eds) *Race and Social Difference*, Harmondsworth: Penguin, pp. 19–43.

UNESCO (1972 [first published in 1964]) 'Proposals on the biological aspects of race', in P. Baxter and B. Sansom (eds) *Race and Social Difference*, Harmondsworth: Penguin, pp. 68–73.

White, J. (1990) 'Yorkshire's biggest test', *The Independent*, 26 May, 29.

Williams, A. (1989) 'Physical education in a multicultural context', in Williams, A. (ed.), *Issues in physical education for the primary years*, Lewes, East Sussex: Falmer Press, pp. 160–172.

Wills, M. (1980) *Physical Education in a Multi-Cultural Society*, Coventry. Elm Bank Teachers' Centre.

Wilson, P. (1991) 'The black man's burden', *The Observer*, 22 September, p. 41.

Yorkshire Television (1990) *Local News*, YTV.

7 In search of the unequivocal Englishman

The conundrum of race and nation in English cricket

Mike Marqusee

In 1980, Roland Butcher became the first product of the great post-war migration of Asians and West Indians to play for the England Test side. Since then, others have followed in a slow but steady trickle. They have been joined in the England ranks by whites from southern Africa, Australia and New Zealand. Unfortunately, this period has also been England's least successful in the international arena.[1] With each setback the efforts to diagnose the malady afflicting English cricket grew more frantic. By 1993, when England were drubbed at home by Australia (and Shane Warne on his England debut) 4–1, some commentators were musing on a possible link between the England side's poor showing on the field and its social composition. Chris Cowdrey, a member of the sanctions-busting Gatting tour to South Africa in 1989, declared that the Test side was 'not English enough'. Neil Foster, another of Gatting's band, complained, 'We don't have a truly English side. We have lost some of our identity.' Reserving most of his ire for the immigrant southern Africans, Foster added, 'At least Lewis and DeFreitas grew up here.'

Foster's 'at least' was a telling phrase, casually qualifying the 'Englishness' of the two black cricketers. David Frith, the editor of *Wisden Cricket Monthly*, one of the English game's two pre-eminent periodicals, made that qualification explicit. English cricket, he said, suffered a 'crisis of identity'. For him the 'at least' applied to Allan Lamb and Robin Smith, whose parents were English. Devon Malcolm, he said, 'acts, thinks, sounds and looks like a Jamaican. This hits the English cricket lover where it hurts.' The arguments about the 'Englishness' of black, Asian and foreign-born cricketers were aired periodically in the cricket press, but received little attention from the outside world until July 1995, when the 'Henderson Affair' became national news, much to the discomfort of cricket authorities and cricket journalists.

The cover of the July 1995 issue of *Wisden Cricket Monthly* (WCM) advertised a feature on 'Racism and National Identity'. Inside was a 2000 word article entitled 'IS IT IN THE BLOOD?' by one Robert Henderson, a former civil servant living on a disability pension in Hoxton, a multi-racial area of inner London. The text was illustrated with photos of Geoff Greenidge (captioned 'the last white player to represent West Indies') and Phil DeFreitas (captioned 'to England at 10').[2]

In the stand-first, David Frith described the article as an examination 'from a cricketing viewpoint – of the sensitive matters of racism and national identity'. In his opening paragraph, Henderson claimed that his chosen topic was 'long overdue for honest discussion', then commenced this discussion with complaints about the West Indies board's alleged discrimination against Asians and Whites. He claimed that 'those who control the first-class cricket of the white Test-playing nations are drawn from the liberal elites' and that under their aegis, 'only one public line on racism in cricket is tolerated, namely that only whites may be racist'. Why was South Africa singled out when so many other nations 'do not have clean racial hands'? 'How many non-Muslims have played for Pakistan, or Tamils for Sri Lanka? ... How many untouchables have played for India?'[3] Henderson concludes that 'racially and culturally determined selection' is ubiquitous and those who deny it are hypocrites.

The rest of the article is devoted to making the case for England itself practising the most rigorous 'racially and culturally determined selection'. Addressing a WCM correspondent who had argued that it was wrong to lump DeFreitas and Ramprakash in with cricket migrants from southern Africa like Smith and Hick, Henderson went out of his way to emphasize his racial preoccupation:

> If I were to take the coward's way, I could point out that DeFreitas came to England at quite an advanced age (around 10) ... I could say, of course, I was not referring to Ramprakash ... because he was born and bred here. But those would be weasel words.

Henderson then quotes Matthew Engel's observation in the 1995 Wisden: 'It cannot be irrelevant to England's long-term failures that so many of their recent Test players were either born overseas and/or spent their formative years as citizens of other countries.' He omits Engel's crucial caveat ('It is not a question of race') and explicitly rejects its inclusiveness: 'An Asian or a negro raised in England will, according to the liberal, feel exactly the same pride and identification with the place as a white man. The reality is entirely different.' Most of the rest of the article is dedicated to proving that blacks and Asians, wherever born or raised, can never be 'culturally' English and can never feel 'a deep, unquestioning commitment to England'.

> Norman Tebbit's cricket test is as pertinent for players as it is for spectators. It is even possible that part of a coloured England-qualified player feels satisfaction (perhaps subconsciously) at seeing England humiliated, because of post imperial myths of oppression and exploitation.

Henderson points to 'the generally resentful and separatist mentality of the West Indian-descended population in England' and urges 'doubters' to:

> Cast their minds back to the riots of the 1980s, take a stroll around Brixton, Deptford, Hackney, Moss Side, St Paul's *et al.*, and think of

Haringey Cricket College which has had few if any white members ... There would seem to be no obvious reason why players such as DeFreitas and Lewis should not share the mentality [of] the general West Indian derived population.

Worse yet, in Henderson's view, is the negative impact 'the interlopers have on the unequivocally English players and consequently on team spirit'. He is certain that 'mixed groups' can never 'develop the same camaraderie as eleven unequivocal Englishmen'. In sum, 'the problem for the England selectors is perhaps similar to that facing England as a nation.' The establishment has 'conspired' to 'remove any sense of pride or sense of place in the hearts of those who are unequivocally English ... Indeed, perhaps even some of the unequivocally English players lack a sufficient sense of pride in playing for England'. In a closing peroration, Henderson proclaims:

> For a man to feel the pull of 'cricketing patriotism' he must be so imbued with a sense of cultural belonging that it is second nature to go beyond the call of duty ... is that desire to succeed *instinctive* [Henderson's italics], a matter of biology? There lies the heart of the matter.

Henderson's piece was a catalogue of racist sophistries, full of misinformation and leaps of logic, not least the leap from culture to biology in the final paragraph (and in the headline[4]). The method in his madness was the deployment of a definition of 'culture' so elastic as to enable him to slide easily from race to nation and back again. In doing so he mirrored in distorted form arguments made by multi-culturalists and anti-racists – a characteristic of racist discourse in the 1990s, in Britain and elsewhere. Henderson's language and conclusions were extreme, but his chain of reasoning, his unspoken assumptions about what constitutes 'races', 'cultures' or 'nations', were commonplace, and not only in the cricket press.

On the 2nd July, a story about Henderson's piece appeared on the *Observer's* front page under the headline 'Cricket world divided by 'negro' loyalty row' (The *Observer*, 2 July 1995). Sports correspondent Kevin Mitchell reported that the WCM office had been 'inundated with calls and letters' complaining about 'IS IT IN THE BLOOD?' Frith confessed he was surprised by the reaction but defended the article: 'Some people are scared [of this issue]. It's healthier out in the open...' Mitchell also sought a comment from Matthew Engel, editor of *Wisdens Cricketers' Almanack*, a member of the WCM editorial board, and widely regarded as one of cricket's most liberal and worldly voices:

> I can't go along with everything that Mr Henderson says, as I'd never heard of him before, but the question of nationality and sport is a legitimate one, as anyone observing Wimbledon or Test cricket can see. There is a problem of how you marry the wider question of race and nationality into

the narrow issue of sporting patriotism. I'm not sure it helps if you scream 'racist' when someone makes a contribution to that debate.[5]

In the next day's *Guardian*, Paul Foot decried Henderson's case as 'quack segregationist "science" of the type which flourished under the Third Reich.' Responding to Engel's statement in the *Observer*, he added, 'I'm not sure it helps either if liberal journalists respond to the most blatant racialism by covering up for it.' Extraordinarily, Engel had seen Foot's column before it went to press and was able to reply in his own column in the same paper on the same day. Here he defended Frith's right to 'edit as he sees fit'. The Henderson article was 'a curious one'. It was 'strange that he should use the word "negroes", which is now widely regarded as offensive outside far right-wing political circles.' Engel dismissed Henderson's mutterings about 'instinct' and 'biology' as 'drivel', but went on to argue that there is a 'difference between team games and individual sports'. Foot had derided Henderson's claim that a dressing room of 'six Englishman, two West Indians, two Southern Africans and a New Zealander' could not develop 'the same camaraderie as eleven unequivocal Englishmen'. Here, insisted Engel, it was Foot who was 'talking drivel'. He argued that 'teams that flog their guts out for their country habitually do better than collections of individuals whose sole aim is to further their own careers. This is one of the reasons England cricket teams lose more often than they win.'

For Engel, this failing was one facet of a broader problem with British identity. Recalling the way Michael Slater kissed the Australian insignia on his helmet after scoring his maiden Test century at Lord's in 1993, Engel declared: 'It is hard, no, impossible to imagine either Graeme Hick or Phil DeFreitas doing the same – in the unlikely event of them summoning the resolution to produce a similar performance.'[6] Engel also dismissed Foot's invocation of Linford Christie's success on the track by claiming there was a fundamental difference between individual and team sports. The implicit argument seemed to be that a 'foreigner' (however defined) might well succeed in English or British colours at the 100 metres or singles tennis or boxing, but as a member of a football or cricket or rugby team (hard to say where Britain's 4 × 400 relay team would fit in) he or she would be likely to detract from the cultural cohesion necessary for victory.

The only practical upshot of Engel's analysis (one which he would certainly oppose) would have been a programme to screen out players with insufficient commitment to the national cause. National identity and national commitment seem self-evident categories to many sports commentators, but the impossibility of devising an unbiased measurement of either quality suggests that, as so often, the self-evident is merely the illusory.[7] Defending his *Guardian* article, which took many readers by surprise, Engel was later at pains to insist that the 'legitimate debate' he sought was one arising from professional sportspersons competing under flags of convenience, people like Greg Rusedski, Zola Budd, Graeme Hick or Robin Smith. 'Like many people in cricket, I am concerned that it is too easy for players to choose which Test team they will represent, even if their connection with the country is marginal.' But by yoking together DeFreitas and Hick, Engel himself blurred the critical dividing line between the two very different 'debates'. And it was surely telling that in the 'debate' which ensued there was not a single specific proposal for an amendment to the existing eligibility rules. In the absence of such a proposal, what was the point of this 'legitimate debate'?

Of course, there is a fundamental distinction between the white 'mercenaries' and DeFreitas or Malcolm or the vast majority of Asian and black cricketers earning a living in the English first-class game. These players were either born in Britain or came here with their parents as children. They did not come to England to play cricket. But as soon as 'Englishness' is defined not by simple quantifiable rules of birth or residence, the line dividing these two groups is blurred. The search for 'cultural cohesion' opens a Pandora's Box. The fact that this search was promulgated in the *Guardian*, and by Matthew Engel, whose coverage of the South African affair had won him admirers among cricket fans alienated by the casual racism of more traditional commentators, indicates that confusions about race and nation, and unexamined assumptions about 'national identity' are widespread, and by no means confined to *Daily Telegraph* readers and writers. In the weeks that followed, it was often reported (*Telegraph*, *Guardian*, *Times*, Press Association reports) that the Henderson piece had precipitated a furore because it had suggested that 'foreign-born' players lacked commitment to England. Such a suggestion was in itself offensive to many, but it was not the core of what Henderson was arguing, and the reluctance of reporters and sub-editors to acknowledge the racial component in the article revealed not only a hesitancy in addressing the 'touchy topic' of skin-colour but also a larger and deeper bewilderment over the shifting boundaries of races, nations, and cultures.

Nonetheless, condemnation of the Henderson article poured in from all quarters. Black sports stars found nothing ambiguous in it, and could see no justification for printing it. 'It's not part of a legitimate debate,' said Victor Ubogu, 'It's crap' (*Caribbean Times*, 7 July, 1995). They saw no reason why their commitment to the sides they played for should be questioned or why they should have to prove their national loyalty. In an editorial, *The Times* deplored the 'ugly article' and 'the irresponsibility of the magazine's editor' in giving credence to an analysis as 'impoverished and execrable' as Henderson's (*Times*, 6 July, 1995). Norman Tebbit was quick to draw a distinction between Henderson's views and his 'cricket test', whose aim, he insisted, was to promote 'national integration'.[8] He called Malcolm and DeFreitas 'nothing but a credit' in their efforts for the national side. Malcolm and DeFreitas themselves wasted no time on interviews and initiated a libel action. England captain Mike Atherton told journalists during the truncated third test at Edgbaston that he had resigned from the WCM Editorial Board, 'I disapprove not only of the views expressed in the article but also its inclusion in the magazine' (*Observer*, 9 July, 1995).

Frith found himself at the centre of a national controversy, his editorial policy under a type of scrutiny with which he was entirely unfamiliar. On 7th July, in a statement issued through the Press Association, he admitted publication of Henderson's article was an 'error of judgement' and offered 'unreserved apologies to all whose sensibilities have been offended'. He had hoped the article would be 'a springboard for beneficial debate' and blamed the furore it had caused on 'distortions in certain sections of the media'. He told Kevin Mitchell, 'I've been up there like a dart board on Henderson's behalf and I've had enough of it' (*Observer*, 9 July, 1995). The August issue of WCM included two pages of letters critical of Henderson and articles by Brearley and Gower debunking Henderson's unreal view of top-class sporting competition. 'The unconscious is a hybrid and elusive beast,' wrote Brearley, 'Mr Henderson's attempts to expose it in others reveal more about his than theirs.' Gower was equally derisive: 'Without being unpatriotic, I think the notion of "national pride" has been over-rated ... Motivation comes from many sources, and a player's determination to do well is an individual quality.'

Frith's editorial was headlined 'Who needs ancestors?' (a reference to Voltaire: 'Whoever serves his country well has no need of ancestors'). If it was an apology, as Frith claimed, it was curiously worded. 'Robert Henderson's article did not place a question mark beside foreign-born England cricketers. It was already there. Reservations have rumbled round the cricket grounds and in the sports columns of the newspapers for several years.' His purpose in publishing Henderson, Frith now claimed, was to 'dismiss' these reservations 'so that cricketers and other sportsmen could be cleansed of suspicion about commitment.' He attributed the negative public reaction to 'the somewhat cold nature of Mr Henderson's language' and blamed the press for shifting 'the grounds of debate from national identity exclusively to race'.[9] Frith then quoted with approval Bill Deedes, the former *Daily Telegraph* editor, who had loftily declared that commentators had all got 'the wrong end of the stick' in the Henderson affair. Sounding increasingly like a *Private Eye* parody of himself, Deedes explained, 'It is cosmopolitanism, not colour, which dilutes loyalty.' Neither Deedes nor Frith seemed to be aware that 'cosmopolitanism' was the charge levied by Nazi propagandists against Jews and leftists, whose loyalties, they claimed, were not exclusively to the German nation-state.

The Henderson Affair fascinated the media. Its elements were sensitive and sensational: race and national identity, Englishness and cricket, the hallowed name of Wisden. Pundits had a field day. Within the cricket world there was shock and confusion. No one wanted to be associated with Henderson, and very few were prepared to defend Frith's editorial choices. But the overall tone was defensive. Many writers, commentators, administrators and players were deeply uncomfortable at the sudden and unexpected spotlight thrown on their little world, a world in which assumptions about race and nation had hitherto remained unexamined. Tim Rice was outraged when he received an appeal from Hit Racism for Six, a group founded in the wake of the Henderson Affair to campaign against racism in cricket.[10] Rice accused the group of creating a problem where none existed. Cricket, he claimed, was 'one of the least racist features of British society'. Most cricket correspondents were at pains to insist that Henderson was merely an aberration and had received far too much attention. Few were prepared to ask why and how an article so openly racist in tone and content, so deeply offensive to so many lovers of the sport, had come to appear (prominently) in one of the game's most respected publications.

When Frith launched WCM in 1979 it was welcomed by younger cricket fans as a sharper and more up-to-date alternative to *The Cricketer*, which had been going since the twenties. But in the decade that followed, Frith had used its pages to wage bitter battles against the anti-apartheid movement and its boycott of South Africa, against Pakistani swing bowlers and Pakistani fans, and, most notoriously, against West Indian fast bowlers. The July 1995 issue which carried the Henderson piece also carried a review by Frith himself of *Real Quick*, a book celebrating the West Indian masters of pace.[11] In the course of the review Frith disparaged the famous four-prong attack as 'morally indefensible'. His verdict on the achievements catalogued by the authors was tersely dismissive: 'Holding was usually magnificent – as was Wes Hall before him – and Garner and Ambrose were fortunate to be endowed with such long limbs. That will suffice.'

An indefatigable correspondent, Robert Henderson had for some time been bombarding the good and the great of the cricket world with letters and essays expounding his views and statistical tables purporting to support them. According to Henderson, Frith had made contact with him after seeing one of his broadsides, and had invited him to contribute to WCM. The result was an article, published in 1991, entitled 'A Fundamental Malaise', in which Henderson argued that cricketers ought to possess 'an instinctive allegiance to a culture' and questioned Nasser Hussain's right to play for England because of a statement he had made to the effect that he felt 'Indian'. The article elicited a letter of complaint from Nasser's mother, Shireen Hussain, to which Henderson replied: 'It is essentially an aesthetic judgement. The inclusion of South Africans, West Indians and an Indian in recent XIs offends my sense of rightness or proportion, just as a badly-drawn picture or self-conscious acting performance does.'

In 1993, he sent out an analysis of 'England Qualified Interlopers Test records', sub-divided into 'colour players' (Cowans, DeFreitas, Hussain, Ramprakash, Small, Malcolm, Lawrence) and 'white players' (Caddick, Hick, Lamb, Smith). He provided a further county-by-county breakdown of 'foreign personnel', among whom he classified 'White players with little or no British childhood experience' and 'those with Negro or Asian blood wherever born' (he was also careful to segregate 'white South African' from 'coloured South Africans' (Nigel Felton and Damien D'Oliveira).[12] A number of leading figures in the cricket world, including former Test players and senior cricket correspondents, responded to this document by writing politely to Henderson expressing 'interest' or 'sympathy' or averring 'I agree with you up to a point'.[13] Henderson claimed that 'two thirds of all the national newspaper cricket writers' shared his views and was enraged at what he saw as their pusillanimity in not coming to his aid in his hour of need. Of course, he was wildly over-eager to snatch at any sign of approbation or even mere forbearance as proof that his views had been endorsed in full. Nonetheless, the reluctance of so many educated people to decry explicitly racist views when confronted with them indicates how widespread and deeply rooted racist assumptions remain, at least in the higher echelons of the cricket world.

In 1994 Frith had written to Henderson: 'How can a true Englishman ever see this as his representative side despite all the chat about the commitment of the immigrant?'[14] As Frith himself has noted with some irritation, this sentiment was by no means confined to contributors to WCM. Reporting England's victory over West Indies in the Lord's Test of 1995, the *Independent* commented: 'What made it additionally pleasing was that England's attack did not for once look like a United Nations strike force. Not since the Old Trafford Test of 1989 ... have England fielded five bowlers (or any amount come to that) with undiluted allegiance to the country they were representing' (*Independent*, 27 June 1995).

Throughout the summer of 1995, the question of national allegiance dogged Andrew Symonds, Gloucestershire's six-hitting prodigy. Symonds, black and Birmingham-born, had moved to Australia at 18 months of age. Under ICC rules he was eligible to play for both England and Australia, but earlier in the year he had told British journalists, 'I'm a fair dinkum Aussie.' There was much debate about whether he should or should not be selected to play for England. Graham Gooch, who in 1982 had abandoned the England cause for three years to play in South Africa, complained that Symonds had no commitment to 'the English way of life'. He drew a contrast with his friend Allan Lamb, whose commitment to this way of life was evinced, Gooch argued, by his love of fishing and hunting (*David Gower's Weekly*, BBC Radio Five, 6 July 1995). Symonds wanted to keep his options open (not least so that he could continue to play for Gloucestershire, which would become difficult if he were reclassified as an overseas player), but by selecting him for that winter's England A-tour, the cricket authorities forced him to choose.

The *Guardian's* cricket writers described Symonds' choice as a matter of 'conscience', as if it would have been somehow immoral or dishonest for Symonds to opt to play for England. Although the writers' intention was to highlight an alleged loophole in the qualification rules, the effect was to place a cricketer's inner motivations, his sense of self and his social identity, under outside scrutiny. The common ground between the *Guardian* writers and Henderson was the assumption that 'Englishness', and with it the right to play for England, was an identifiable personal characteristic, something existing in a realm more substantive than that of technical criteria relating to birth, parentage or residence. In the end, Symonds rejected the England offer and returned to Australia. In December, the TCCB altered its eligibility rules. From now on players with dual nationality would have to sign a declaration that they had no 'desire or intention to play cricket for any country outside the European Community'.[15] After all the agonizing, the authorities could come up with nothing more than a loyalty-oath – a confession that in the face of a globalized economy and migrant workforces, they were no longer able to demarcate clearly the English from the not-English.

Nonetheless, the belief that Englishness is a fixed cultural attribute deeply implanted in those who are deemed English remains widespread among cricket commentators (among many others). Indeed, it seems that ever-increasing exposure to global competition (sporting and otherwise) is only adding to the potency of this myth. Commenting on the 1995 Benson and Hedges final, John Woodcock, one of the country's most experienced observers of the game, compared Mike Atherton's 93 off 141 balls for Lancashire (who batted first and won) to Aravinda da Silva's 112 off 95 balls for Kent (who lost):

> English commitment and Sri Lankan artistry were on show ... vigilance and genius, the Occident and the Orient ... two contrasting cricketing cultures ... you really need to be born on the sub-continent to play exactly as da Silva does, with eyes that flash and wrists that are naturally supple and feet that need no telling ... Englishmen have to work harder to break the mould.

Woodcock's admiration for da Silva was heartfelt, but his praise was, unintentionally, double-edged. It was the long-discredited duality of nature and nurture, spontaneity and deliberation, East and West, and it obscured far more than it revealed. Cricket writers relish archetypes – the beefy fast bowler, the diminutive keeper, the phlegmatic opening batsman, the cavalier strokemaker, the temperamental left arm spinner – but, when transferred to the international arena, these archetypes all too easily degenerate into mere racial or national stereotypes. And the tragedy of the stereotype is that it occludes our view of reality. It severs us from the glorious unpredictability of human diversity. Da Silva's batsmanship, even in the frenetic one-day arena, is for the most part correct, classical and every bit as calculated as Atherton's. And his daring shot-making in that Benson and Hedges final owed far more to the fact that his team were chasing a sizeable target than to genetic or cultural factors. Woodcock was so besotted by the lure of the cricketing Orient that he simply could not see what was in front of his eyes. In wandering from the individual to the national to the cultural to the racial without breaking stride, he displayed – in relatively benign form – many of the intellectual habits which also shaped Frith's and Henderson's less generous effusions.

It is important to note, however, that cricket commentators were not the only ones preoccupied with English national identity and its cultural attributes. Even as the Henderson Affair was swirling through the sports pages, the National Curriculum chief Nick Tate was voicing concerns about the dilution of British national identity. 'We've become apologetic about the majority mainstream culture ... we belong to one country and if membership of it is to mean anything we have to have a common culture' – a culture which in his view was explicitly 'Christian'. Chris Woodhead, the former Chief Inspector of schools, agreed. 'A clear sense of national identity gives a country collective strength.'

Like Henderson, Bill Deedes and many others, Woodhead proclaimed himself strongly opposed to 'some watered-down cosmopolitan mish-mash'. Tate, Woodhead, Frith, Deedes (not to mention Henderson): none of them could grasp the underlying truth that the unresolved conflicts within the nation are the nation, and the only vigorous nation is one that is in formation, merrily borrowing from all and sundry.

Meanwhile, unimpressed by Frith's editorial, Malcolm and DeFreitas pursued their legal action against WCM. In September of 1995 the magazine's lawyers read out a statement in the high court in which they apologized for printing the article, disassociated the magazine 'entirely from the allegations' made by Henderson, and agreed to pay 'substantial damages' to both plaintiffs. Damages were also subsequently paid to Chris Lewis. David Graveney, Secretary of the Professional Cricketers' Association (and organizer of Mike Gatting's 1989 sanctions-busting tour to South Africa), had advised Malcolm and DeFreitas not to sue. Undeterred, the two players sought and received assistance from the Professional Footballers' Association, a body both more independent of management and less frightened of the issue of racism than the PCA.

> 'I felt strongly that this sort of thing must be brought out into the open and dealt with before it takes root,' said Malcolm. 'Look at the problems football has with racism. I had a chance to do my bit to stop that happening in cricket. Too many things have been swept under the carpet in the past but the problem is there, eventually the bump under the carpet gets so big you fall over it.'
>
> (Interview with Rob Steen, *Inside Edge*)

Malcolm started playing cricket seriously only after his move from Jamaica to Sheffield at the age of 15. Not surprisingly, at every stage of his subsequent career, he has been a late starter. Thanks to Sheffield's Caribbean Sports Club, he was able to progress into the local leagues, but because of Yorkshire CCC's 'Yorkshire-born only' rule, he ended up signing for Derbyshire. His 9 for 57 against South Africa at the Oval was often cited during the Henderson Affair as some kind of scientific, and therefore decisive, refutation of Henderson's arguments. But the triumphant flourishing of Malcolm's match-winning effort raised more questions than it answered. It still harked back to the quaint notion that people's loyalties can be tested and proven, as if by some inquisitorial trial: throw him in at the Pavilion end and see if he takes wickets. If he does, he's a loyal black, but if he doesn't? Is the 'Englishness' of those who fail to deliver on the big occasions somehow 'equivocal'?

As so often in this debate, people were desperately seeking some measurement, some standard, of that notorious will o' the wisp, national identity. And as ever, when people seek certainty in a realm of ambiguity, their attempts to impose standards merely reveal their own prejudices. In his autobiography, Frith agrees that at the Oval Malcolm 'was totally committed to England's cause, even though he was Jamaican born and even though he told *The Cricketer* in an April 1995 interview that his heroes were Viv Richards, Michael Holding and Richard Hadlee, and that his favourite music was rhythm and blues, soul, funk and reggae'.[16] Frith seemed oblivious to the fact that Malcolm shares his musical preferences with millions of white English youths.

In January 1996 Frith was sacked by the WCM management. In his autobiography he portrays himself as the victim of 'a collaborative manoeuvre' and inveighs against those who shared his (or Henderson's) views but ran for cover when the spotlight fell on WCM. Matthew Engel, in his editor's notes to the 1996 *Wisden Cricketers' Almanack*, conceded that WCM had 'made the mistake' of publishing Henderson's article. Nonetheless, he still insisted that 'it is reasonable to believe that not everyone who has chosen to regard himself as English has done so out of any deep patriotic commitment'. Therefore, 'the qualification rules should be tightened'. He did not say how. As for Robert Henderson, who felt he had been crucified merely for saying what others were thinking, in early 1997 he was investigated by police for sending 'race hate' letters to Tony and Cherie Blair. Officers from the Met told the Mirror, 'the language is very basic, direct and insulting' (*Mirror*, March 1997).

Notes

1 Between 1878 and 1980, England won 36 per cent and lost 25 per cent of Test matches played; between 1980 and 1993, it won 21 per cent and lost 38 per cent.
2 All quotations from 'Is it in the blood?' are taken from *Wisden Cricket Monthly*, July, 1995.
3 The answer, in all three cases, is a few, but not enough.
4 Henderson says the headline was written by Frith.
5 So far the only public statements about the issue had come from Frith and Henderson. So just who was doing the 'screaming'?
6 In the *Financial Times*, Michael Spinaker responded: 'DeFreitas has lived in England since the start of secondary school. Are these not a cricketer's formative years? And if it is the years before that are formative, would Engel accept as English a player who had lived in Australia since, say, the age of 10? I doubt it.'
7 The saddest aspect of the Engel analysis is its assumption that diversity – racial, cultural, national, even linguistic – is an insuperable obstacle to the forging of a common purpose on the field of play. Across Western Europe all the big football clubs are not only multi-racial, but multi-national, and often polyglot. This has not inhibited them on the field nor has it diminished the fervour of supporters. The great West Indies sides of the 70s and 80s comprised players from as many as seven different countries, as well as players with diverse racial, cultural and religious associations. Of course, there were tensions among them. But when the tensions were transcended, the unity in diversity of the team was clearly a source of inspiration. It has been to the West Indies team's advantage that it represents an aspiration towards West Indian unity, a desire to fashion a broader, more inclusive identity. It has been to the England team's disadvantage that just about the only time English national identity is invoked, as in the Henderson Affair, it is with the purpose of excluding someone because of his colour or country of origin.
8 For an account of the 'Tebbit test' and its impact on the cricket world, see my book *Anyone But England: Cricket, Race and Class*, Two Heads, 1998 (revised edition).

9 Henderson himself told the *Evening Standard*, 'Personally I would not select Asians or blacks. It is a particular problem with team sports.'

10 In July and August 1995 Hit Racism for Six circulated a four-point anti-racist declaration; although its contents were innocuous and it was supported by mainstream figures from the church, politics, and entertainment, only a tiny handful of cricketers and cricket writers were prepared to sign it. For more on Hit Racism for Six, see 'Race and Cricket in England Today', published by Hit Racism for Six, with the assistance of the Churches Commission for Racial Justice, 1996.

11 *Real Quick*, by Alastair McLellan and Michelle Savidge, 1995.

12 Copy of document in author's possession.

13 Henderson later circulated copies of these letters to the media, hoping to prove his contention that he was the victim of hypocrisy. Anyone who has read these letters can be in no doubt that a large number of prominent figures in the cricket world were prepared to indicate some degree of support for some of Henderson's views. I have omitted their names from this account here not merely to spare their blushes, but because I do not believe an argument about who is or is not 'a racist' among well-known cricket figures is pertinent or productive. The point is rather how Henderson's views formed part of a broader stream of assumptions permeating much of the cricket world and of British society and media.

14 Letter circulated by Robert Henderson.

15 Britain's membership of the European Union has caused dilemmas for cricket authorities. Under the rules governing the movement of labour within the EU, the restrictions on overseas players cannot be applied to EU nationals (hence Dutch or Danish or Irish cricketers are not classified as 'overseas players' in county cricket). As long as England remains the only significant cricket power in Europe, this dilemma will cause few headaches. Unlike football, cricket's international domain is circumscribed by the legacy of the British empire. This historical burden plays a major role in shaping the manifestations of racism in the game.

16 David Frith, *Caught England, Bowled Australia: A cricket slave's complex story*, Eva Press, 1997.

8 Sport, racism and the limits of 'colour blind' law

Simon Gardiner and Roger Welch

Introduction

The phenomenon of racism in society has long been a focus of social policy and legal intervention. This has included attacking practices and procedures that have been judged to be discriminatory in social spheres such as employment and education. The scourge of racial incitement – verbal and physical – has been challenged through both non-legal and legal approaches. The tragic killing of Stephen Lawrence in South London in 1993, the subsequent inability to bring the perpetrators to justice and the Official Inquiry which reported in 1999, highlighting the allegations of the racist practices of the police, have become a focal point in discussing the problem of racism in contemporary Britain.

A major issue is how to respond to, and effectively challenge, racism. What role does the law play? The enactment of aggravated race crime offences in the Crime and Disorder Act 1998 is a specific approach. It reflects developments in the United States during the past few years where there has been a proliferation of 'hate crime' laws aimed at confronting racist acts. Legislative provisions have both created dedicated race assault offences and considered racism as an aggravating factor. In Britain evidence shows significant increases in racist attacks and incidents. For instance Home Office figures showed 12,222 racial incidents recorded by the police in 1995/96 (Home Office 1997), which had nearly doubled by 1999/2000 to 47,810 (Home Office 1999). Similarly, the British Crime Survey, the national victim survey that has been produced every two years since 1984, is considered to provide a more precise figure for the actual level of crime. It indicates consistently that a more accurate figure for racially motivated crime is *in excess of ten times* that of official police figures. A focus on the more extreme and criminal forms of racism does however lead to the danger of failing to acknowledge the more subtle and pervasive forms of societal racism (see Goldberg 1997).

This chapter will primarily focus on the ways that the law has been used as a mechanism of regulation in confronting racism in sport. In confronting racism in sport, we will question the assumption that 'more law' is the most effective tool in fighting manifestations of racism. In regulating racism in society as a whole, the law can, at best, be seen as having been peripheral in Britain. We would argue that as a mechanism of regulation it has largely failed to be an agent of positive change. It may have highlighted incidents of racism, but has often lacked efficacy in reducing the phenomenon of racism and impacting upon structural racism.

In order to explore these issues about the role of law in combating racism within society generally, and sport in particular, we will compare the situation in Britain with that of the United States. Here, due to the historical experiences of slavery, 'Jim Crowism', and the Civil Rights movement, such questions have been addressed more fully. A stated objective in the U.S. has been how to create a society where 'colour doesn't matter' (Williams 1992, 1997). The problem with legal regulation is that the law is 'colour blind' in so far as it requires all individuals to be treated equally irrespective of race, nationality or ethnic grouping. Thus it fails to reflect the reality that minority groups in society suffer specific forms of oppression which cannot simply be overcome by legislative requirements for equal opportunities.

The focus will primarily be on football as it is widely seen to be the 'national game' and is therefore clearly focused within the contemporary gaze of the media and public, though cricket will also be considered. Its significance is that in being the archetypal 'English game' it arguably exhibits important underlying discourses concerning nationalism, racial distinctions and prejudice.

Sport, society and the law

Whether sport is merely a reflection of society, a sort of microcosm of wider society, or is fundamentally a separate sphere of social interaction, divorced from the normal rules of societal behaviours, is clearly a complex sociological question. Whilst George Orwell's view that sport is 'war minus the shooting' correctly highlighted the political significance of sport, it clearly failed to appreciate the fact that sport is seen by many to simply be a way of entering into another world. A comparison between the law's intervention in society generally and sport in particular can nevertheless be a useful way of examining such contradictions.

However such a comparison can be problematic. Some may question whether a victim's plight concerning racism in sport, particularly in high-paid elite professional sport, is really anything that we should care too much about. Is being called a 'nigger' or 'black bastard' on a sports field equal to the manifestation of racism felt by those in Britain's deprived inner city areas? But the same social ills that pervade general life are still clearly found in sport. Racism, in terms of limited work opportunities for ethnic minority employees, verbal abuse and harassment are realities in the sporting world too.

So an analysis of how the law should operate is useful. In any discussion on legal regulation, a distinction should be made between the law providing a remedy of compensation for acts of racism in terms of the denial of an individual's right, and the prohibition of racism through regulation and penalizing sanctions. The former is the ambit of the civil law, the latter the criminal law.

Both, of course, are located within a paradigm of legal liberalism: the law priori-
tizing the individual and basing liability, blame and fault formally on the individual. In the context of racism, the emphasis on individual responsibility for
racist activities runs the risk of obfuscation of its social causes. It is not primarily
an issue of individual responsibility and blame; it is a societal failure and responsibility that lies with us all.

This can be illustrated by the use of the law to provide compensatory
remedies, reactive solutions to acts of racial discrimination 'to past wrongs.' Individual acts are emphasized whether it is in the fields of education or of employment. Such provisions have little impact upon social and institutional structures
and practices that discriminate. As a form of social justice there are persuasive
arguments that have not been put into meaningful legal form in Britain, for proactive 'affirmative' legal intervention to bring about positive change.

Contextualizing sports racism

In sport, racism is a continuing problem that deservedly needs to be highlighted.
It reveals itself, for example, in sportsmen and women being vilified by, and
having limited job opportunities in, the sports industry. In professional sport, the
media have played a role in highlighting such tensions. There have been allegations in recent seasons that football players such as Ian Wright and the ex-Ports-
mouth striker, Paul Hall, continue to be the victims of racist abuse on the field
of play. In the 1996–97 season, Nathan Blake refused to play for Wales after the
manager, Bobby Gould, had allegedly made racist statements about opponents in
the dressing room (see Mitchell 1997). This last incident is especially revealing,
as initially Gould was not even capable of understanding that he had voiced sentiments which could be construed as racist.

In cricket, recent incidents have included criticisms of the ex-England cricket
manager, Raymond Illingworth, concerning his alleged comments against Devon
Malcolm. Earlier, in 1995, an article by Robert Henderson in *Wisden Cricket
Monthly* led to a general furore when the author suggested that Asian and black
cricketers playing for England did not try as hard as their white counterparts, as
they supposedly lacked the biological traits deemed necessary to play Test
cricket. Devon Malcolm and Philip DeFreitas, two of the black cricketers mentioned in the article, won substantial damages after issuing writs for libel. The
editor, David Frith, was almost alone in justifying the publication of the article
when he stated: 'The aim was to launch a constructive debate ... reservations
(about non-English players) have rumbled around the cricket grounds and in
the sports columns of the newspapers for several years' (Frith 1995).

Henderson's view that black players who play for England, such as Malcolm
and DeFreitas, do not have as much commitment is as prejudiced as the former
Conservative MP Norman Tebbit's infamous invention of the 'Cricket Test' –
ethnic minorities in England cannot call themselves English unless they support
England at cricket and not the teams from where they have migrated from. The
Henderson episode led to the formation of a fans-based campaigning group

(cricket's equivalent to football's *Kick it Out*) called '*Hit Racism for Six*' (see Hit Racism for Six 1996). The continuing tale concerning match fixing and allegations of cheating against Pakistan cricket and cricketers is another example of an underlying narrative of racism within cricket (see Fraser 1995). These issues were raised in the High Court in the Imran Khan v Botham and Lamb libel case in 1997, with allegations of racism bandied about alongside the debate about whether picking of the seam of a cricket balls amounted to cheating (see Marqusee, this volume).

Defining racism within a legalistic discourse

Defining racism within society, and in sport, is problematic. Though it has operational difficulties, Cashmore's (1996) suggestion that racism can be defined as 'prejudice coupled with power', is useful. This is because it highlights the fact that certain minority groups often lack power within society. Though they may have prejudiced views, if they lack the institutional power to put such views into effect, it makes little sense to talk of subordinated groups expressing 'racism' in the same way as dominant groups.

In Britain, different statutory agencies have their own social construction of the problem of racism in terms of causality and prescription. As Bowling states, 'the process of naming the problem is not simply a matter of semantics but reflects the intensely political process of conceptualization' (Bowling 1998: 23). This includes local authority agencies such as housing, education and social services departments. Additionally, the police's definition can illustrate that these individual perspectives reflect very clearly the different discourses prevalent in each agency. Since 1986, the police forces in England and Wales have used the Association of Chief Police Officers' (ACPO) definition of a 'racial incident' as being: 'Any incident in which it appears *to the reporting officer or investigating officer* that the complaint involved an element of racial motivation or any incident which includes an allegation of racial motivation' (Brennan 1999: 26, emphasis added). By contrast the Stephen Lawrence Inquiry Report considers a more radical and subjective approach by recommending, 'A racist incident is any incident which is perceived to be racist by the victim or any other person' (The Stephen Lawrence Inquiry 1999: recommendation 12).

The law has attempted, often with little success, to provide some precision in defining racism (on legal regulation of racism generally, see Hepple 1968; McCrudden 1982; Gordon 1982; Commission For Racial Equality 1990; Solomos 1993). As we will argue later, the Race Relations Act 1976 provides a guide to what amounts to racial discrimination. The Public Order Act 1986 defines the crime of incitement to racial hatred, but no guidance is provided as to what words or behaviour are required. Under the Crime and Disorder Act 1998, assaults can be dealt with in a more serious form if they are seen as being 'racially aggravated'. This occurs if either a) at the time of committing the offence, or immediately before or after doing so, the offender demonstrates towards the victim of the offence hostility based on the victim's membership (or presumed membership) of a racial group; or h) the offence is motivated (wholly or partly) by hostility towards members of a racial group based on their member-ship of that group.

The second test is essentially the main target of this new offence – where the motive of an assault is racial. The first test does not require the proving of a racial motivation, and is likely to be more commonly used as the basis of a prose-cution (see Leng, Taylor and Wasik 1998 for further analysis). This requires 'demonstrated racial hostility'. As Jepson argues, this will need a change in the police definition of a racial incident. The police will now need 'to look for and identify objective factors that relate to racial hostility' (Jepson 1998: 1838).

This problem of perspectives is evidenced by the police view of racial inci-dents as 'events'. Crime is not an event, but a social process which includes a number of social events each of which is inextricably bound up with the other. The Stephen Lawrence Inquiry Report notes: 'racism in general terms consists of conduct or words or practices which disadvantage or advantage people because of their colour, culture, or ethnic origin. In its more subtle form it is as damaging as in its overt form' (The Stephen Lawrence Inquiry 1999: Para 6.4). The Report also considered at some length the meaning of institutional racism. One supported view was that it is: 'not solely through the deliberate actions of a small number of bigoted individuals, but through a more systematic tendency that could unconsciously influence police performance generally' (The Stephen Lawrence Inquiry 1999: Para 6.5).

Such definitions, of course, have been put forward before. In his report into the Brixton riots, Lord Scarman responded to the suggestion that 'Britain is an institutionally racist society,' in this way:

> If, by [institutionally racist] it is meant that it [Britain] is a society which knowingly, as a matter of policy, discriminates against black people, I reject the allegation. If, however, the suggestion being made is that practices may be adopted by public bodies as well as private individuals which are unwit-tingly discriminatory against black people, then this is an allegation which deserves serious consideration, and, where proved, swift remedy.
> (The Scarman Report 1981: Para 2.22, p 11)

Legal definitions are always problematic. If drafted too widely, they lack preci-sion and are open to numerous alternative constructions; if too narrowly, tech-nicalities and distinctions can be argued; lawyers are masters at the art of mystification. The reality of the language of the law is of course, that it is based upon contingency. In attempting to define a complex social phenomenon such as racism, a goal of providing a workable legal meaning is highly ambitious.

The specificity of sports racism

Similarly, racism in sport should be perceived as a social process. Two main manifestations of racism in sport will be examined in the rest of the chapter.

Spectator racism has been identified as a problem for many years. Football, not surprisingly, has been the main area of activity but other sports, particularly cricket, have also been subject to this problem. The second main area concerns employment opportunities where structural and institutional practices discriminate against ethnic minorities. In the sports industry there are many examples where choices are made not to employ or promote individuals based on their race.

Spectator racism: the continuing problem of football

Spectator racism in football continues to occur. However, there is persuasive evidence that a long way has been travelled from the 'bad days' of the 1970s with a decline in the overall frequency, and a significant decrease in the amount, of racist chanting. This can be claimed to be a success for the various anti-racist initiatives that have taken place within football such as the publication of anti-racist fanzines by supporters of particular clubs; *'Let's Kick Racism out of Football'* campaign conceived in 1993 by the Professional Footballers Association and the Commission for Racial Equality (later reconstituted as *Kick it Out* – see McArdle and Lewis 1997; Garland and Rowe 1999 for an evaluation); and outside legal intervention.

Certainly there is a dominant discourse within the Football Association that the problem is decreasing, if not completely eradicated. There is, however, strong evidence that incidents of racist activity are still perpetuated by individuals and small groups that operate 'in complex and often contradictory ways ... racist abuse in grounds occurs in an intermittent fashion' (Back, Crabbe and Solomos 1998: 84). That is, the location and form, or the articulation of racism, has changed – it is however unclear whether the extent of the underlying problem has altered significantly. Caution is vital in alluding to a perception that the overall problem has reduced. The causality of racism is complex, as are the solutions. Many argue that racism in football is a reflection of general societal-wide racism. As Bowling says: 'The historical records show that violent racism waxes and wanes with social, economic and political forces ... [W]e must hope ... no one becomes complacent during those periods when the extent and ferocity of violent racism wanes' (Bowling 1998: 317).

The Football Task Force interim report, *Eliminating Racism from Football* (1998), as one of its key recommendations asks the Government to amend the Football Offences Act 1991 as a matter of urgency to make it an offence for individuals to use racist comments inside football grounds. This has been enacted with section 9 of the Football Offences and Disorder Act 1999 which amends the offence of indecent or racist chanting at designated football matches which is contained in section 3 of the Football Offences Act 1991. The effect of the amendment is that an individual who engages in such chanting on their own can commit the offence (see Gardiner 1999). Under the 1991 Act, chanting was defined as the 'repeated uttering of any words or sounds in concert with one or more others.' The Cantona Affair in 1995 when the Manchester

United player attacked a Crystal Palace supporter, Matthew Simmons, high-lighted the perceived limitations of this section. Simmons, who had taunted Cantona with racist insults, was not charged under the Football Offences Act due to his lone action – but he was however charged and convicted with other public order offences (Gardiner 1998). In the aftermath, there were many calls for the legislation to be strengthened by allowing for the 'individualizing' of this offence.

The 1999 Act is the third dedicated piece of legislation for the regulation of football stadia. The first was the Football Spectators Act 1989, the second the Football Offences Act 1991 and, as with the 1999 Act, they all have their origins in the recommendations of the Taylor Report based on the Hillsborough disaster (Taylor 1990). The Report considered that the provisions of the Public Order Act 1986 concerning 'threatening, abusive or insulting words or beha-viour' did not adequately cover indecent or racialist chanting.

Section 3 of the 1991 Act has been little used suggesting that it has been used primarily *symbolically* as an official indication that something was being done. Until early 1998, there were only about eighty convictions. In the season 1998–99 there were thirty-three convictions. One of the major problems is the issue of policing even though closed circuit television cameras are used to aid identification of perpetrators during matches. The individualiz-ing of the offence would arguably be even harder to enforce with police and ground stewards finding it difficult to identify the cries of a lone racist. As Parpworth argues: 'There is a certain futility in creating statutory offences which are effectively moribund due to difficulties associated with detection' (Parpworth 1993: 1016).

Football stadia have become one of the most overtly regulated public spaces. There is an increasing danger that this regulatory approach to social problems by the use of the law will create increasingly anodyne environments where freedom of expression and movement is overtly suppressed through the law. 'Panic law' is invariably bad law (on the legal regulation of football see Green-field and Osborn 1996, 1998; Redhead 1995). At best it can play a minor role as a part of a quasi-regulatory approach that attempts to engage effectively with the roots of racism in football and society generally, and treats racism as a problem of social policy.

Spectator racism: it's just not cricket

Cricket spectating has also increasingly fallen under the gaze of both those who disapprove of the increasing 'footballization' of cricket fans, the so-called 'Barmy Army' phenomenon, and those who are challenging the events that go on at some grounds. The home of Yorkshire cricket, Headingley, and its Western Terrace particularly, has been identified as having a specific problem with racism. It is an area that facilitates relaxed spectating, beer drinking, good humour and player-worshipping. However over recent years, it has increasingly witnessed incidents involving groups of individuals in ugly racist scenes. At the

Nat-West Cup semi-final match in 1996, Northamptonshire Indian test bowler, Anil Kumble, at a stage when Yorkshire were heading for defeat, was pelted with bananas when he fielded on the boundary. Similarly as former *Observer* sports editor, Alan Hubbard, recounts:

> David 'Syd' Lawrence recalls that when he played at Headingley they called him 'nigger, black bastard, sambo, monkey, gorilla, and threw bananas'. He also received a letter with a Yorkshire postmark which read: 'Don't shout yer mouth off, nigger, you won't be welcome next time. Nig, nog.'
>
> (Hubbard 1996:12)

The problem may not be perceived to be as great as that in football. Certainly there have been few calls for the extension of legislation such as the Football Offences Act to cricket and some attempts have been made to address the problems. Yorkshire County Cricket Club has, uniquely for a county and Test venue, a policy and ground rules that specifically ban racist chanting and abuse. It has also re-planned the operations of the stewards and redesigned the seating on the Western Terraces with greater space and access and monitoring with CCTV.

The major question, then, is what is the most effective way to regulate spectator racism generally in those sports where it is seen as a problem? What role does the law have to play? It is contended that the law may have a complementary role to play, along with other quasi-legal and non-legal methods, but it certainly cannot act as a substitute for or in isolation of them.

United States comparison

In the United States, the regulation of spectator racism that impacts upon the sports arena has not been through the criminal law. Title VII of the Civil Rights Act of 1964 outlaws discrimination in employment because of an individual's race. It includes not only discriminatory treatment that leads to economic loss but psychological and emotional harm experienced in the workplace. The harassment in question must be 'sufficiently severe or pervasive to alter the conditions of employment and create an abusive working environment'.

Phoebe Weaver Williams recognizes that although: 'sports employers, like other employers, are not directly responsible for the behaviour of third parties, e.g. fans and spectators, they are nevertheless required to eliminate racial harassment in the workplaces of their professional athletes' (Weaver Williams 1996: 312). Issues relevant to this include the extent of the employer's control and any other legal responsibility the employer may have with respect to conduct of such non-employees. Weaver Williams recognizes that much more needs to be done to clean up what she views as the 'racially polluted environments' of the sports arena (we will explore comparisons with US sports legal experience more fully later in the chapter).

Racism in the sports workplace

The other significant social field for racism in sport is the workplace. Difference in work opportunities for ethnic minorities has long been identified. In Britain, nearly 20 per cent of professional footballers are of Afro-Caribbean origin. However the 'glass ceiling' of structural barriers obstructs the ability of those from ethnic minority groups to rise into positions of influence and power in football administration and management. Moreover, there is the widely held perception within professional football that the game does not provide a suitable career for members of the Asian community (see Chaudhary, 1994).

As far as the workplace is concerned, the Race Relations Act 1976 has provided support for those who suffer discrimination. Under section 1 of the Act, 'a person discriminates against another in any circumstances if . . . on racial grounds he treats that other less favourably than he treats or would treat other persons'. Section 3 defines 'racial' as covering 'colour, race, nationality or ethnic or national origins'.

Racial vilification in the football industry

The case of *Hussaney v Chester City FC and Kevin Ratcliffe* in 1997 provides an example of how the provision operates. James Hussaney won an action for racial discrimination against Chester City FC. Hussaney was an apprentice at Chester and had played for the youth and reserves team. On 29 January 1997, when he was due to play for the Chester City Reserves against Oldham Athletic Reserves, he was called a 'black cunt' by the first team manager, Kevin Ratcliffe, who was also due to play for the reserves. Hussaney had put the wrong sized studs into Ratcliffe's football boots. Hussaney made a formal complaint to the club. Shortly after this, during spring 1997, Hussaney was informed he would not be offered a professional contract. The club agreed that Ratcliffe made the alleged racial abuse, but denied it amounted to racial discrimination. Ratcliffe made some attempts to provide an apology to Hussaney. The industrial tribunal held that the abusive language amounted to discrimination by both Ratcliffe and the club on grounds of race and made a compensatory award of £2,500 for injury to feelings. The tribunal found, however, that the failure to offer a professional contract was made 'purely on footballing grounds'.

Unexceptionally, the Football Association failed to carry out an inquiry, viewing this incident as essentially an internal one for Chester FC (see McArdle, 1998). In 1999, Ratcliffe continued to be manager of what now is a financially struggling club. This inaction by the FA belies their Anti-Discrimination Policy for Football which states:

> The FA will not tolerate sexual or racially-based harassment or other discriminatory behaviour, whether physical or verbal, and will work to ensure that such behaviour is met with appropriate disciplinary action in whatever context it occurs (paragraph 4).[1]

Can a more direct legal response be made to this structural racism? Another measure proposed by the Football Task Force's report, *Eliminating Racism from Football*, is that the Professional Footballers Association (PFA) and the League Managers Association should:

> 'recommend inserting an anti-racism pledge in player's and manager's contracts with breaches incurring severe sanctions (fines or dismissals)' (Football Task Force 1998: para. 4(b)25).

Related to this is a call on the Football Association (FA) to amend its disciplinary rules so that racist abuse on the field of play is recognized as a 'distinct offence punishable by separate and severe disciplinary measures'. Racist abuse by one player to another should also be automatically treated as a red card offence by referees. The report and these proposals are explicitly built on the experience of the *Kick It Out* Campaign, which also calls for disciplinary action to be taken against players who engage in racist abuse.

Racial harassment and abuse can occur in two contexts – within a club and between players of opposing teams on the field of play. Stipulating that racism is a breach of contract will be of symbolic and cultural significance in the first context but will make relatively little difference from a legal perspective. This is because, as illustrated by Hussaney above, case law under the Race Relations Act 1976 (and the similarly worded and interpreted Sex Discrimination Act 1975) make it clear that clubs, as employers, will incur liability if they fail to protect players and their employees in general from racist harassment by colleagues or those in managerial positions. This statutory position is reinforced by the Code of Practice and Notes on Contract, which is given to all professional footballers and trainees.

Technically, there is still some doubt that a 'mere' racist insult uttered in jest or in the 'heat of the moment' constitutes racial harassment (see *De Souza v Automobile Association* [1986] IRLR 103).[2] A suitably worded clause in footballers' contracts could (and should) clarify that a verbal racist insult or 'joke' constitutes a breach of contract, and thus a disciplinary offence.

To avoid statutory vicarious liability, as imposed by section 32 of the Race Relations Act, clubs should provide and enforce written rules, preferably as part of equal opportunities policies and procedures, which prohibit racial harassment and impose penalties up to and including dismissal of guilty employees. One problem with vicarious liability is that it can only be imposed if the guilty employee is acting within the scope of his or her employment. The landmark decision by the Court of Appeal in *Tower Boot Co v Jones* ([1997] IRLR 168), in reversing an Employment Appeals Tribunal decision to the contrary, clarified that the common law approach to this restriction on vicarious liability is not appropriate in applying the Race Relations Act.

Thus clubs are still potentially liable if they fail to protect players from racism which occurs, for example, as part of so-called 'locker-room' behaviour which, it could be argued, is outside the common-law concept of a player's scope of employment. It is often this form of racism which is the most insidious in the perpetuation of a racist culture which in itself is, at the very least, a contributing factor in deterring members of ethnic minorities from pursuing a career in professional football. If this is no longer true with respect to members of the Afro-Caribbean community it would still appear to be the case with respect to members of the Asian community. One of the points highlighted by the Football Task Force's report is that there are no top-flight Asian footballers, despite the huge enthusiasm for the game amongst Asian children (see Chaudhary 1994; Bains and Patel 1996).

Clubs which dismiss employees who are guilty of racial harassment will be safe from incurring liability for unfair dismissal providing they act consistently against offenders, and proper procedures, such as the conducting of a reasonable investigation, the convening of a formal disciplinary hearing and the provision of rights of appeal, have been followed. Another practical outcome of making racism a breach of contract will be that it will facilitate, although not require, clubs defining racism as gross misconduct which, if proven, will result in summary, i.e. instant, dismissal.

However, the major lacuna with respect to the Race Relations Act is that it does not require employers to take disciplinary action against employees who engage in racist behaviour towards individuals outside of the employing organization. This is especially important in professional football as it is clear that the problem of racism is significantly more important with respect to players of opposing teams on the field of play. This is partly because a player, who as an individual is racist, will be less inhibited about expressing his/her racism to an opponent than against a team-mate. It is also partly because racism is used as a cynical and calculated act of 'gamesmanship' to wind up an opposing player to put him/her off their game and/or provoke him/her into committing a foul which results in the victim of racism rather than its perpetrator being sent off. In the analogous context of homophobia, this 'tactic' is exemplified by the much publicized incident between Robbie Fowler and Graeme Le Saux in the latter part of the 1998–99 season (see Whelan 1999).

The measures proposed by the Football Task Force should operate in a two-pronged and mutually reinforcing manner. First, referees will be obliged to send off players who are guilty of racism during the course of a game. Second, clubs can regard such players as having acted in breach of their employment contracts and can take disciplinary action against them accordingly. The fact that racist players have been sent off and consequently damaged their teams' prospects of success will, hopefully, encourage their clubs to subject them to disciplinary proceedings. Similarly, clubs will begin to demand that referees are consistent in regarding racism as a red card offence. Anti-racist clauses in managers' contracts will also deter the more cynical managers (should they exist) from encouraging their players to engage in racist 'gamesmanship'.

In conclusion, it is certainly conceivable that the inclusion and enforcement of anti-racist clauses in players' and managers' contracts will combat racism on the field of play, as well as within clubs themselves. In turn, this could contribute to a further reduction in the racist culture that traditionally has pervaded professional football, not least on the terraces and in the stands, as supporters follow their player role models in renouncing overt racist conduct.

Therefore, inserting clauses in players' contracts may well contribute to making participation in the professional game more attractive to individual members of minorities. However, the limits of legal regulation are exemplified by the fact that this will do very little, if anything, to counteract the view apparently held by many managers, coaches and scouts that professional football is not a viable career option for young persons from the Asian community. Only when attitudes based on this perception begin to alter significantly, will the aspirations of the Task Force for the establishment of professional football as a truly multicultural sport be met.

The US experience: affirmative action

The position in UK sports employment can be compared to the position in the United States. In *Black and White: Race and Sports in America*, Kenneth Shropshire provides a detailed analysis of the position of ethnic minorities, particularly African-Americans in the United States' sports industry. He examines their opportunities in terms of employment in 'front office' position and in terms of ownership of sports franchises. In front office positions he includes chief executive offices, head coaches, team doctors, lawyers and accountants. In terms of sports franchise ownership in the States in 1994 in football, baseball and basketball, only seven were African-Americans out of 275 who had interests (Lapchick and Bennedict 1994). This is of course in the context of very high levels of representation of African-Americans in American amateur and professional sport. Lapchick (1995) shows that whilst African-Americans comprise 12 per cent of the population, 80 per cent of National Basketball Association players are black, 68 per cent in the National Football League and 19 per cent in Major League Baseball. As an icon, Michael Jordan illustrates the apparent black meritocracy that has been created in US professional sport. This 'success' though, clearly has a wider ideological function. As Weaver Williams states, African-Americans:

> have not only played their sports well, they have excelled at America's game. Their successes 'fax' to us America's message: if you are truly talented, work hard, have something of value to offer, and function from an 'individualistic' perspective rather than a victim perspective, our society will award you in a 'colourblind' fashion.
>
> (Weaver Williams 1996: 289)

But Shropshire (1996: 2) further identifies the close link that can be made between racism in sport and in society generally. Citing high profile incidents in the United States such as the beating of Rodney King by members of the Los Angeles Police Department, and the police misconduct and racism that was established in the O.J. Simpson trial, he concludes that 'prospects for solving the race problems of the United States, particularly discrimination against Afro-Americans, are dismal' (Shropshire 1996: 2). The racist killing of James Byrd in Texas in 1998 (an African-American dragged to death behind a pick-up truck by white supremacists) and the continued 'race hate' killings in America can be added to this list (see Kettle 1999; Campbell 1999).

Positive discrimination or affirmative action has developed as a legally enforceable policy to attack historical structural racism in the United States (see Kennedy 1986; Williams 1997; West 1993; Marable 1995). Four typical forms of affirmative action can be identified: the concerted recruitment of an under-represented group; the institution of training programmes, such as diversity and sensitivity training; the modification of employment practices that promote the under-utilization of under-represented individuals; and the most popular con-ception of affirmative action, the preferential hiring and promotion of under-represented groups. Shropshire asserts that in the United States, 'the last and most extreme version is not needed in sports at this time. What are needed in sports are strategies to open the hiring networks' (Shropshire 1996: 84).

Certainly, whatever its potential merits, affirmative action has not as yet changed the position for African-Americans with respect to their lack of repre-sentation in the upper echelons of sport. As in the UK, the glass ceiling remains for most members of ethnic minorities.

Conclusion

The role of the law in regulating racism needs to be situated in the context that the parameters of legal regulation from other non-legal normative mechanisms are unclear. The danger is that the law too easily becomes the primary regula-tory mechanism to be used to provide remedies. However it is increasingly argued, particularly by Alan Hunt (1993), that law is best understood in con-temporary society, not in the classic formulation of English jurisprudence as a collection or model of rules, but as a form of 'governance' or regulation. He stresses that this occurs not only through law but other quasi-legal and non-legal mechanisms. Law is increasingly interwoven with other mechanisms and not distinct in terms of regulation.

Hunt uses the work of the French philosopher Michel Foucault as the basis of this perspective concerning the sociology of governance. He sees Foucault's con-tention that though law was important in the pre-modern world as a form of control, in modern society (from the end of the eighteenth century), law has largely given way to 'governance' and 'policing', a more complex multidimen-sional form of regulation. One of Foucault's most persistent influences on politi-cal philosophy are his ideas on discipline and surveillance, in that, increasingly, the State uses bodies of knowledge to intervene as a form of power. As Hunt says: 'the picture that he is taken to have painted is of ever extending and ever more intrusive mechanisms of power that insert themselves into every nook and cranny of social and personal life' (Hunt 1993: 288).

One aim of this is the stated goal of increasing 'normalization' and the search for new sites of disciplinary intervention. Can racism in sport be seen as one of these sites needing regulation? Is the discourse of anti-racism a means of sanitizing football culture generally? There is a lack of specificity concerning racism; the focus is now more widely on the regulation of a number of anti-social activities (see Back, Crabbe and Solomos 1998).

A major issue with the intervention of the law into new areas of social life, and in this case sporting arenas, are the dangers of juridification, where what are intrinsically social relationships between humans within a 'social field' become imbibed with legal values and become understood as constituting a legal relationship; that is, social norms become legal norms (see Bourdieu 1987). If a dispute then befalls the parties, a legal remedy is seen as a primary remedy. This will invariably change the nature and perception of the dispute and the relational connection between the parties. As Foster (1993) argues:

> Juridification ... at a simple level, merely reproduces the traditional idea of private and public realms, with private areas increasingly being subject to public or judicial control, a move from voluntarism to legalism. But it offers also a more complex version which stresses the interaction as legal norms are used to reorder the power relations within the social arena.
>
> (Foster 1993: 105)

So what future does the law have to play in the fight against sports racism? In terms of employment, in the present political climate in Britain it is unlikely that any meaningful affirmative action, even if desired, is likely to occur. Formal barriers to participation in sporting activity is not a problem in the vast majority of major sports in Britain and the United States. This can be contrasted with post-apartheid South Africa where formal quotas for non-white players have been implemented and seen as essential in rugby and cricket, after considerable government pressure (see Chaudhary 1999). In Britain, there may well be increasing calls for quotas especially in terms of progression of those from ethnic minorities to get into these 'front office' positions. However, again their legal position is uncertain.

In the context of spectator racism, more legal intervention and criminalization seems likely in the near future. However echoing Francis's comment on legal intervention concerning societal racism: 'Rather what is needed is a genuine commitment from Government and existing agencies to an imaginative use of existing powers, coupled with the continuing development, monitoring and evaluation of extra-legal provision' (Francis 1994: 16).

Racism in sport is a reflection and representation of societal racism generally. The law has a supportive role to play alongside other solutions to the complex issue of racism. The formalism of legal intervention however lacks the subtlety to bring about real lasting social change. An array of interconnected non-legal, quasi-legal and legal instruments is needed. Effective and real implementation of such measures is the key to bring about real change. In the context of bringing about transformation in the practices of the police, the Stephen Lawrence Inquiry Report suggests that close monitoring of performance indicators is needed to assess the impact of the many recommendations. It is essential that changes primarily come from within. Sports governing bodies therefore need to begin to assume greater responsibility over dealing with the problem of racism in their back yards and promote policies that provide meaningful opportunity for all in sport. As Patricia Williams (1997: 26) warns: 'I think one of the greatest obstacles to progress at the moment[is] the paralysing claim that racism *has* no solution.'

But what role does law have to play? We have argued in the past that the use of legal prohibition is unlikely to be the best solution (Gardiner 1996, 1998; Gardiner *et al.* 1998). Indeed, there is a strong argument that the use of legislation can be seen as diverting attention and resources from educational and social policy initiatives, which might more successfully eliminate the causes of the problem. The process of legalization and possible criminalization of problems, such as racist hate speech, can often be used to deflect political responsibility away from its being a failure of social policy towards being seen as an issue based on individual responsibility and wickedness. In many ways 'colour doesn't matter' in sport, but as this book clearly shows, there is much to be done. Legal provisions have a role to play, but it should not be at the expense of forgetting the importance of other non-legal social practices.

Notes

1   By way of comparison, in Australia, similar but formally enforced 'anti-vilification' codes have been introduced. In 1995, the Australian Football League (AFL) introduced racial and religious vilification rules covering club players, directors, officers and employees including coaches. Complaints are initially subject to a conciliation process, but if it remains unresolved, progress to an AFL Tribunal. In 1998, the Australian Cricket Board (ACB) introduced similar rules. However these are limited to players who are participating in a match played under the auspices of the ACB.

2   This case concerned a claim brought by a black employee who overheard her manager refer to her as 'the wog'. In rejecting her claim, May LJ stated: 'Racially to insult a coloured employee is not enough by itself, even if that insult caused him or her distress' (at pp. 106–07). This decision has never been overruled, although it has been implicitly doubted by cases concerning sexual harassment which have involved interpretations of parallel provisions contained in the Sex Discrimination Act 1975. See as examples: *Porcelli v Strathclyde Regional Council* [1986] IRLR 134 and *Wileman v Minilec Engineering* [1988] IRLR 144.

Bibliography

Back, L., Crabbe, T., and Solomos, J. (1998) 'Racism in Football: patterns of continuity and change', in A. Brown (ed.) *Fanatics! Power Identity & Fandom in Football*, London: Routledge.

Bains, J. and Patel, R. (1996) *Asians Can't Play Football*, Birmingham: Asian Social Development Agency.

Bourdieu, P. (1987) The Force of Law: towards a sociology of the juridical field, 38 *Hastings Law Review*, 814.

Bowling, B. (1998) *Violent Racism*, Oxford University Press.

Brennan, F. (1999) Racially Motivated Crime: the response of the Criminal justice system, *Criminal Law Review* January, 17.

Campbell, D. (1999) 'Hate spawned on the Fourth of July', *The Guardian*, 6 July.

Cashmore, E. (1996) *Making Sense of Sport* (2nd ed.), London: Routledge.

Chaudhary, V. (1994) 'Asians can play Football too', *The Guardian*, 17 August.

—— (1999) 'End of the Lillywhite rainbow', in *The Guardian*, 26 February.

Commission For Racial Equality (1990) *Second review of the Race Relations Act 1976*, London: CRE.

Football Task Force (1998) *Eliminating Racism from Football*, A report by the Football Task Force submitted to the Minister for Sport on Monday 30 March 1998.

Foster, K. (1993) 'Developments in Sporting Law', in L. Allison (ed.) *The Changing Politics of Sport*, Manchester University Press.

Foucault, M. (1977) *Discipline and Punish: the Birth of the Prison*, London: Penguin.

Francis, P. (1994) 'Race Attacks: do we need new legislation?', *Criminal Justice Matters* 16.

Fraser, D. (1995) 'Balls, Bribes and Bails: the Jurisprudence of Salim Malik', *Law and Popular Culture Research Group Working Papers*, Manchester Metropolitan University.

Frith, D. (ed.)(1995) *Wisden Cricket Monthly* August.

Gardiner, S. (1996) 'Racism as Hate Speech', *Criminal Justice Matters*, 23.

—— (1998) 'The Law and Hate Speech: Ooh Aah Cantona' and the Denomination of 'the Other' in A. Brown (ed.) *Fanatics! Power, Identity & Fandom in Football*, London: Routledge.

—— (1999) 'The Continuing Regulation of Football Supporters: The Football Offences and Disorder Act 1999', *Sports Law Bulletin*.

Gardiner, S., Felix, A., James, M., Welch, R., and O'Leary, J. (1998) *Sports Law*, London: Cavendish.

Garland, J. and Rowe, M. (1999) 'Selling the Game Short: An Examination of the Role of Antiracism in British Football', *Sociology of Sport Journal*, 35.

Goldberg, D. (1997) *Racial Subjects: Writing on Race in America*, London: Routledge.

Gordon, P. (1982) 'Racial Discrimination: Towards a Legal Strategy', *British Journal of Law and Society*, 127.

Greenfield, S. and Osborn, G. (1996) 'After the Act? The Reconstruction and Regulation of Football Fandom', *Journal of Civil Liberties*, 7.

—— (1998) 'When the Writ Hits the Fan: panic law and football fandom', in A. Brown (ed.) *Fanatics! Power Identity & Fandom in Football*, London: Routledge.

Hepple, B. (1968) *Race, Jobs and the Law in Britain*, Allen Lane: Penguin Press.

Hit Racism for Six (1996) *Hit Racism For Six: Race and Cricket in England today*, London: Roehampton Institute.

Home Office (1997) *Racial Violence and Harassment: A Consultation Document*, September, appendix B.

Home Office (1999) *Race and the Criminal Justice System*, London: Home Office.

Hubbard, A. (1996) 'Racism In Sport: malignant malady that lingers on', *The Observer* 18 August, 12.

Hunt, A. (1993) 'Law as a Constitutive Mode of Regulation' in *Explorations in Law and Society: Towards a Constitutive Theory of Law*, London: Routledge.

Jepson, P. (1998) 'The Definition of a Racial Incident', *New Law Journal*, 11 December, 1838–1839.

Kennedy, R. (1986) 'Persuasion and Distrust: a Comment on the Affirmative Action Debate', 99 *Harvard Law Review*, 1327.

Kettle, M. (1999) 'US shows fast growth in race hate groups', *The Guardian*, 24 February.

Lapchick, R. and Bennedict, J. (1994) *Racial Report Card*, Boston: North-Eastern University, Centre for Study of Sport in Society.

Lapchick, R. (1995) *1995 Racial Report Card*, Boston: North-Eastern University, Centre for Study of Sport in Society.

Leng, R., Taylor, R., and Wasik, M. (1998) *Blackstone's Guide to The Crime and Disorder Act 1998*, London: Blackstone Press.

Lester, A and Bindman, G. (1972) *Race and Law*, Allen Lane: Penguin.

Marable, M. (1995) *Beyond Black and White: Transforming African-American Politics*, London: Verso.

MacPherson, Sir W. (1999) *The Stephen Lawrence Inquiry: Report on the Inquiry by Sir William Macpherson of Cluny* Cm 4262, London: HMSO.

McArdle, D. (1998) 'In My Opinion', *Sports Law Bulletin*, 1(2), March/April, 2.

McArdle, D. and Lewis, D. (1997) *'Kick Racism Out of Football'*: A Report on the Implementation of the Commission for Racial Equality's Strategies, Centre for Research in Industrial and Commercial Law, London: Middlesex University.

McCrudden, C. (1982) 'Institutional Discrimination', 2 *Oxford Journal of Legal Studies*, 303.

Mitchell, K. (1997) 'Gould has the Gift of the Gaffe', *The Observer*, April 6.

Parpworth, N. (1993) 'Football and Racism: a Legislative Solution', *Solicitors Journal*, October 15, 1016–17.

Redhead, S. (1995) *Unpopular Cultures*, Manchester University Press.

Scarman, Lord (1981) *The Brixton Disorder: Report on the Inquiry by Lord Scarman*, London: HMSO.

Shropshire, K. (1996) *In Black and White: Race and Sports in America*, New York University Press.

Solomos, J. (1993) *Race and Racism in Britain*, London: Macmillan.

Taylor, Mr Justice (1990) *The Hillsborough Stadium Disaster* (Cm 962), London: HMSO.

Weaver Williams, P. (1996) 'Performing in a Racially Hostile Environment', *Marquette Sports Law Journal* 6(2), 287.

West, C. (1993) *Keeping Faith: Philosophy and Race in America*, London: Routledge.

Whelan, C. (1999) 'Nowt so queer as footballers', *The Observer*, 7 March.

Williams, P. (1992) *The Alchemy of Race and Rights*, Cambridge, Mass: Harvard University Press.

—— (1997) *Seeing a Colour-Blind Future: The Paradox of Race*, London: Virago.

Part III

Challenging discourses/ contesting identities

9 Playing their own game
A South Asian football experience

Sanjiev Johal

Introduction

When, in 1998, the pop group *Cornershop* reached the top of the British charts singing about 'A Brimful of Asha', only a select minority of those discerning pop music consumers who bought the single fully understood or even referentially appreciated the song's somewhat esoteric celebration. 'A Brimful of Asha' was the band's founder member, lead singer and song writer Tjinder Singh's personalized tribute to one of Bollywood's[1] greatest female vocalists Asha Bhosle. Whilst the eponymous recipient of this musical homage may have remained an obscure, indeed anonymous, lyrical figure for most people who experienced the song, the ethno-specific, or rather culture-specific, theme and language of the song did not preclude its massive chart success.[2] The British popular music scene can boast an innovative and insurgent contribution being made to the industry by British Asian artists. As well as those already mentioned, others such as Apache Indian, Sonia (lead singer of indie band *Echobelly*) Talvin Singh (winner of the 1999 Mercury Music Award), *Black Star Liner*, Bally Sagoo, *Asian Dub Foundation* are all recognized performers from across the musical generic spectrum, and all of whom variously bask in the ephemeral glow of pop's transient glory.

The wide world of television outwardly broadcasts its own visible/visual multi-culturalism. From newscasters, reporters and presenters to soap-opera characters, actors and comedians, South Asians command a relatively pervasive presence on television screens across Britain. In the professional sporting arena the English Test cricket team has called upon the respective talents of Mark Ramprakash and Nasser Hussain (awarded the England captaincy in 1999) – both players of 'mixed race' parentage with fathers who are of South Asian descent.[3] Sport completes a self-ordained holy pop-cultural trinity that also embraces television and popular music, and each member of this triumvirate (to differing degrees) can point to a particular participation and contribution by British South Asians. However, football, arguably sport's most emergent global marker, has historically and contemporaneously refused to admit its expansive popularity amongst Britain's varied South Asian communities. Indeed the authoritative gatekeepers of British football have blindly shackled, and at times culpably ignored, the input and ambition that these communities harbour toward the national game.

When Jas Bains (1995) deployed that much vaunted British penchant for irony in the title of his report *Asians Can't Play Football*, his satirical assertion was somewhat lost on many of those for whom the report would have been of greatest benefit, i.e. the controlling football authorities. For many, the title merely served to crystallize an ill-conceived and erroneous sporting axiom, the mechanics of which the body of the report successfully evinced. More recent work (Bains and Johal 1998; 1999) has illustrated that South Asians in Britain can and do play football, and that they enjoy a multifarious association with the sport that cuts across the playing, spectating and commercial aspects of the game. In this chapter I will examine the principal forms by which South Asian football and South Asian footballers have been denied recognition, development and access by and to the predominantly white-controlled world of British football. In the course of such an examination, the implications of this exclusion will also be drawn out through an overview of the establishment of all-South Asian teams, the Asian Games tournaments, and the Khalsa Football Federation. The first-hand accounts of South Asian players will be used to highlight a common experience of racism endured by many South Asian teams and players, but without assigning racist sentiments to all white teams and players. With the subject of South Asians and sport receiving minimal sociological enquiry, such treatment must first be redressed by situating existing studies within their appropriate spheres. With such a task in mind, the tendency to view South Asian association with sport in recognized and officially demarcated arenas is challenged, and the case to look beyond the mainstream of sporting/leisure pursuits is put forward.

Studies of South Asians and sport

Most discussions concerning race, racism and sport in Britain have largely tended to concentrate the dialectic within a black, African-Caribbean discourse (Carrington 1983; Cashmore 1981, 1982, 1983, 1990; Jarvie and Reid 1997; Lashley 1980, 1990; Maguire 1991; Orakwue 1998). The paucity of material concerning South Asian involvement in British sport has contributed to the general lack of informed understanding about the subject. The work that does exist in this field is predominantly, if not entirely, located within the established, quantifiable, institutionalized domains of sport and leisure (Carrington *et al.* 1987; Carroll 1993; Dixey 1982, Fleming 1989, 1994, 1995; Lyons 1989; McGuire and Collins 1998, Verma and Darby 1994). Much of this existing work obeys a heavy male bias, predominantly focusing on male sports activities. School sports, physical education, organized extra-curricular sport, regional local-authority leisure providers and sports clubs represent the recognized arenas in which the participation (or non-participation) of South Asians is viewed and critically ordered. Fleming's (1995) *Home and Away: Sport and South Asian Male Youth* is the most detailed and self-reflexive of these works for he recognizes the measuredly confined parameters of his study (his research was set in a north London multi-racial comprehensive school in which Bangladeshi-Muslims constituted the majority within the group of South Asian male pupils). His fastidious insistence on making explicit the heterogeneity of South Asians enabled him to avoid the pitfalls of a 'false universalism' (a term Fleming borrows from Eisenstein [1984]), a critical understanding and premise which is sadly absent from much of the earlier (and some more recent) studies carried out in this field.[4]

Defining labels

In popular and academic debates focused around sport and race, and in particular football and race, the term race is reduced to, or conflated with being black. This reductive proclivity may in fact have political precedence whereby a consensus has emerged amongst race equality professionals and activists, 'that the term "black" should be used to describe all those who because of their race are unfavourably treated within British society' (Modood 1988: 397). The absence of any significant number of South Asians from the most exposed echelons of professional British sport is in stark contrast to the highly prominent visibility of an African-Caribbean/black-British presence, a presence that is never more pervasive and potent than when it takes the form of the England football team captain, as Paul Ince and Sol Campbell have been on infrequent occasions. Thus when referring to black footballers, a particular racialized image-identity is assigned, for as Modood states, the term black 'has a historical and current meaning such that it is powerfully evocative of people of sub-Saharan African origins, and all other groups, if evoked at all, are secondary' (1994:89).

Reference to South Asians and football remains an esoteric enigma. 'South Asian' is effectively a nomenclatural indulgence of academia that necessarily differentiates the peoples of the Indian sub-continent (or those of sub-continental origin) from those originating from or resident of south east Asia encompassing China, Japan and associated regions. They are both convenient umbrella terms that themselves allow for a degree of slippage and over-simplification. 'Asians and football' in the British context has little to do with those players from Japan, China or North or South Korea. The 'Asian identity' invoked here is one with 'some share in the heritage of the civilization of the old Hindustan prior to British conquest. Roughly, it is those people who believe that the Taj Mahal is an object of their history' (Modood 1988: 397). However, such an attempt to draw together a markedly divergent number of disparate groups cannot be unproblematically adopted. As Chetan Bhatt points out, Modood, in trying to decouple Asianess from blackness, inadvertently essentializes South Asian identity with such a definition (1994, 1997). Indeed the Taj Mahal as a symbol of Moghal rule in India represents Moghal domination over a variety of religious and ethnic groups on the subcontinent. Punjabi Sikhs in particular endured a volatile and often hostile relationship with Moghal rulers, and fought a series of bloody wars to preserve their own Sikh religion and identity. Contemporaneously, the Sikh

Golden Temple at Amritsar stands as the definitive edifice which serves to emblematize and embody a specific Sikh heritage. 'British Asian' or 'Asian' are the more widely used and accepted group labels that refer to people of Indian sub-continental descent, particularly within the more populist circles such as British football. The signing in the late 1990s of Chinese international players by First Division club Crystal Palace has engendered a particular 'Asian' involvement in the professional game, hence it is necessary for the purposes of this paper to retain the narrower nomenclature of South Asian.

(In)visible players

The perceived absence of South Asians from professional football is a subject that has received a fair deal of media and public attention (BBC TV 1991; Datar 1989; Bose 1996), yet the superficial and mono-directional perspective of the coverage has far from ameliorated the general ignorance about the topic, it has, instead, created a somewhat facile pseudo-rationale that begins to address the negativities of the issue without evincing their consequences. These negativities must represent a point of departure before any consequential effects can be drawn out.

It has been the case for a number of years now that many people, especially those within the governing bodies of football and the various gatekeepers to the professional ranks, have used the 'invisibility' of South Asians in professional football to arrive at the simplistic assertion that this British ethnic minority has no great interest or aptitude for the sport. By limiting their own (and the popular imagination's) line of vision narrowly to the recognized professional arenas, they have rendered themselves, and many others, blind to the peripheral existence of a vibrant South Asian footballing culture. It is a culture, however, that is founded on and maintains a near-unilateral male bias. The subject of South Asian women and sport is possibly one of the most under-researched areas of social enquiry, with only a handful of works available (Dixey 1982; Hargreaves 1994; Verma and Darby 1994). In India, women's *kabaddi* is as big a sport in terms of spectating as the more ubiquitous men's game. It has to be said that 'women's' *kabaddi* is in fact played by girls and is part of the schools' physical education curriculum in many states. There is also a history of women's football in India, the infrastructure of which predates the men's semi-professional Philips League (Bains and Johal 1998: 194). In Britain, South Asian girls and young women are not readily associated with sport or physical leisure activity. However, the specific targeting of South Asian women and girls by leisure providers has shown that informed provision of sport/leisure activities is actively received and consumed by this often neglected section of the population. In cities such as Birmingham, Leicester and Bradford, South Asian women and girls are actively engaging in the whole process of deciding upon and implementing desired sport and recreation facilities (*ibid.*: 194–210). Such projects that consider the implications of the environment in which sport and leisure can take place, are endeavouring to confirm Dixey's assertion that it is 'not physical activity *per se* which is objectionable on cultural grounds, but the setting or context in which that activity takes place' (1982: 114).

The broad topic of South Asians and sport has occupied only a tangential space in enquiries relating to ethnicity and/or sport. The *Asians Can't Play Football* report distinguishes itself as a vital and informed interjection within this specific debate that has (until very recently) been afforded only generalized, facile conjecture. From their extensive research – that included the contribution of professional football clubs, South Asian players (at various levels and of various ages), coaches, teachers, referees and community and youth development officers – the report's authors somewhat presciently uncovered a culpable order of ignorance and thinly disguised (often nakedly explicit) racism that had proscribed any sustained South Asian progression in the game. Some of the key findings showed that over half the professional club officials surveyed deemed football not to be popular among South Asians in Britain; a statistic which lost any credence it may have had in the response of young South Asian players who were avid followers of the game and held obdurate ambitions to pursue the sport professionally (Bains 1995:5). The ignorance of recognized football officials further extended to their adherence to, and reproduction of, negative stereotypes of South Asians as a mass homogenized community. A popular and enduring myth of South Asian physical inferiority, with its associations of stamina and strength deficiencies, continues to predominate amongst such putative experts (see Fleming, this volume). As indeed misconceptions of the role of religion and culture (often regarded as interchangeable) in the lives of South Asians have resulted in a defensive closing of gates by their keepers, namely scouts, coaches and community officers. Remarks such as 'You hear about Asians (sic) stopping practice to say their prayers' and '. . . they don't like open changing rooms, their ethics don't allow it' (Bains 1995: 6) are sadly reflective of an anachronistic ideology that is perpetuated by the exclusive bastion of British football itself.

The absence of South Asian players from the game has to be set alongside the limited opportunities available to them. From the comparatively small number of South Asian players who have had trials, apprenticeships or even full-time contracts with professional clubs, the majority have reportedly encountered various obstacles that have hindered their advancement. Subjection to overt racist abuse from coaches, players and spectators is a primary common denominator for many of these would-be footballers, whilst being made to feel isolated from the rest of the team or group is another shared experience that is effected through more subtle means, such as exclusion from after-training socializing and ritual young male bonding. The *Asians Can't Play Football* report goes on to describe how this ostracization is compounded by many coaches' tangible indifference toward South Asian players, simply going through the motions of including them in training without providing the essential support, encouragement and constructive criticism that other white players received. 'Problematic cuisine' is also cited as a detrimental aspect of South Asian culture that precludes the sporting success of the diverse members of that culture (*ibid.*). This seems one of the more ludicrous objections since curry is now recognized as one of Britain's national dishes (particularly popular amongst footballers). The 'hot dish of vindaloo' was even deployed during the 1998 World Cup as a rousing nationalistic football anthem which pointed to the common appeal of curry through the infectious chant, 'we all love vindaloo'. Thus curry, interestingly, is used in an attempt to lyrically unite English football fans – a distinctively South Asian cultural product usurped by non-South Asians to symbolize a particular, and unequal, version of English diversity. More widely, South Asian cuisine in Britain is marked by its popularity, indeed is purportedly devalued because of its popular appeal. It has become subsumed into mainstream culture and its putative association with drinking copious amounts of lager and 'new lad' culture has denied it due credibility and indeed respected culinary status (Alibhai-Brown 1999).

With such fallacious conceptions of ethnicity and such myopic visions of the future of British football, the defenders of the game's monolithic faith have clearly limited the 'pool of talent' that these shores have to call upon. Many club officials (coaches, scouts, managers, community officers) are guilty of illegitimately espousing the ideology of football's inherent 'colour blind' principle which allows for any (male) player to reach the highest levels of the sport regardless of colour, creed, religion or ethnic affiliation. This type of naïve, quixotic thinking is deemed to be substantiated by the disproportionately high numbers of black professional footballers. This argument denies the heterogeneity of Britain's various ethnic minority communities and the different histories, life experiences and points of exclusion that constitute their social, political and economic position in this country. As Fleming (1995) states, 'the experiences of racism in sport are experienced differently by different ethno-cultural groups, and they respond to it in different ways' (p. 42). This is particularly pertinent when it serves to rationalize conventional abstract conjecture which holds aspirant South Asian footballers as subject to the same modes of discrimination and prejudice as the pioneer black players in British football (cf. Brown 1972). It also disclaims the massive discrimination that persists in denying Britain's black population opportunities in other professional spheres and in education. In the same instance, the relative success of some South Asian groups in vocational fields such as the legal profession, medicine, the media, commerce and business, has been used against them as an indictment of their lack of interest in sport and a more pressing motivation toward social and professional advancement (Cashmore 1990; Robinson 1990; Ballard 1994; Fleming 1995; Benson 1996). It must be noted that such relative social success is more apparent in South Asians of Indian descent as compared with the Bangladeshi and Pakistani communities, with the class locations of these groups impacting on any drive towards social mobility. The type of ethnic 'vocational stacking', mentioned above, has been evident in schooling where African-Caribbean youngsters who show a particular aptitude and excellence in any sport, are actively encouraged to pursue that sporting interest, often at the expense of their education (Hayes and Sugden 1999). Conversely, South Asians have not been regarded by physical education teachers as possessing any great sporting or physical abilities and have instead received greater encouragement in matters more scholarly (Fleming 1995: 38). By adopting this kind of rationale PE teachers have failed to recognize, nurture and promote the soccer talents of young aspiring South Asian football enthusiasts. They are subsequently removed from, or denied access to, the progressive levels of competition and coaching that young white (and black) school-level players (a level that is still male dominated) enjoy. This order of exclusion is replicated and perpetuated through junior county football, amateur and non-League games, semi-professional football through to the privileged echelons of the full professional ranks.

Recent soccer history does offer a handful of names that signal a South Asian participation in top-flight football (see Dimeo and Finn, this volume). Some of these names in fact reveal a greater truth about the society in which the game exists. In the late 1990s, Derby County Football Club had a gifted young South Asian player (Amrick Sidhu) who promised to make a sustained impact on their first team.[5] Naseem Bashir was briefly on the books of Reading Football Club in the late 1980s, but a regular first team place was not forthcoming. The players who did manage to impose themselves upon first teams were Roy Smith who played for West Ham in the mid 1950s, Paul Wilson who played under Jock Stein at Glasgow Celtic and possibly the most famous footballer of South Asian descent, Ricky Heppolate, who played for Preston North End, Chesterfield, Orient, Peterborough United and Crystal Palace. The names of these three players betray their ethnic origin, moreover, their names disclose the extent to which their ethnicity, their South Asian heritage has been 'compromised', indeed forsaken, during the course of their (and their families') respective quests for socio-cultural alignment. All three footballers are of mixed race parentage, a syncretic proclivity that extends to more than one generation of their familial genealogies. Heppolate, as the most travelled and renowned of this trio, is a very apposite illustration of how football welcomes those who can fit into the accepted convention of what it is to be British and what it takes to be a footballer. He speaks no sub-continental language, only English, he does not practise or adhere to any of the religions of that region, was raised in a very 'white' environment with little South Asian influence and has 'no emotional attachment to the country of his birth (India)' (Bains 1995:11 [parenthesis added]).

Heppolate's story bears remarkable similarity to that of Chris Dolby. Dolby was born to South Asian parents but adopted by white parents as a baby. Raised in Yorkshire in a mainly white domestic environment without the exertion of any aspect of any South Asian custom or tradition, Dolby went on to join first Rotherham, then Bradford as a professional footballer (*ibid.*). It was only the colour of his skin that gave superficial testament to his ethnic origin. When the most notable players to have made the grade in British professional football seem to share a common, distinct non-South-Asian-ness, it seems to suggest that to become a footballer in Britain one does not necessarily have to be white, rather one must be seen as being white, seen as being British, in a cultural, and thus a perceived ideological, context.

Beyond the sporting stereotype

Modern football represents a global phenomenon that continues to colonize new sporting outposts. The 1998 World Cup in France included more competing nations than ever before, some taking part in their first competition. Although the game's inceptive English heritage is widely pronounced and proudly guarded, its near ubiquitous popular appeal has created specialized footballing cultures in various sections of the globe. Media commentary (particularly in television coverage) of France '98 demonstrated how specific capacities, traits and qualities have been manufactured to become synonymous with the character of certain nations and their representative teams and players. Hence South American teams and players were often referred to as skilful, naturally gifted and exhibitionists, whilst simultaneously being fiery, temperamental and unpredictable. North African teams were perceived as being somewhat light-weight and lacking in physical power. Other African national football teams such as Nigeria and Cameroon were naturally athletic, strong runners but with little organization and discipline, whereas the Scandinavian teams were very disciplined, possessing great power, little flair but stern commitment to shape and style (or lack of it). Such comments were present in much of the media (not solely television) coverage of the World Cup in France.[6] Their roots lay in popularized stereotypic characteristics that are ascribed to nations and national character. International football affords such reductive clichés an arena in which they can be 'legitimately' deployed and indeed one in which it thrives. Its perverse logic implicates arbitrary character or even physiological traits as 'naturally' belonging to certain unashamedly generalized groups, hence when the football players of Cameroon are referred to as 'athletic and undisciplined', this is a specificity of an extrapolation that posits all the people of Cameroon, and by further implication, all the people of Africa (for other African teams were subjected to the same order of ascribed representation) as being of the same ilk and cast from the same mould.

The standard stereotype of South Asian people, is, by contrast, one of the submissive, naturally placid and physically frail individual. The effeminacy of such a stereotype is not incidental and is fully drawn out in the caricature of the exoticised, submissive, sexually elusive South Asian (young) woman. As Brah (1993) states, 'Whether she is exoticised, represented as ruthlessly oppressed in need of liberation or read as a victim/enigmatic emblem of religious fundamentalism, she is often presumed to be the bearer of 'races' and cultures' (p.447).[7] In footballing terms, South Asians have typically had to struggle to alleviate the ingrained notion that they possess no understanding or capability for the sport. This is in spite of an historical precedence that was set when, in 1911, a bare-footed Bengali Indian team defeated the British military's East Yorkshire regiment team by two goals to one in the final of the Shield competition (Mason 1992). The magnitude of this victory was passionately encapsulated in a local Calcutta newspaper *Nayak* which exultantly declared:

It fills every Indian with joy and pride to know that rice-eating, malaria-ridden, bare-footed Bengalis have got the better of beef-eating, Herculean, booted John Bull in that peculiarly English sport.

(*ibid.*, p. 150)

Unfortunately this sporting victory proved to be an isolated moment in Indian history and the image of a passionate footballing people never managed to transcend that moment, not even on the sub-continent itself. Not surprisingly, South Asians in Britain have had to fight for the right to be perceived as footballing protagonists:

> unlike their Afro-Caribbean counterparts, there was no evidence of Asian role models, no players of international repute whom white British people could identify with. Whilst Afro-Caribbean immigrants also encountered problems when playing in white football teams, they were undoubtedly assisted in their ability to converse in the same language, the wearing of similar clothes and the worshipping of the same nominal God.

(Bains and Johal 1998: 51)

Playing for keeps

Sport had initially been recognized by the first generation of South Asian immigrants in Britain, as an effective means of maintaining ethno-cultural solidarity in the face of geo-political and social dislocation. Sport was also regarded as an 'important vehicle to channel the energies and ambitions of an Asian youth being nakedly exposed to a nation where sport was an integral part of the cultural fabric' (*ibid.*), as well as performing the important function of developing 'strong community networks … and consolidating fragile confidences and restoring morale' (*ibid.*). To this end, by 1963 a Sikh temple in Smethwick in Birmingham organized the first Asian Games tournament which saw teams representing the cities of Coventry, Wolverhampton and Birmingham competing in *kabaddi*[8] and volleyball matches. The Sikh heritage of these 'tournaments' (as they are popularly known) is further evidenced by their official title as the Shaheed Udham Singh Games, or the Shaheedi Games. This title is homage to the Punjabi Sikh martyr who was hanged following the assassination of former Governor of the Punjab Sir Michael O'Dwyer in 1940. Udham Singh held O'Dwyer personally responsible for the massacre of five hundred men, women and children at Jallianwala Bagh in the Sikh holy city of Amritsar. From their beginnings in Smethwick in the mid 1960s, these tournaments grew to become annual national sporting events in the Punjabi social calendar, spreading as far south as Gravesend, Southall and Barking, through various locations in the Midlands such as Wolverhampton, Coventry, Leamington Spa and Birmingham and up to the North reaching Leeds and even across the border into Glasgow. As the sites for the tournaments grew so too did the sports they embraced. Along with the enduringly popular *kabaddi* and volleyball, weightlifting, tug-of-war, hockey and various athletic events were all added. It is necessary to state that these tournaments were distinct masculinized sites in which men, young and old, indulged themselves in sportive and other hedonistic pursuits, notably the excessive consumption of alcohol. The occasion of the tournament was however a social event that brought families and friends from various parts of the country to one place at one time, and thus, while male members of families went to the tournaments, the female collective organized their own social agenda.[9] However, as one sport in particular began to assume greater popularity, it necessitated its own tournament, and its own organization. Football was very much an intrinsic player in the South Asian sporting scene.

For those male members of the diasporic South Asian communities who wanted to play football in an organized and competitive environment, there was little opportunity for them to seamlessly merge into the insular fabric of local-league amateur football. With the indigenous white community harbouring a great deal of hostility and manifest resentment toward any foreign immigrants (Holmes 1991), penetrating into the ranks of local all-white football teams was a near impossible and often perilous endeavour. With the increase in numbers of younger South Asians in Britain and the concurrent surge in the intensity of their footballing passion, it was inevitable that they would take responsibility for themselves and pursue the charge of formulating their own all-South Asian football teams. In heeding the admonishing caveats of 'false universalism's' logic, it must be stressed here that the pioneering South Asian football teams and clubs, as well as the *kabaddi* and volleyball teams, were predominantly made up of Punjabi Sikhs mostly of the *Jat* caste.[10] Indeed it remains true to say that the majority of all-South Asian football teams in Britain represent the Punjabi Sikh community although increasingly caste differentiation is decreasing in its significance. The distribution and settlement patterns of the various South Asian communities have seen particular groups establish themselves in particular regions of the country, with greater Pakistani (predominantly Mirpuri) concentrations in the Yorkshire region, and a stronger Bengali Muslim presence in neighbouring Lancashire. The West Midlands is home to many Punjabi Sikhs with a smaller Hindu population. London and its surrounding areas have an assortment of South Asian communities resident in various locations in varying concentrations (Ballard 1994, Clarke *et al.* 1990). With the predominance of particular South Asian groups in certain regions, any all-South Asian football teams from that region will reflect the ethnic specificity of its South Asian populace. However, what unites these teams, more than a false notion of ethnic homogeneity, is the common experience of racism, and a particular racism that is parasitically exacted through football.

For South Asian football teams in Britain, racial abuse is not an uncommon violation. Individual accounts of such incidents are as alarmingly manifold as they are invidious. Football matches between all-South Asian teams and all-white teams are immanently infused with a confrontational charge. The volatility, indeed naked hostility of this charge, may be strategically played out underneath the game's open aggression, combativeness and vigour (especially in British amateur leagues). On frequent occasions however, this legitimized belli-cose veneer is penetrated to reveal an underlying order of blind hatred and ignorant fear. Whilst it would be foolish to suggest that every footballing clash between white and South Asian teams is nothing more than sublimated race war, competitive football has provided a symbolic arena in which the competi-tive interaction of an imperious 'host' community with a minoritized foreign 'other' often occurs (cf. Carrington 1998; Westwood 1990). But this is not a fair competition. Football is an English sport that these shores 'gave' to the rest of the world. It is seen as part of the nation's fabric. For foreign groups entering this country, it is wrongly assumed that the game has to be an acquired passion not a naturalized hereditary legacy, thus, falsely, asserting a controlling distance between non-indigenous British groups and football. This quasi-rationale is then used to place South Asians below the indigenous white community in terms of footballing acculturation, and this is the same mode of (ir)rationalization used by those who were happily oblivious to the irony of the rhetorical statement that 'Asians can't play football'.

This merry oblivion is also in evidence when real incidents of racial abuse during football matches involving South Asians are brought to light. It is still the common perception that racism in football is nothing more than a bit of harmless chanting or verbal 'stick' from the terraces. Actual accounts of physical threat such as that suffered by Nelson's leading South Asian (Pakistani) team Paak FC, dispel such naivete:

> The away team was in their changing room and we could hear them shouting things like, 'We can not lose to these Pakis' ... 'Let's show the Pakis how to play' and another shouted, 'Come on let's break their legs' ... I remember looking at the referee hoping he would take some action. Within the first few minutes Tariq (Paak mid-fielder) went down the middle and these three opposition players, I mean three of them all went in to tackle him. When they caught up with him we thought Tariq had broken his leg. We couldn't believe it when the ref waved play on. I ran up to the referee and all he said was that they played the ball. How could that explain the stud marks all down Tariq's side? We knew then that the referee would be too frightened to take action against them. Eventually the ref gave us a penalty and there was a near riot on the pitch. The referee just took off and said he was going home. We persuaded him to come back on, but within ten minutes, after another tussle, he walked off again. This time he didn't return. To make matters worse we were fined for our part in the incident.

> (Bains and Johal 1998:181)

Bains (1995) summarizes the experience of racism that South Asian players have encountered and how they are reacting against such abuse:

Evidence of racism toward Asian players is still very apparent. Although two-thirds of Asian footballers claim to be subjected to regular forms of racism – an extraordinarily high level of abuse – what is most disturbing is the common perception amongst our respondents that referees and league management committees still offer them little or no protection. Over the years some Asian footballers have begun to change their image from being 'soft-touches' to people who can 'look after themselves.' For the most part verbal abuse continues and it is up to the footballing authorities at local and national levels to stamp it out.

(Bains 1996: p. 27)

Attempts by South Asian players to join white teams at local league level have been met with various forms of resistance. Such opposition from some white teams has taken the more obvious form of racially motivated, hostile exclusion, and also, a more tacit, non-welcoming exclusionary policy. A cautious, occasionally deliberate, reticence on the behalf of some South Asian players, has served to maintain a distance between certain South Asian footballers and white teams. The racist tendencies of particular members of a club/team can influence the overall composition of the team and its strategy in terms of using and accepting various players. The more powerful and influential such members are, the greater control they will have over team personnel.

It must be stressed that clearly not all white teams and players can be marked as racist by particular experiences pronounced by non-white players/teams. White teams and communities are also diverse and may include individuals who are distinctly anti-racist or who do not subscribe to more overtly racist sentiments. Just as it is vital to avoid falsely universalizing the South Asian population, the same critical recognition must be afforded to the white population. Those South Asian players accepted by white team-mates as part of the team, have to contend with the fact that being the only 'non-white' face in a predominantly white team, gives some opposition players greater licence to subject them to the full torrent of their ignorant abuse. All-South Asian teams constitute more than just a 'bunch of lads' starting their own football team. Such teams represent safe, de-pressurized, sites that allow South Asians to play the game and also proffer the opportunity to effect positive interaction with non-South Asian teams in a competitive environment. In the recent past when such positive interaction with white teams was not forthcoming, there was significant growth in the number of all-South Asian football teams being established, although South Asian leagues were not so readily inaugurated. This numerical increase then necessitated the formal regulation and governance of the Khalsa Football Federation, a voluntary Sikh organization that reflected the predominance of Punjabi Sikh teams in Britain. Although the Khalsa Football Federation now enjoys a mutually co-operative relationship with the Football Association, it is a relationship that remains informal and non-committal, a stance largely sustained by FA myopia. With many of these teams affiliated to local county FA's and playing against a variety of white, black, South Asian and mixed teams, the Khalsa Football Federation recognized the intra-ethnic rivalry that had formed amongst South Asian football teams from across Britain. To satisfy the competitive ambitions of such rivalries, and to increase the number of competitions open to South Asian teams, the Federation inaugurated football into the established sporting sphere of the Shaheedi Games tournaments.

The growing professionalization of *kabbadi* and the separate burgeoning of South Asian football, have engendered two distinct sporting events, the football tournament and the *kabaddi* tournament. Although they take place at the same time of year (every summer), occasionally at the same venue (depending on size and facilities), they are run by separate governing organizations. The Shaheedi Games have latterly been assigned the name 'Asian Games' to appease local councils and open them up nominally to the whole of the localized British South Asian populations. Every year ten Asian Games football tournaments take place in Birmingham, Coventry, Bradford, Barking, Leamington Spa, Gravesend, Derby, Reading, Slough and Wolverhampton. Up to a thousand adult and youth footballers can be involved during a single event. Yet, despite this vast array of footballing talent on display, the tournaments have failed to attract the attention of professional football club representatives. There are three perceptible reasons for such oversight. First, the tournaments receive minimal advertisement outside the confines of South Asian communities. Second, club scouts state the problems of assessing relative abilities of players in an environment where overall standards are difficult to gauge. They also argue that most of the better players are too old to be seriously considered by professional clubs. Third, South Asians in Britain are still perceived as being an insular community and the idea of all-South Asian tournaments seemingly reiterates such a view. South Asian footballers are therefore regarded as being happier and more comfortable playing in their 'own' company. The exclusivity of the Asian Games is used as further 'proof' of this line of argument. However:

> such a position overlooks the specific history and social and cultural context of these tournaments. What it also does is to ignore the obvious enthusiasm of the players who play in mainstream football as well as the Asian Games. Indeed it speaks volumes for these players' love of the game that they are prepared to play all year round year after year. It's an enthusiasm for football that one would struggle to find in other communities.
>
> (Bains and Johal 1998: 57)

Conclusion

There is an almost Machiavellian tautology that operates whereby South Asians are forced into creating their own mono-ethnic football teams in order to protect themselves from racial abuse and still partake of the sport. The failure of British football's gate-keeping bodies to effect positive access for South Asians into the game gives further impetus to their enforced mobilization. Once football hungry South Asians established their own association with the sport in this country, their ingenuity, their enterprise and their obvious passion for football is then used as an illicit pretext to espouse old notions of generalized South Asian insularity and impenetrability. With the governing authorities of football opening their eyes and minds to a hitherto (for them) clandestine soccer culture, South Asian footballers' contribution to the various levels of British football must receive due recognition and reward. The Football Association's 'Working Party on Asians in Football' is placing a formal concentration on developing measures to tap into and encourage the South Asian footballing population. Professional clubs are attempting to establish more effective 'Football in the Community' programmes that reach all sections of local communities by developing closer links and more specialized schemes. Leicester City Football Club, Sheffield United and West Ham United are amongst the more prominent clubs that have specifically geared 'Football in the Community' schemes that are targeted at local South Asians. Gordon Taylor, Chief Executive of the Professional Footballers Association, has stated that with clubs spending millions in the transfer market, 'what we need to do is to plough some of that money back through 'Football in the Community' schemes and target it towards developing Asian (sic) football' (Bains and Johal 1998: II).

Whilst this belated recognition of a South Asian footballing passion and penchant is undoubtedly encouraging, the specific schemes that attempt to develop South Asian football talent must not fail to recognize all such players no matter what their abilities and relative merits may be. There will of course be an elite of South Asian players who possess the required abilities to succeed in the professional game, but, just like the rest of the population, there are many more South Asian football enthusiasts who play and enjoy football without being necessarily equipped to make the professional grade. Football scouts ranging from non-league and professional clubs have a reduced inclination to dismiss South Asian players, teams, games and tournaments in the quest to promote 'home-grown' talent in the face of growing foreign influence in British teams, and the under-achievement of the English national team. But any such pursuit of selecting, developing and harnessing elite talent, particularly with regard to South Asian players, must maintain an informed commitment to those who play football without a view to professionalism, indeed, those who represent the footballing majority.

Notes

1 Bollywood is the popularized term used to identify the populist commercial film industry of Mumbai (formerly Bombay), India.
2 The song contained Punjabi words and phrases and was only commercially successful on second release after being re-mixed by Norman Cook. *Cornershop*, *Babylon Zoo* and *White Town* are three recent chart-topping bands which are all fronted by singer-song-writers of South Asian origin (Tjinder Singh, Jas Mann and Jyoti Mishra respectively).
3 The inclusion of these players and others such as Min Patel, Ronnie Irani and Vikram Solanki in the England Test cricket team, does not disguise or obscure the fact that access to organized cricket and the recognition and support of cricketing authorities

have not been forthcoming for members of Britain's various ethnic minority communities. Indeed racial prejudice and discrimination have served to maintain distinct
'cricket cultures' which are largely based on ethnic lines. See Khan (1996); Long *et
al.* (1997); McDonald and Ugra (1998); Williams, J. (1994); and also Carrington and
McDonald (this volume).

4 See Rhaval, S. (1989) for a critique of Eurocentric studies of South Asian lifestyle
patterns.

5 Jas Jutla is another talented footballer of South Asian descent, who in the late 1990s
was plying his trade for Scottish League Division One outfit Greenock Morton,
having been released by Glasgow Rangers (see Bains and Johal 1998).

6 Neil Blain *et al.* discuss the manner in which such national identities and characteristics are assigned to sports players by the various continental media; see Blain *et al.*
(1993: 55–87).

7 For more detailed accounts of the self-perceived image-identities of young South
Asian women see Bhachu (1991); Brah (1996); and Drury (1996).

8 *Kabaddi* is the popular Indian tag sport which involves two teams of usually ten
players. Each team has a set of raiders and a set of defenders. It is the raiders' aim to
approach the opposition defenders whilst constantly making it apparent that he is not
taking pause for breath by continuously voicing the word *'kabaddi'*, and to make
contact, just to touch one of the defenders and run back to his own team line before
any or all of the defenders prevent him from doing so and causing him to exhale. If
the raider manages to retreat to his line without having his breathing broken, then
any defender that he made contact with is automatically ruled out of the game, or as
is more popular in this country, points are awarded for each defender that has been
contacted, so the defenders continue to play.

9 The importance of tournaments in the lives of Punjabi Sikh women is further
explored in Bains and Johal (1998).

10 For a detailed account of the various Punjabi Sikh castes and their Indian origins as
well as the history of Sikh patterns of immigration and re-settlement, see Ballard
(1990; 1994).

References

Alibhai-Brown, Y. (1999) 'The Raj lives on in our restaurants', in *The Independent* 25
March.
Bains, J. (1995) *Asians Can't Play Football*, Midland Asian Sports Forum.
Bains, J. and Johal, S. (1998) *Corner Flags and Corner Shops – The Asian Football Experi-
ence*, London: Victor Gollancz.
—— (1999) *Corner Flags and Corner Shops – The Asian Football Experience* (Second
Edition), London: Phoenix.
Ballard, R. (1990) 'Migration and kinship: the differential effect of marriage rules on the
processes of Punjabi migration to Britain', in Clarke, C., Peach, C. and Vertovec, S.
(eds), *South Asians Overseas*, Cambridge: Cambridge University Press.
Ballard, R. (ed.) (1994) *Desh Pardesh – The South Asian Presence in Britain*, London: C.
Hurst & Co. Ltd.
BBC Television. (1991) *Black Britain*, BBC 1.
Benson, S. (1996) 'Asians have culture, West Indians have problems: discourses of race
and ethnicity in and out of anthropology' in Ranger, T., Samad, Y. and Stuart, O.
(eds), *Culture, Identity and Politics*, Hants: Avebury.
Bhachu, P. (1991) 'Culture, ethnicity and class among Punjabi Sikh women in 1990's
Britain', in *New Community*, Volume 17, No. 3.
Bhatt, C. (1994) 'New Foundations', in Weeks, J. (ed.) *The Lesser Evil and Greater Good*,
London: Rivers Oram Press.

168   *Sanjiev Johal*

—— (1997) *Liberation and Purity*, London: UCL Press.
Blain, N., Boyle, R. and O'Donnell, H. (1993) *Sport and National Identity in the European Media*, Leicester: Leicester University Press.
Bose, M. (1996) *The Sporting Alien English Sport's Lost Camelot*, Edinburgh: Mainstream Publishing Company Ltd.
Brah, A.K. (1993) 'Race and culture in the gendering of labour markets: South Asian young Muslim women and the labour market', in *New Community*, Volume 19, No. 3.
—— (1996) *Cartographies of Diaspora: Contesting Identities*, London: Routledge.
Brown, D. (1972) 'Where are Britain's coloured stars?', in *Football Association News*, December.
Carrington, Ben (1998) 'Sport, masculinity and black cultural resistance', in *Journal of Sport and Social Issues*, Volume 22, No.3.
Carrington, Bruce (1983) 'Sport as a sidetrack. An analysis of West Indian involvement in extra-curricular sport', in Barton, L. and Walker, S. (eds), *Race, Class and Education*, London: Croom Helm.
Carrington, Bruce, Chivers, T. and Williams T. (1987) 'Gender, leisure and sport: a case study of young people of South Asian descent', *Leisure Studies*, Volume 6, No. 3.
Carroll, B. (1993) 'Factors influencing ethnic minority groups' participation in sport', *Physical Education Review*, Volume 16, No.1.
Cashmore, E. (1981) 'The black British sporting life', *New Society*, 6 August.
—— (1982) *Black Sportsmen*, London: Routledge & Kegan Paul.
—— (1983) 'The champions of failure: black sportsmen', *Ethnic and Racial Studies*, Volume 6, No.1.
—— (1990) *Making Sense of Sport*. London: Routledge.
Clarke, C., Peach, C. and Vertovec, S. (eds) (1990) *South Asians Overseas*, Cambridge: Cambridge University Press.
Datar, R. (1989) 'An elusive goal for the East End Pele', *The Guardian*, 28 June.
Dixey, R. (1982) 'Asian women and sport, the Bradford experience', *British Journal of Physical Education*, Volume 13, No. 4.
Drury, B. (1996) 'The impact of religion, culture, racism and politics on the multiple identities of Sikh girls', in Ranger, T., Samad, Y. and Stuart, O. (eds) *Culture, Identity and Politics*, Hants: Avebury.
Eisenstein, H. (1984) *Contemporary Feminist Thought*, London: Allen & Unwin.
Fleming, S. (1989) 'Sport and Asian youth culture', Paper presented at British Sociological Association Workshop, Sport and Ethnicity, University of Warwick.
—— (1994) 'Sport and South Asian youth: the perils of 'false universalism' and stereotyping', *Leisure Studies*, Volume 13, No.3.
—— (1995) *Home and Away: Sport and South Asian Male Youth*. Hants: Avebury.
Hargreaves, J. (1994) *Sporting Females: Critical Issues in the History and Sociology of Women's Sport*, London: Routledge.
Hayes, S. and Sugden, J. (1999) 'Winning through "naturally" still? An analysis of the perceptions held by physical education teachers towards the performance of black pupils in school sport and in the classroom', in *Race, Ethnicity and Education*, Volume 2, No. 1.
Holmes, C. (1991) *A Tolerant Country? Immigrants, Refugees and Minorities in Britain*, London: Faber and Faber.
Jarvie, G. and Reid, I. (1997) 'Race relations, sociology of sport and the new politics of race and racism', *Leisure Studies*, Volume16, No. 4.
Khan, A. (1996) 'Welcome to the Quaid-I-Azam League' in *Hit Racism for Six: Race and Cricket in England Today*, London: Wernham.
Lashley, H. (1980) 'The new black magic', *British Journal of Physical Education*, Volume 11.
—— (1990) 'Black participation in British sport: opportunity or control', in Kew, F. (ed.) *Social Scientific Perspectives on Sport*. Sports Science Education Programme, Leeds, BASS monograph No. 2.

Long, J., Nesti, M., Carrington, B. and Gilson, N. (1997) *Crossing the Boundary: A study of the nature and extent of racism in local league cricket*, Leeds: Leeds Metropolitan University.

Lyons, A. (1989) *Asian Women and Sport*, Birmingham: West Midlands Regional Sports Council.

Maguire, J.A. (1991) 'Sport, racism and British society: a sociological study of England's elite male Afro-Caribbean soccer and rugby union players', in Jarvie, G. (ed.), *Sport, Racism and Ethnicity*, London: Falmer Press.

Mason, T. (1992) 'Football on the Maidan: cultural imperialism in Calcutta', in Mangan, J.A. (ed.), *The Cultural Bond – Sport, Empire, Society*, London: Frank Cass.

McDonald, I. and Ugra, S. (1998) *Anyone for Cricket?* London: University of East London.

McGuire, B. and Collins, D. (1998) 'Sport, ethnicity and racism: the experience of Asian heritage boys', *Sport, Education and Society*, Volume 3, No. 1.

Modood, T. (1988) ''Black', racial equality and Asian identity', *New Community:* Volume 14, No. 3.

—— (1994) 'The end of a hegemony: the concept of "black" and British Asians', in Rex, J. and Drury, B. (eds), *Ethnic Mobilisation in a Multicultural Europe*, Research in Ethnic Relation Series. Hants: Avebury.

Orakwue, S. (1998) *Pitch Invaders The Modern Black Football Revolution*, London: Victor Gollancz.

Rhaval, S. (1989) 'Gender, leisure and sport: a case study of young people of South Asian descent: a response', *Leisure Studies*, Volume 8, No. 3.

Robinson, V. (1990) 'Boom and gloom: the success and failure of South Asians in Britain', in Clarke, C., Peach, C. and Vertovec, S. (eds) *South Asians Overseas*, Cambridge: Cambridge University Press.

Verma, G.K. and Darby, D.S. (1994) *Winners and Losers: Ethnic minorities in Sport and Recreation*, London: Falmer Press.

Westwood, S. (1990) 'Racism, black masculinity and the politics of space' in Hearn, J. and Morgan, D. (eds) *Men, Masculinities and Social Theory*, London: Unwin Hyman.

Williams, J. (1994) 'South Asians and cricket in Bolton', *The Sports Historian*, Number 14.

10 Reconceptualizing race, gender and sport

The contribution of black feminism

Sheila Scraton

Introduction

A decade ago, Susan Birrell (1989, 1990: 186) argued for 'a broadening of our theoretical frameworks and theorizing difference within the field of gender and sport'. Ten years on, there appears to be little evidence that feminist sport theorists, or indeed sport sociologists in general, have risen to this task particularly concerning the complex relationships between race, gender and class. It remains the case that most research and writing tends to concentrate on sport as a key institutional site for the construction of gender (Birrell 1988; Birrell and Cole 1994; Hargreaves 1994; Hall, 1996) or the relationship between race and sport (Cashmore 1982; Carrington, Chivers and Williams 1987; Jarvie 1991). In the former, the emphasis is predominantly (although not exclusively) on white sportswomen, and in the latter, black sportsmen. Not only is there a serious lack of information on black women's experiences of sport but there have been few attempts to provide a critical analysis that 'listens to' the writings and autobiographies of black women both inside and outside sport (Birrell 1990).

Sport sociology and feminist sport scholarship in the UK have been virtually silent about the experiences of black women in sport and sport as a racialized and engendered arena. White women, who have dominated feminist sport discourse, have failed to address sufficiently the marginalization of black women and have failed to seriously interrogate their own whiteness. I place myself within this dominant white feminist sport discourse and the following discussion is a reflexive consideration of why this position is untenable and contradicts the fundamental definition of feminism as anti-oppressive and committed to challenging the marginalization of *all* women. We, as white feminists, are in a privileged position and cannot simply hide behind guilty and apologetic statements (De Groot 1996). Sporting feminism cannot analyse sport without fundamentally challenging it as a racialized arena, recognizing difference as a key theoretical and political challenge.

Beyond the world of sport, theorizing difference has been high on the agenda of feminist thought for the past two decades. During this time there has been an abundance of work theorizing 'difference' initiated by black feminists[1] (Anthias and Yuval-Davis 1993; Bhavnani and Phoenix 1994; Brah 1996; Collins 1990;

hooks 1984, 1989, 1991; Mirza 1997) and more recently within the debates around postmodernism and poststructuralism (Butler 1990; Elam 1994; Probyn 1994, 1996; Spivak 1992). In addressing the invisibility and marginalization of black women in feminism, Mirza argues:

> The invisibility of black women speaks of the separate narrative construc-
> tions of race, gender and class: it is a racial discourse, where the subject is
> male; in a gendered discourse, where the subject is white; and a class dis-
> course, where race has no place.
>
> (Mirza 1997:4)

Collins (1990) argues powerfully for the need to understand interlocking, multiple axes of oppression or what Brah (1996) refers to as the 'intersectionality' of social identities rather than additive models. Race does not simply increase oppression as it is 'added to' other sites and discourses of subordination and oppression such as gender, sexuality and class. Rather it must be viewed that multiple axes of oppression qualitatively challenge the whole nature of oppression and should be viewed in relation to sources of resistance, identity, support and creativity (Maynard 1996; Glenn 1999). In addition, black British feminists have strongly argued that being a woman, being black and being British has a *particular* historical location within patriarchy, colonialism and post-colonialism (Mirza 1997). Race and gender are not predetermined categories but are socially constructed within specific historical contexts (Glenn 1999).

Applying this to sport, it becomes obvious that sport cannot be understood outside its historical location similarly sustained and reproduced by forms of social domination articulated around and through discourses of race, gender and class. The following discussion aims to reassert Birrell's call to look towards broadening our frameworks and to providing more theoretically sophisticated analyses of race, gender, class and sport. This chapter will concentrate specifically on sport, gender and race within the British context. I will argue that we need to look beyond sport theorizing and learn from the theoretical and empirical contributions of black feminists who are raising crucial theoretical questions while providing rich ethnographic and autobiographical accounts of their lives and experiences. However, despite the productiveness and excellence of much of the work by black feminists discussed above, none of this work has paid serious attention to how sport as a cultural practice maintains, challenges and reproduces discourses of difference and its place more generally within (black) women's lives. Unless sport scholars engage with the theoretical debates around difference, representation, identity, marginalization and oppression and locate sport in different women's experiences and lives, then black women will remain at the periphery and theorizing will continue to consider gender and race as separate fields of enquiry. We need to move towards an integrative framework in which gender, race and class are seen as relational and mutually constituted through processes of racialization and engendering, with sport acknowledged as a key institutional site for these processes.

Sports feminism: three decades of white theorizing?

The contribution of sports feminists to an understanding of sport as a gendered cultural form is considerable (Birrell and Cole 1994; Hall 1996; Hargreaves 1994; Theberge 1987). Over the past three decades we have progressed from the early distributive studies of women and sport to relational analyses of gender and sport and increasingly to more sophisticated analyses of gender, sexuality and sport (Hall 1996). Exciting, innovative work has looked at the construction of gendered and sexualized bodies in and through sport (Markula 1995; McDermott 1996; Obel 1995); sexual abuse and violence in sport (Brackenridge 1997; Brackenridge and Kirby 1997); homophobia and lesbianism (Cahn 1996; Griffin 1992; Lenskyj 1991); men, masculinities and sport (Curry 1991; Messner 1992; Messner and Sabo 1990); feminism, sport and consumer power (Cole and Hribra 1995) and so on. This latter article is interesting as it is located in post-feminist debates around individual choice, physical empowerment and the contribution of trans-national capitalism in the form of *Nike* to a discourse of 'just do it' aimed at women. However, as acknowledged by the authors, this discourse relates to a white, Western, privileged position that provides no critical questioning of the place of Third World women as the producers of sporting goods in an oppressive capitalist patriarchy. Many of the current issues addressed in sport, while being central to a critical feminist project and/or engaged with contemporary post-structuralist debates, in the main, remain ethnocentric. That is they view sport through a 'gender lens' (Feree, Lorber and Hess 1999) of white women's experiences, so that black women continue to be unknown and unheralded (Oglesby 1981).

In attempting to overview the work by and on black women, culture, racism and sport, it becomes glaringly obvious that there is little to review. In North America, Yevonne Smith's (1992) article is one of the few accessible, published feminist works by a black sports scholar that theorizes the invisibility and absence of black women in the sporting world. Like Birrell (1989, 1990) she argues that most of the work has been categoric (emphasizing differences between categories such as research into the different socialization into sport of black and white children) or distributive, providing statistics on inequality of opportunity, access and distribution of resources. In the early 1990s it was acknowledged that there was little or no research that looked at social and cultural contexts and the connections between the micro level of the individual and the macro social level.

In Britain, it is *even* difficult to find levels of research that could be labelled categoric or distributive. Furthermore the relational research that was developing in the 1980s on gender, ethnicity and race has tended to present a simplistic additive theoretical model of black (or South Asian) women's experiences of sport (for example, Bruce Carrington *et al.* 1987). Sadhna Raval (1989) provides one of the first critiques from the position of a South Asian woman in challenging the appropriateness of white, male academics researching the sporting and leisure experiences of black and South Asian women. In her view their conclusions pathologise South Asian culture, universalize South Asian women and fail to provide an adequate acknowledgement of the complex relationships between race, ethnicity, gender and class. These arguments are taken up by Tessa Lovell (1991: 59) who argues for a recognition of differences between women, through an exploratory investigation into 'the role of sport in the lives of some South Asian and Afro-Caribbean women, and how racism impinges on their experiences'. Her research points to the significance of power and control in sport and the ways sport is tied to concepts of gender and culture. This latter point would appear to be crucial for it begins to raise the issue of the racialized engendering of sport and how this is experienced by different individuals and groups of women. This has been further developed into the field of physical education and sport by the work of Tamsin Benn (1996) on teacher education and Hasina Zaman (1997) on the perceptions of Muslim young women of Islam, well-being and physical activity. Both these articles point to a major issue being the definition of sport as Western and masculine. Hargreaves (1994) in her important contribution to the history and sociology of women's sports is one of the few white sport feminists who does provide a brief account of racism and women's sport. She argues coherently that British sport policies reflect 'white' culture steeped in tradition, values and practices that are inappropriate for a modern multiracial society. However, even her limited engagement with black women and sport simply reflects the paucity of work in the area and the need for a more integrated and detailed engagement with issues relating to race, gender and sport.

As can be seen, the majority of research on women, gender and sport has remained centrally concerned with white women. A few black researchers are moving the debates forward but their work remains very much on the periphery. As will be discussed below, this not only reflects that the power of the academy in feminist sport studies remains very much in the hands of white women but also that little (if any) of the work by black feminists addresses sport as a central area of debate and analysis. I would argue, therefore, that a key task for feminist sport studies is to 'listen to' the writings and experiences of black feminists and apply these theoretical and empirical concerns to the development of critical sport studies.

Race and sport: from black men to racialized masculinities

Just as the majority of feminist work on gender and sport has focused on white sportswomen so it has been recognized for some time that the majority of work on race and sport has focused on black sportsmen (Archer and Bouillon, 1982; Carrington and Wood 1983; Cashmore 1982; Fleming 1989, 1994; Jarvie 1991; Cashmore and Troyna 1982). These writers and researchers primarily represent work conducted in Britain focusing on a range of issues including stacking, apartheid, unequal participation, ethnographic studies, PE, youth sport and so on. It is not difficult to find reference to work in Britain or North America on race and sport but, as alluded to in the introduction, the unifying feature is that when a racial discourse is studied the subject is male (Mirza, 1997).

However, there is some indication that some work on race and sport is beginning to look more critically at the inter-relationships between race, ethnicity, sport *and* gender. Sport as an important institution for the maintenance and reproduction of hegemonic masculinity is well documented (Hall 1996; Hargreaves 1994). Hegemonic masculinity (white, Western, heterosexual, middle-class, able-bodied) marginalizes both women and other subordinated masculinities (Connell 1987, 1995). Certainly there have been important contributions by pro-feminist male writers on the stabilization and reproduction of this hegemonic masculinity by sport through its construction of the powerful, muscular body (Messner and Sabo 1990; Messner 1992). These writers are beginning to critically examine gender, race and class in an attempt to look at the complex intersectionality of these relations of power. For example, Dworkin and Messner (1999: 343) argue that 'young men from race- or class-subordinated backgrounds disproportionately seek status, respect, empowerment and upward mobility through athletic careers'. Although it is acknowledged that very few actually become top-level professional athletes, those that do are celebrated as providing exemplary images of an extreme muscular athletic masculinity. Yet this image of athletic masculinity is not only about being 'a man', a dominant powerful image seen in opposition to a subordinate femininity, it is also a racialized image that distinguishes between black athleticism and white athleticism. Black sportsmen, particularly African Caribbean sportsmen, are often depicted as muscularly powerful yet as almost dangerous with a potent sexuality (Majors, 1990). In Richard Majors' work, sport is considered as an important site for black men to adopt a 'cool pose'. This is identified as a means of self-expression which can act as a response and resistance to the limitations and constraints imposed by institutional racism in other contexts. However, as pointed out in the research, although a 'cool pose' in and through sport can be seen as a form of resistance it also potentially reinforces a marginalized, racialized, low-status position in society. Achieving 'success' as an athlete, or the space for self-expression and the construction of a challenging identity, may appear to be a resistance to race and class locations but 'this agency operates largely to *reproduce* – rather than to *resist* or challenge – current race, class and gender relations of power' (Dworkin and Messner 1999: 344). Thus, sport is not only concerned with preserving notions of male identity and power, it is also implicitly concerned with the preservation of white superiority, white identity and forms of white, male power.

Ben Carrington's (1998; 1999) work on race, racism and cricket in Britain is a recent example of the development of a critical engagement with the complexities of black masculinity and sport. His ethnographic research provides rich, empirical data on a black cricket club in a northern city. He draws on the influential work of C.L.R. James (1963) who argues that cricket has provided one of the few cultural forms where Caribbean players can unite to resist white supremacy and oppression. As such cricket is a site that challenges and resists racism

not only within sport but within broader social, political and economic structures. Yet C.L.R. James' analysis, whilst being powerful in relation to racism and
sport as resistance, has no acknowledgement of the gendered relations that are a
part of this resistance. In Carrington's study it becomes clear that to only see
cricket as a site of black cultural resistance to racism does not recognize that
this is a form of black, *male* resistance often dependent on gendered power relations that not only leave intact *male* power in this specific context but also con-
tributes to the further silencing of the needs and voices of black women.

It is clear, therefore, that there is some new and exciting work on black masculinities that identifies sport as a site for the resistance to racism (Carrington
1998); sport as popular culture in the form of media sports texts that present
powerful competing discourses of masculinity, race, sexuality and class (Baker
and Boyd, 1997); and sport as a site of masculine self-expression for black males
that can provide some means of resistance but can also serve to reinforce and
lock them into their marginalized positions in a racist society (Majors 1990). All
these examples represent important inroads into our understandings of masculinities particularly in relation to the complex interweaving of race, gender, sexuality and class. However, as implicitly acknowledged in Carrington's work and
explicitly articulated by Messner in his fascinating discussion about racialized
masculinity politics:

> in foregrounding the oppression of men by men, these studies risk portray-
> ing aggressive, even misogynist, gender displays primarily as liberating forms
> of resistance against class and racial oppression ... What is obscured or
> even drops out of sight is the feminist observation that these kinds of mas-
> culinity are forms of domination over women.
>
> (Messner 1997: 77)

Michael Messner is one of the few male sport scholars to recognize that men,
who are seriously engaging with a radical critique of masculinity, must centralize
the work of black feminists and utilize the theoretical frameworks offered in
their writings and analyses. In this sense, he is stating categorically that 'the
humanization of men is intricately intertwined with the empowerment of
women' (Messner 1997: 110).

Black feminism: reshaping the debate

As evidenced in the previous two sections there is little work that could be
defined as offering a black feminist perspective in sport studies. Indeed, it seems
that sport studies, with a few exceptions, have remained largely oblivious to the
contribution that black feminist thought and activism have made during the
past decade or two. Susan Birrell (1990: 193) in her analysis of 'Women of
color, critical autobiography and sport' concludes that 'we need to increase our
awareness of issues in the lives of women of color as they themselves articulate
these issues'. She is one of the few sport feminists to have recognized that 'we

cannot remain in our old theoretical homes' (p. 195). The task she set was to reread the themes that dominate the discourses of black women using both discourse analysis and cultural theory, thus attempting to connect the subjective with structural relations of power. This, as yet, has not happened although we now have a wealth of literature from black British feminists that can support our engagement with these issues. We cannot afford to let another decade pass before we radically challenge our current theorizing from a position of privilege in sport studies.

Since the 1980s, black British feminists have provided black, female-centred autobiographical reflections and ethnographic studies that have added to our empirical knowledge and highlighted flaws in our theorizing (Afshar 1994; Bhattacharyya 1998; Brah 1994, 1996; Mirza 1997; Bhavnani and Coulson 1986; Ifekwunigwe 1999; Simmonds 1997). Significantly, these autobiographical and ethnographic accounts have been situated in women's position within post-colonial migration. The accounts of these British black women provide a challenge to normative discourse, articulate different knowledges and reveal their multiple and complex experiences. The project of black feminism:

> asserts and reclaims our agency in the telling of who we are. Our voice, our being and our very presence within the patriarchal imperialist project of sexualized racialization is to actively contest the system of which we form a part.
>
> (Mirza 1997: 6)

This project helps to reveal the distorted ways that dominant groups have constructed their assumptions and the complexities, contradictions and power relations among different women. Universal theories of domination that have been at the foundation of modernist feminism are revealed as inadequate for understanding difference, multiple subjectivities and agency. Yet, there is no move into a total postmodern celebration of 'otherness', difference or local experience. In much of the work of black feminism, experience is firmly located in materiality. There is no abandonment of the 'real world' of discrimination and oppression but a concern to map the micro-local experiences onto a macro-institutional and material inquiry of racism. Avtar Brah (1994: 169) epitomizes this approach suggesting that, 'the micro world of individual narratives constantly references and foregrounds the macro canvas of economic, political and cultural change'. In her discussion of young South Asian Muslim women and the labour market, Brah (1994) outlines a framework that looks at the interconnectedness of the micro and the macro. Although applying this theoretical framework to the racialized gendering of labour markets, Brah suggests that it could have wider applicability. Developing her analysis further she identifies the interconnectedness of structure, culture and agency arguing that these formations are 'inextricably linked' (*ibid.*: 152). She suggests that within this framework, structure and culture are not separate or fixed. Economic and political structures emerge and change over time and both respond to and shape cultural meanings. Applying her analysis to black women and sport the following questions are immediately raised:

- to what extent and in what ways do social representations construct black women as a racialized category and how do these stereotypes serve to structure their position in sport?
- what are the processes whereby sport becomes racially gendered?
- how do women position themselves with respect to such discourses?
- what light do women's personal accounts throw on the way in which discursive significations are implicated in their personal and social identities?

(adapted from Brah 1994: 153)

The following discussion suggests ways in which Brah's theoretical framework could be applied to a more critical understanding of sport as a racialized and engendered arena. In doing so the concept 'black women' is deconstructed to explore more fully difference within sport while at the same time being constructed to recognize collective experiences of silencing and marginalization experienced by black women both within and in relation to sport. Or as Mirza (1997: 21) puts it, the strategic use of multiplicity and contingency can be seen as a hallmark of black British feminism, which demonstrates 'that you can have difference (polyvocality) within a conscious construction of sameness (i.e. black feminism)'.

Grounding women's experiences of sport in the historical perspective

A historical perspective is crucial to black British feminist thought. Locating women's experiences in colonialism, imperialism and migration is imperative, for this background frames black communities and is inherently tied to the development of British sport. However, such an analysis must also include a recognition that racism, colonialism and imperialism are all important elements in the maintenance of gender relations in sport. Although we have some knowledge about the historical development of sport as an institution producing and reproducing patriarchal relations of domination (Hargreaves 1979; Mangan 1981; Mangan and Park 1987), there is an absence of historical material that considers sport as inherently racialized as well as gendered. Black women are almost totally invisible within sport histories (as to a large extent are black male athletes). As yet, we have no knowledge as to whether this invisibility reflects a total absence from sport or whether the existing histories that have concentrated on competitive, male sport simply ignore women's existence in other important contexts of physical activity (Vertinsky and Captain 1998). It would appear that 'hidden histories' have become written out of, and marginal to, the 'official story' of British sports. There is a crucial need to find 'black voices' in the histories of sport together with the task of disclosing sport's historical role in the construction of white identities (Ware 1992).

If we are to understand black women's relationship to sport we need to consider the structural relations of immigration and women's position as gendered and racialized subjects within particular class locations. It is easy to presume that 'cultural reasons' result in black women remaining outside sport, yet this requires far deeper interrogation particularly in relation to different ethnic backgrounds, different generations and the specific social and economic climate of both Britain and the institution of sport. Black feminists have argued powerfully that the impact of immigration legislation has resulted in the social construction of black people as 'problematic' with black women seen as 'dependents'. As discussed more fully in the next section, this social construction has important implications for the images and ideas people hold about black women, not least in important contexts that both directly and indirectly impact on women's access to sport.

Similarly, it is all too easy to consider sport primarily in relation to participation. While access and opportunity are important issues that highlight discrimination and black women's marginalization from the sporting world as athletes, it is important to consider their position (or lack of position) as coaches, administrators, teachers, and managers. How far is this exclusion part of a patriarchal discourse implicitly tied to racialized discourses? We need to interrogate institutional racism and sexism, learn more about sporting cultures and listen to the experiences of women in both competitive and recreational sport. We do have knowledge that suggests that women (read as white women) are crucial in the servicing of sport but analyses of the development of capitalism, particularly the restructuring of global national economies, require in-depth analysis of black women's position in the production of sporting goods both within Britain and as female labour in Third World countries that directly service British sport (Cole and Hribra 1995).

An historical perspective on the development of sport in Britain requires its location within a hegemonic masculinity that is white, heterosexual, middle-class and able-bodied. Currently, critical analyses locate sport within a patriarchal discourse that emphasizes gender, or a racial discourse that emphasizes race and ethnicity. We need to move towards analyses of sport that recognize the intersectionality of race, gender and class and that are located within *specific* historical contexts.

Images and representations both within and outside sport

Racialized discourses intertwined with discourses of gender and class serve to construct and represent black women in particular ways. This is the case in sport and throughout many aspects of black women's lives. Specific ethnographic studies in Britain have provided insights into the impact of images and representations on black women's experiences and opportunities. These 'pictures' of black women's lives offer quite a different story from the dominant universal stereotypes that are based on cultural and religious constraint. For example, Brah (1996) highlights the fact that South Asian family life is often misrepresented which has consequences for how their leisure (and sport) is perceived and policies enacted. Brah claims that too much attention has been focused on 'the family' and not enough attention has gone into addressing South Asian women's experiences more widely. In many ways this explains the lack of attention given to South Asian women and sport and physical activity. There is an assumption that a perceived absence from sport exists because of cultural and family constraint. One of the dominant stereotypes is that South Asian women are passive and subordinate especially within the family context. However, if women's lives are qualitatively considered through ethnographic study, there develops a portrait of their lives that features a complex myriad of experiences. The worlds they inhabit are highly differentiated dependent on factors such as country of origin, regional location, class position in the subcontinent as well as in Britain, marital status, age, rural/urban and so on (Afshar 1994; Brah 1994; Woolett *et al.* 1994). In the everyday lives of these women these factors, together with others, are not separate but are intersecting and interwoven.

It is this complexity that must be interrogated if we are to understand both involvement in and absence from sport. An example of this from recent research is the response of a South Asian woman who was articulating a problem that she had in taking her daughter swimming. The comment, taken at face value, appeared to reinforce the stereotypical notion that South Asian girls and women are constrained from taking part in swimming because of 'cultural or religious constraint'. However, when this was followed up and discussed in more detail, the reason was revealed to be a concern that is shared by many women about the exposure of her body because it was not the 'acceptable' feminine size and shape (Scraton and Watson, 1998). Her concerns were not totally divorced from her identity as a Muslim woman but this was subsumed by a more powerful vulnerability about her appearance as a woman. The extent to which this was circumscribed by Western patriarchal definitions of 'an appropriate feminine attractiveness' would require detailed analytical consideration.

There is no doubt that there is a powerful discourse of 'cultural constraints' that has impacted on analyses of race, gender and sport. Brah highlights the fact that the 'cultural constraint' most often discussed in relation to Muslim women is the institution of 'purdah', which she defines as 'a series of norms and practices which limit women's participation in public life' (Brah 1994: 158). However, again the complexity and fluidity of this practice are highlighted as its patterns and observance are shown to vary in different contexts. It is intricately tied, also, to a patriarchal discourse, thus it is neither static nor fixed. As Brah points out:

> What is particularly relevant is the specific ways in which 'purdah' manifests itself differently among different Muslim and other South Asian communities in Britain and the extent and manner in which it articulates with other British patriarchal ideologies and practices.
>
> (Brah 1994: 158)

In considering difference in relation to gender, race and sport we need to recognize diversity amongst groups such as Muslim women and South Asian women that still are universalized in much of our analysis. By investigating difference we recognize the multiplicity of subject positions that women hold while recognizing that these are embedded in discourses and a materiality that can produce universal effects and common experiences. As Rasool (1997) argues, a homogenized dominant view of 'black' contrasts with the rich tapestry of black experience grounded in different diasporas. It is this 'rich tapestry' of black experience in and with sport that can then be located and 'mapped' onto material and structural processes.

Agency and self-determination

The richness, creativity and self-determination of black women's lives have been ignored generally within feminism and specifically within the study of sport. There has been a concentration on constraints and barriers, with black women often pathologised into a position of 'victim'. However, as black feminists have recorded their struggles and resistances it becomes obvious that there must be a shift from black women as 'object' of research to black women as 'subject' (hooks 1989). Critical autobiographies of black women relocate their experiences at the centre of analysis. These studies focus on different groups of women, defined and racialized as, for example, South Asian (Afshar 1994; Brah 1994; Parmar 1982) and African Caribbean (Bryan *et al*. 1985; Mirza 1992). We need to know from black women how they experience sport as a competitive and/or a recreational activity and as part of a National Curriculum in school. This needs to focus not only on the barriers and constraints that they face from racist sporting and educational institutions together with the racialized images and representations that attempt to define their participation, but also on the meanings that sport holds for them, including friendships and community networks, negotiations around racialized engendered spaces and enjoyment and pleasure gained in active recreation.

White feminist sport scholars have been interested in how ideologies of femininity, defined in terms of heterosexual attractiveness, are central to definitions of female physicality (Scraton 1992) and how exercise has come to be used in the social construction of the 'ideal feminine body' (Markula 1993). Recently there has been important work that focuses on sport and physical activity as a site for the empowerment of women through an active physicality that challenges patriarchal definitions of femininity (Gilroy 1997; McDermott 1996). However, sport is not only implicitly related to the production, reproduction of and resistance to, an engendered body powerfully articulated by discourses of heterosexual attractiveness. These bodies are also racialized bodies that are intricately related to discourses of *white* heterosexual attractiveness. Rarely is this acknowledged in the work of white feminists. As Weekes (1997: 114) argues: 'Though femininity is bound up with heterosexuality and the ability of women to appear attractive to men, black women occupy a differential racialized space within and against these constructions'.

Currently, we have little acknowledgement in the sports world of, for example, the 'fitness boom' and aerobics as a racialized engendered space. We have little knowledge of the meaning and importance attached to physical well-being, fitness, exercise and health by different women (Zaman 1997). Partly this is associated with the lack of critical engagement with 'whiteness' as a racial category that needs to be deconstructed and understood. Too often issues to do with race, gender and sport are seen to relate solely to 'black women and sport' rather than a critique of whiteness in theorizing and practice. Not least, there needs to be a questioning of the significance of sport and physical activity in the diverse lives of different women. It is no coincidence that until recently feminists outside the academic area of sport have seen sport and physical activity as having little relevance to feminist politics and activism. Sport is defined as 'male' and of minor significance in comparison to issues such as violence against women, work and the labour market, education and schooling etc. However, as the body has taken on increased significance within feminist discourse so the relationships between body, physicality, sexuality, exercise and physical activity have begun to be viewed as having some relevance to a broader feminist project. There remains much work to be done on the racialization and sexualization of female physicality, images and representations and black women's self-perceptions. Furthermore, just as many white feminists, who have not formerly been involved in sport, find themselves enjoying physical activity and exercise as an important aspect of their identities as strong, capable women so, too, may black women find in physical activity an expression of themselves that has the potential to be empowering and pleasurable. Sport theorists, policy makers and providers simply do not have the knowledge that is needed to support equitable and appropriate provision of opportunity for *all* women.

'Unlearning one's privilege' (Landry and Maclean 1996)

Increasingly there is a need for studies of the 'unmarked' such as masculinity and whiteness (Glenn 1999). Already, as discussed earlier, there are some excellent contributions to feminist debate from pro-feminist men attempting to 'unmask' masculinity in the sports arena (Messner 1992; Messner and Sabo 1990). As yet whiteness has received little attention especially as engendered whiteness. Such a focus represents a challenge to assumptions that race is about minority experiences or that whiteness is 'raceless' (Dyer 1988). White *is* a racial category albeit a privileged one that has gone unexamined (Bonnett 2000; Frankenberg 1993; Wong 1994). Furthermore, just as black feminists have sought to locate their lives and experiences in a historical discourse of migration, colonialism and postcolonialism, so it is crucial that white researchers and sport scholars locate themselves within their cultural, political and social history (Dyer 1997; Wray 1999). Sport feminism is epistemologically located within white feminism, primarily researching the activities and experiences of white women. This locates 'whiteness' at the centre and thus marginalizes or 'others' black women, albeit that this is largely an unconscious and unintentional action. 'Naming whiteness' allows it to be displaced from its central unmarked and undefined position (Frankenburg 1993). However, I would introduce a word of caution here in that to simply 'name' our power as white women does not fundamentally reduce the powerful oppressive racism experienced by the black community. As Sivanandan (1985) argued in the early days of 'race aware-ness training' (RAT), there is a danger that this simply allows white racism to 'name' itself but without having to fundamentally change practice or challenge the structures that support its existence.

Within sport, the notion that white is 'raceless' has allowed the majority to maintain their central position by feeling 'unable' to research an issue that is 'other' to themselves. Researching difference raises difficult methodological issues that we cannot ignore (Maynard 1994; Maynard and Purvis 1994; Phoenix 1994). However, it is important that difference is not only defined as experiential diversity but is seen as relational and fundamentally tied to relations of power. Analysing the gendered whiteness of sport would identify the struc-tural advantages that are historically located in the institution of sport as well as challenging white women to examine themselves in relation to both black women and men. As Maynard (1994: 20) acknowledges, we need to focus on the 'taken-for-granted everydayness of white privilege' as well as the situations in sport where it is more directly expressed. It involves problematizing the term 'white' and recognizing, also, that we need to go beyond a simple dualistic understanding of white-black:

> It should not be forgotten, for instance, that it is not necessary to be black to experience racism, as the Jews and the Irish and the current events in Europe testify. Further, the meanings of the categories of black and white are not constant. Those labelled one way under certain socio-economic conditions may find the label changes under others.
>
> (Maynard 1994: 21)

Conclusions

Black feminists have produced rich empirical knowledge from autobiographical and ethnographic accounts and have challenged the epistemology of white feminism. Sport is a significant cultural and social arena and impacts on people's lives through competitive or recreational participation, as spectators, via the media, in schools and education, in relation to health and exercise, the body and physicality and in the consumption and production of sporting goods. Yet, as sport sociologists, our critical sport analysis has paid little attention either to the experiences of black women or the racialization and engendering of sport. As yet, there have been few attempts to relate the epistemological and metho-dological concerns of black feminists and the knowledge that they have produced, to a political and theoretical understanding of race, gender and sport.

As we read and 'listen to' the writings of black feminists it becomes obvious that it is insufficient to rely on additive models of oppression that simply 'add to' the existing canons of knowledge that constitute our understanding of sport (De Groot 1996; Birrell and Cole 1994). We need to shift the focus to place the present and past of black women at the centre and question the construction of whiteness and the privileges that it holds. Too often the study of race and sport or black women and sport concentrates on constraints. Although identifying constraints and barriers may be important for a liberal agenda of equal opportunities, this emphasis does little to challenge the ethnocentrism and androcentrism of sport.

I have argued that the work of black feminism is useful in suggesting theoretical models that help to view difference as more than experiential diversity and a celebration of multiculturalism. It is not enough to rely on localized studies that emphasise the *effects* of race and ethnicity. These need to be mapped onto broader social and historical processes. As bell hooks (1991: 260) succinctly argues we should not separate the 'politics of difference' from the 'politics of racism'. The autobiographical studies of British black feminists have pointed to the complexities of black women's lives and the multiple overlapping axes of class, race, gender and sexuality. In their work the interconnectedness of structure, culture and agency is explored in ways which provide useful models that have application to the study and analysis of sport. We need to move beyond the separate approaches that view sport through a 'gender lens' or a 'race lens' (Feree, Lorber and Hess 1999) to an integrated analysis that will 'invoke some measure of critical race/gender reflexivity into mainstream *[sport]* academic thinking' (Mirza 1997: 5).

Note

1   I acknowledge the complex debates around terminology. Use of the term black is inherently problematic as it serves to homogenize diverse groups yet identifies the collective challenge made by feminists to the hegemony of white western women's perspectives. Throughout this article I shift terminology to reflect its usage by particular feminist writers, researchers and activists.

References

Afshar, H. (1994) 'Muslim women in West Yorkshire: Growing up with real and imaginary values amongst conflicting views of self and society' in H. Afshar and M. Maynard (eds.) *The Dynamics of 'Race' and Gender: some feminist interventions*, London: Taylor and Francis, pp. 127–150.

Anthias, F. and Yuval Davis, N. (1993) *Racialized Boundaries: Race, Nation, Gender, Colour and Class and the Anti-racist Struggle*, London: Routledge.

Archer, R. and Bouillon, A. (1982) *The South African Game: Sport and Racism*, London: Zed Books.

Baker, A. and Boyd, T. (1997) *Out of Bounds: Sports, Media and the Politics of Identity*, Indianapolis: Indiana University Press.

Benn, T. (1996) 'Muslim women and Physical Education in Initial Teacher Training', *Sport, Education and Society*, vol. 1, no. 1, pp. 5–21.

Bhattacharyya, G (1998) *Tales of Dark-Skinned Women: Race, Gender and Global Culture*, London: UCL Press.

Bhavnani, K. and Coulson, M. (1986) 'Transforming socialist feminism: the challenge of racism', *Feminist Review* no. 23.

Bhavnani, K. and Phoenix, A. (1994) *Shifting Identities, Shifting Racisms: A Feminism and Psychology Reader*, London: Sage.

Birrell, S. (1988) 'Discourses on the gender/sport relationship: From women in sport to gender relations', *Exercise and Sport Science Review*: 16, pp. 459–502.

—— (1989) 'Racial relations, theories and sport: suggestions for a more critical analysis', *Sociology of Sport Journal* 6, pp. 212–227.

—— (1990) 'Women of color. Critical autobiography and sport' in M. Messner and D. Sabo (eds) *Sport, Men and the Gender Order*, Champaign, IL: Human Kinetics.

Birrell, S. and Cole, C. (eds) (1994) *Women, Sport and Culture*. Champaign, IL: Human Kinetics.

Bonnett, A. (2000) *White Identities: Historical and international perspectives*, London: Prentice Hall.

Brackenridge, C. (1997) 'Healthy sport for healthy girls? The role of parents in preventing sexual abuse in sport', *Sport, Education and Society*, Vol. 3, no. 1, March.

Brackenridge, C. and Kirby, S. (1997) 'Playing safe: assessing the risk of sexual abuse to young elite athletes', *International Review for the Sociology of Sport*, 32, 41, pp. 407–418.

Brah, A. (1994) 'South Asian young Muslim Women and the labour market' in H. Afshar and M. Maynard (eds) *The Dynamics of 'Race' and Gender: Some Feminist Transformations*, London: Taylor and Francis, pp. 151–172.

—— (1996) *Cartographies of Diaspora: Contesting Identities*, London: Routledge.

Bryan, B., Dadzie, S. and Scafe, S. (1985) *The Heart of the Race-Black Women's Lives in Britain*, London: Virago Press.

Butler, J. (1990) *Gender Trouble: Feminism and the Subversion of Identity*, London: Routledge.

Cahn, S. (1996) 'From muscle moll to the butch ball player: mannishness, lesbianism and homophobia in US Women's Sport', in Vicinus, M. (ed.) *Lesbian Subjects: A Feminist Reader*, Indianapolis: Indiana University Press, pp. 41–65.

Carrington, Ben (1998) 'Sport, masculinity and black cultural resistance', *Journal of Sport and Social Issues*, 22, August, pp. 275–298.

—— (1999) 'Cricket, Culture and Identity', in Roseneil, S. and Seymour, J. (eds) *Practising Identities: Power and resistance*, London: Macmillan.

Carrington, Bruce, Chivers, T. and Williams, T. (1987) 'Gender, leisure and sport: a case-study of young people of South Asian descent', *Leisure Studies*, vol. 6, no. 3, September, pp. 255–280.

Carrington, Bruce and Wood, E. (1983) 'Body talk: Images of sport in a multi-racial school', *Multiracial Education*, Vol. 11, 2, pp. 29–38.

Cashmore, E. (1982) 'Black Youth, Sport and Education', *New Community*, vol. 2, Winter.

Cashmore, E. and Troyna, B. (eds) (1982) *Black Youth in Crisis*, London: Allen Unwin.

Cole, C. and Hribra, A. (1995) 'Celebrity feminism: Nike style, post Fordism, transcendence and consumer power', *Sociology of Sport Journal*, 12, pp. 347–369.

Collins, P. H. (1990) *Black Feminist Thought: Knowledge, Consciousness and the Politics of Empowerment*, Boston: Unwin Hyman.

Connell, R.W. (1987) *Gender and Power*, Stanford, CA: Stanford University Press.

—— (1995) *Masculinities*, Sydney: Allen and Unwin.

Curry, T. (1991) 'Fraternal bonding in the locker room: A profeminist analysis of talk about competition and women', *Sociology of Sport Journal*, 8, pp 119–135.

De Groot, J. (1996) 'Anti-colonial subjects? Post-colonial subjects? Nationalisms, ethnocentricisms and feminist scholarship', in M. Maynard and J. Purvis (eds), *New*

Frontiers in Womens' Studies: Knowledge, Identity and Nationalism, London: Taylor & Francis.

Dworkin, S. and Messner, M. (1999) 'Just Do ... What? Sport, bodies, gender' in M. Ferree, J. Lorber, B. Hess (eds) *Revisioning Gender*, London: Sage.

Dyer, R. (1988) 'White'. *Screen*, 29, pp. 44–64.

—— (1997) *White*, London: Routledge.

Elam, D. (1994) *Feminism and Deconstruction*, London: Routledge.

Feree, M., Lorber, J. and Hess, B. (1999) *Revisioning Gender*, London: Sage.

Fleming, S. (1989) 'Asian lifestyles and sports participation' in Tomlinson, A. (ed.). *Youth Cultures and the Domain of Leisure*, Eastbourne: LSA, pp. 82–98.

—— (1994) 'Sport and South Asian youth: the perils of 'false universalism' and stereotyping', *Leisure Studies* 13, pp. 159–173.

Frankenberg, R. (1993) *The Social Construction of Whiteness: White Women, Race Matters*, London: Routledge.

Gilroy, S. (1997) 'Working on the body: links between physical activity and social power' in G. Clarke and B. Humberstone (eds) *Researching Women and Sport*, London: Macmillan.

Glenn, E. (1999) 'The social construction and institutionalization of gender and race: an integrative framework', in M. Feree, J. Lorber, and B. Hess (eds) *Revisioning Gender*, London: Sage.

Griffin, P. (1992) 'Changing the game: homophobia, sexism and lesbians in sport', *Quest*, 44, 2, pp. 251–265.

Hall, A. M. (1996) *Feminism and Sporting Bodies: Essays on Theory and Practice*, Champaign, IL: Human Kinetics.

Hargreaves, J. (1979) 'Playing like gentlemen while behaving like ladies', unpublished MA Dissertation, University of London.

—— (1994) *Sporting Females: Critical Issues in the History and Sociology of Women's Sports*, London: Routledge.

hooks, b. (1984) *Feminist Theory: From Margin to Center*, Boston, Massachusetts: South End Press.

—— (1989) *Talking Back: Thinking Feminist, Thinking black*, Boston: South End Press.

—— (1991) *Yearning: Race, Gender and Cultural Politics*, London: Turnaround Press.

Ifekwunigwe, J (1999) *Scattered Belongings: Cultural Paradoxes of Race, Nation and Gender*, London: Routledge.

James C.L.R. (1963[1994]) *Beyond a Boundary*, London: Serpent's Tail.

Jarvie, G. (ed.) (1991) *Sport, Racism and Ethnicity*, London: Falmer.

Landry, D. and Maclean, G. (eds) (1996) *The Spivak Reader*, London: Routledge.

Lenskyj, H. (1991) 'Combating homophobia in sport and Physical Education', *Sociology of Sport Journal*, 8, pp. 61–69.

Lovell, T. (1991) 'Sport, racism and young women' in G. Jarvie (ed.) *Sport, Racism and Ethnicity*, London: Falmer.

Majors, R. (1990) 'Cool Pose: black masculinity and sports' in M. Messner and D. Sabo (eds) *Sport, Men and the Gender Order*, Champaign, IL: Human Kinetics.

Mangan, T. (1981) *Athleticism in the Victorian and Edwardian Public School*, Cambridge: Cambridge University Press.

Mangan, J. and Park R. (1987) *From 'Fair Sex' to Feminism*, London: Frank Cass.

Markula, P. (1993) 'Looking good, feeling good: Strengthening mind and body in aerobics', in L. Laine (ed.) *On the Fringes of Sport*, pp. 93–99, St. Augustine, Germany: Academia.

—— (1995) 'Firm but shapely, fit but sexy, strong but thin: the postmodern aerobicizing female bodies', *Sociology of Sport Journal* 12, pp. 424–453.

Maynard, M. (1994) '"Race", gender and the concept of "difference" in feminist thought' in H. Afshar and M. Maynard (eds) *The Dynamics of 'Race' and Gender*, London: Taylor Francis.

—— (1996) 'Challenging the boundaries: Towards an anti-racist Women's Studies' in M. Maynard and J. Purvis (eds) *New Frontiers in Women's Studies: Knowledge, Identity and Nationalism*, London: Taylor & Francis.

Maynard, M. and Purvis, J. (eds) (1994) *Researching Women's Lives from a Feminist Perspective*, London: Taylor & Francis.

McDermott, L. (1996) 'Towards a feminist understanding of physicality within the context of women's physically active and sporting lives', *Sociology of Sport Journal* 13(1), pp. 12–30.

Messner, M. (1992) *Power at Play: Sports and the Problem of Masculinity*, Boston: Beacon Press.

—— (1997) *Politics of Masculinities: Men in Movements*, California: Sage.

Messner, M. and Sabo, D. (1990) *Sport, Men, and the Gender Order: Critical Feminist Perspectives*, Champaign, IL: Human Kinetics.

Mirza, H. (1992) *Young, Female and Black*, London: Routledge.

—— (1997) (ed.) *Black British Feminism: A Reader*, London: Routledge.

Obel, C. (1995) 'Collapsing gender in competitive body building: Researching contradictions and ambiguity in sport', *International Review for the Sociology of Sport*, 31, 2, pp. 185–202.

Oglesby, C. (1981) 'Myths and realities of black women in sport,' in T. Green, C. Oglesby, A. Alexander, N. Frank (eds) *Black Women in Sport*, Reston, VA: The American Alliance for Health, Physical Education, Recreation and Dance.

Parmar, P. (1982) 'Gender, race and class: Asian women in resistance' in Centre of Contemporary Cultural Studies, *The Empire Strikes Back*. Birmingham: CCCS.

Phoenix, A. (1994) 'Practising feminist research: the intersection of gender and 'race' in the research process' in M. Maynard and J. Purvis (eds) *Researching Women's Lives from a Feminist Perspective*, London: Taylor & Francis.

Probyn, E. (1994) *Sexing the Self: Gendered Positions in Cultural Studies*, London: Routledge.

—— (1996) *Outside Belongings*, London: Routledge.

Rasool, N. (1997) 'Fractured or flexible identities? Life histories of "black" diasporic women in Britain' in H. Mirza (ed.) *Black British Feminism: A Reader*, London: Routledge.

Raval, S. (1989) 'Gender, leisure and sport: a case study of young people of South Asian descent – a response', *Leisure Studies*, Vol. 8, pp. 237–40.

Scraton, S. (1992) *Shaping up to womanhood: Gender and girl's physical education*, Buckingham, England: Open University Press.

Scraton, S. and Watson, B. (1998) 'Gendered cities: women and public leisure space in the "postmodern city"', *Leisure Studies*, vol. 17, no. 2, April, pp. 123–137.

Sivanandan, A. (1985) 'RAT and the degradation of black struggle', *Race and Class*, vol. XXVI, Spring, No. 4.

Simmonds, F. (1997) 'My body, myself: how does a black woman do sociology?' in H. Mirza (eds) *Black British Feminism: A Reader*. London: Routledge.

Smith, Y. (1992) 'Women of color in society and sport', *Quest*, 44, pp. 228–250.

Spivak, G. (1992) 'Women's indifference' in A. Parker, M. Russo, D. Sommer and P. Yaeger (Eds) *Nationalisms and Sexualities*, London: Routledge.

Theberge, N. (1987) 'Sport and women's empowerment', *Women's Studies International Forum* 10, pp. 387–393.

Vertinsky, P. and Captain, G. (1998) 'More Myth than History: Representation of the black female's athletic ability', *Journal of Sport History*, vol. 25, no. 3, pp. 532–561.

Ware, V. (1992) *Beyond the Pale: White Women, Racism and History*, London: Verso.

Weekes, D. (1997) 'Shades of blackness: young black female constructions of beauty' in H. Mirza (eds) *Black British Feminism: A Reader*, London: Routledge.

Wong, L. (1994) 'Di(s)-secting and di(s) closing "whiteness": two tales about psychology' in K. Bhavnani and A. Phoenix, (eds) *Shifting Identities, Shifting Racisms: A Feminism and Psychology Reader*, London: Sage.

Woolett, A., Marshall, H., Nicholson, P. and Donsanjh, N. (1994) 'Asian women's ethnic identity: the impact of gender and context in the accounts of women bringing up children in East London', *Feminism and Psychology*, Vol 4, No. 1, pp. 119–132.

Wray, S. (1999) 'Rethinking methodology: the diverse and differing experiences of mid-age women taking responsibility for health and fitness': paper presented to the BSA Conference, University of Glasgow, 6–9 April 1999.

Zaman, H. (1997) 'Islam wellbeing and physical activity: perceptions of Muslim young women', G. Clarke and B. Humberstone (eds) *Researching Women and Sport*, London: Macmillan.

11 Notes from the sports desk
Reflections on race, class and gender in British sports journalism

Emma Lindsey

Introduction

One of the great myths which surrounds sport is that it is an oasis of decency, honour and fair play in the desert of immorality and corruption which lays waste to the outside world. A safe haven of rules sanctified by stopwatches, its boundaries delineated by goals and winning posts; it's no wonder that sport continues to be held up by so many as the one great equalizer which transcends those immutables, race and gender – so long as everyone plays by the rules. But as the perennial drugs scandals in athletics and boardroom backstabbing elsewhere show, rules in sport are just as prone to being bent as the rules in politics and business. Sport mirrors the outside world. I would suggest that it is only within the intensely personal experience of playing sport or watching it, that a romanticized, transcendent view can be justified.

In this chapter I will be lending my insight as a woman who worked on the sports desk of a national newspaper, to give you an inkling about how the media machine works to perpetuate, and indeed helps to create, certain stereotypes which exist elsewhere. I shall be expressing my opinions, which are informed by my perspective as a black woman, about why I think this is the case. Hopefully some of my thoughts on how race is dealt with in the media may go some way in debunking the myth that sport is an oasis. Beyond that I shall be looking at the role of business in the promotion of certain stereotypes, and its ever-tightening grip on sport's future.

Entering the field

I am not nor have I ever been a 'sports nut' but perhaps having been brought up by two armchair sports fanatics, namely my parents, had an effect. Snooker, darts, athletics, boxing, football, rugby – anything with a score – was never too far from the television. Cricket was my mother's favourite, possibly because she was born and raised in Yorkshire. Her ashes are scattered there. In the summer it seemed that she would spend whole days in front of a mute television – she turned the sound down in preference to radio's cricket commentary – watching men in white on a field of green. My father went one better and being an

American Air Force man, would tune into the Armed Forces radio network which was broadcast from Germany, to pick up basketball and baseball games. Machine gun bursts of interference amongst screaming commentary would blare from the radio in the kitchen on Sunday nights, when he did the washing up. Much earlier than that though, aged four, I was allowed to stay up very late one night to watch a man called Muhammad Ali on our small black and white television, sitting next to my mother cheering him on. So despite my decidedly undistinguished school sporting record, you could say some kind of sport was in my blood. Or perhaps not.

I had been working at *The Weekly Journal*, a broadsheet newspaper aimed at the black community, for about a year and a half, writing features and doing a bit of freelancing on the side, when I stumbled upon Chris Eubank and Alan Hubbard. The former is known for his monocle, 'Simply the Best' catchline and ringside posing, the latter for his creativity and ribald humour as (then) Sports editor at *The Observer*. Both men were key figures in my nascent career. I interviewed Eubank about the trauma of putting boxer Michael Watson in a wheelchair after *that* fight in 1991, the cost of his Versace underpants (£80 a pair) and then sent the piece to Hubbard, who published it. Later this was capped by winning an award for a collection of off-beat interviews which, after Eubank, Hubbard had gone on to commission. Under his guidance (and keep in mind Alan Hubbard cut his own literary teeth writing comedy scripts for Galton and Simpson, purveyors of fine lines to Tony Hancock and creators of Steptoe and Son), I learned the ropes of live sport reporting, and an important rule on the planet they call sport: a sense of humour helps.

During the three and a bit years I spent at *The Observer* I was one of a very small band of women writing about sport in national newspapers. I say 'band', but actually there was no particular sense of camaraderie amongst us, born probably of the 'fighting over crumbs' phenomenon. When we did meet at events such as Wimbledon, a nod or a wave might be exchanged from a safe distance, dispersed as we were amongst the mostly male camps of sports journalists. Anyway, thanks to the likes of newspaper doyennes Sue Mott at the *Daily Telegraph*, *The Guardian's* Julie Welch, and television's ace anchorwomen, the late Helen Rollason and the now ubiquitous Sue Barker, the fact of being a woman at sports events was barely an issue most of the time. Yet sometimes being black was.

My first live assignment was to do a 'colour' piece from the 1995 Epsom Derby. This meant describing the atmosphere: the sights, sounds and smells from the historic 'people's race'. But first I had to get in. My arriving very early due to high anxiety – in fact there was still dew on the grass I recall – was not the only thing to trouble the jobsworth at the main gate. He was unable to comprehend that a woman who was black could, at the same time, be a national newspaper sports journalist. Presumably this was the reason he refused to let me in despite my having a press pass and a letter of accreditation. Finally with the aid of his walkie-talkie, he got 'someone upstairs' to ring *The Observer*, to check that I was who I claimed to be. Then he grudgingly let me through. This was my first taste of overt prejudice at journalism's table. The second came at my very first Wimbledon. It was a similar scenario, where the cognition which (usually) occurs when a press officer is handed a piece of paper in exchange for a press badge, took longer than usual. I tell these incidents to gently illustrate that in sport as elsewhere, racist attitudes and assumptions persist despite the best efforts of those who would deny it.

Black athletes, white media

Perhaps nowhere more blatantly so than in boxing where the battle for survival is made manifest; a brute sport which, perhaps because of its elemental nature, has wrung some of the most eloquent communications ever heard in the sports arena from its practitioners and pundits. As Hugh McIlvanney noted: 'For some of us boxing, with all its thousand ambiguities, offers in its best moments a thrill as pure and basic as a heartbeat.' And perhaps it is this purity which allows the struggle of freedom versus oppression around the central fight for power, to be seen. Muhammad Ali saw it clearly, made others see it too and in his halcyon days of reckoning, flaunted his gift. Knowing as he did that the arena of his sport was also the platform for his messages, Ali straddled without effort the chasm that some believe cleaves sport from the broader picture. In the biography *Muhammad Ali: His Life and Times*, Thomas Hauser (1996) put it like this:

> [Ali] altered the consciousness of people the world over. Ali was black and proud of it at a time when many black Americans were running away from their colour. With the exception of Martin Luther King, no black man in America had more influence than Ali during the years he was in his prime.

Ali transformed the traditional role of fighter from bit part to star turn and in February 1964, when he came out of the closet to declare his conversion to Islam, all hell broke lose. American sportswriter Robert Lipsyte remembers the effect Ali had in challenging the way black athletes were supposed to behave and the trouble the white establishment in general, and white sports writers in particular, had in dealing with him:

> The older reporters were saying this is the worst thing that has ever happened to boxing ... This might be the worst thing that ever happened to the youth of America which needs a proper role model ... And this garbage about the heavyweight champion being a role model; basically what they were talking about was the heavyweight champion, usually black, always poor, being a safe role model for the underclass. The heavyweight championship was a way for the white establishment to say to black America 'You should channel your rage and energy into being someone who fights to entertain us within very specific carefully bounded areas ... Choke down your rage at how your people are getting screwed over ... have your pleasures in

stereotypical ways, cars, women, wine, song, ultimately self-destruct and keep our stereotypes in order.' And now all of a sudden these people were stuck with a heavyweight champion [who] understood. 'I don't have to be what you want me to be; I'm free to be me.' And among the things he didn't have to be were Christian, a good soldier of American democracy in the mould of Joe Louis, or the kind of athlete-prince white America wanted.

Fighting talk from Lipsyte but then, the glory days of Muhammad Ali were iconic, inspiring writers' prose to sing, just as much as his actions earned him the moral outrage of others. He spoke of and to a revolutionary spirit.

Frank Bruno, who has been wholeheartedly embraced by the mass media, speaks of and to a more reactionary spirit. Look, at the evidence. For his buf-foonery rather than his boxing skills, it can be argued, Bruno has earned, amongst his WBC and European championship titles, the accolade of 'British Institution'. He has fashioned, unwittingly perhaps, his public persona in a manner that is startlingly reminiscent of 'coon show' characters which were the only roles available for black actors in Hollywood for most of the twentieth century. Film critic Donald Bogle writes:

> In short films created by whites ... black America was a steady line up of stereotypes ... dimwitted, comic ... the stereotypes eased white tensions about black America and put to rest any concern about social/racial inequalities and injustices; at the same time the images served to justify white notions of superiority and power.

At the same time Bruno refuses to talk about race or to 'see' colour which, as Ben Carrington has argued in his essay 'Double Consciousness and the Black British Athlete', enabled him in the face of strong anti-apartheid sentiment to justify his decision to fight the white South African, Gerrie Coetzee during the politically charged 1980s.

But to be fair, Bruno, like entertainers Ainsley Harriott and the exercise guru Mr Motivator, has simply chosen the path of least resistance in order to make his living. The degree to which Bruno has been used as a 'good role model for blacks', is instructive in highlighting how black athletes still have to conform to very narrow definitions of what constitutes good behaviour in order to be accepted. By volunteering to 'act the clown' he inadvertently fills a waiting sub-missive black male role, understood by the millions who buy products which advertisers need to sell and who in turn, know a commodity when they see one. So 'Loveable Frank' ensures his name and income live on after his boxing has gone, helping to sell products from brown sauce to toilet tissue.

Thoughts on Linford

It was generally assumed that being black, I would have more of an 'in' with black athletes than my white counterparts and as far as understanding that race is more or less of an issue for people of colour, depending on variable factors, that supposition was true. But the price for knowing that was the painful discovery that what is expected by black athletes, from black journalists, is an uncritical eye, and an unflinchingly sympathetic view, much in the way one might (in a perfect world) expect unconditional approval from one's parents. Within the context of commenting on competitive sport this view is at best unrealistic. As a journalist confronted with athletic endeavour, your fundamental role is to tell it as you see it and, if lucky enough to be given the freedom, to express opinions and offer comments around it.

One of the first articles I was asked to write after joining *The Observer*, was a piece questioning how much longer the most successful British sprinter of all time, Linford Christie, could keep running. I requested an interview with him several times but was refused so in the end I had to do the next best thing speculate and ask the opinions of other athletes.

> At the fast ripening age of 35, with thirty major international honours to his name and nine gold medals to date ... time could be running out on the man who's made a living out of beating the clock. Four defeats in eight days have posed the question Christie least likes to answer: Just how much longer can he stay on track?
>
> (*The Observer*, 11 June 1995)

As it turned out that question combined with the use of 'legend in his own lunchbox' – an alliterative turn of phrase I was rather pleased with – in the strap running across the top of the piece, caused no end of trouble. Christie saw the piece and flipped. On ITV's *Sport In Question*, the following week, he referred to what I guess must have been my article: 'One of the broadsheet newspapers, they wrote a story about me over the weekend praying for me to retire, you know, what's the point? Do you lot want me to retire? I'm at the stage where I'm so fed up of it all that I can walk out of the sport any day.' And within moments he burst into tears. Although most people reading the article would agree that it was hardly a scathing attack, and certainly *not* a prayer for his retirement, Christie perceived it that way, took it very personally. I know that this is one of the hazards of journalism but I feel that had I been a white journalist, Christie's ill-feeling toward me which he has on several occasions made manifest, would not have been so strong, or at least taken on a different significance. It seems as though being a black woman and having the temerity to pose an awkward question, was viewed as little short of treachery.

Having said all that, Christie's understandable sensitivity about sandwich containers, with its clear inferences to myths about black sexuality, isn't too difficult to understand when seen in the perspective of the following quote from this article about Patrick Ewing, centre for the New York Knicks, in the *Evening Standard*:

There are few occasions when mentioning the colour of a person's skin makes any contribution to what is being said. Then again there are few occasions to match the experience of being a white woman interviewing a 7 ft black man when the chap in question is completely naked ... He looked like some fantastic exhibit at the Natural History Museum.

(*Evening Standard*, December 1997)

This is one of the clearest examples of the worst kind of racist stereotyping and white journalistic fascination with the bodies of the black 'other' I have come across and it was written just a few years ago. Here it is boldly evident that 'Mandingo'-type notions about black male sexuality, prevalent in wider society, are right there in the sports department. But mentioning the fact within the profession of sports journalism is frowned upon. Speaking from my own experience, it has been remarked by colleagues on other newspapers that for the sake of my career I stay away from 'campaigning journalism' and interviewing 'too many' black sports personalities. Perhaps this tendency was shaped by my wanting to play a part in rectifying the way that black people are presented in at least one small area of the media.

Despite blatant and subtle examples of the ongoing objectification of black people within sport, the idea of it as a social leveller persists. Possibly because like sex, the concept sells, (or so we are led to believe) to the extent where the relationship between sport and business is now so close as to be symbiotic. Athletes across the disciplines succeed or fail not according to their sporting ability, but in the first instance, their ability to attract sponsors. So powerful is the notion of sport as a democratizing force, it spawned Nike's hugely successful 'Just Do It' campaign. Those three words touched a nerve which feeds the dream everyone wants to believe but the facts of capitalist life mean that some have more of a chance of that dream coming true than others. A Nike poster in circulation in 1998 showed a young black boy smiling rapturously, mid-way through kicking a football. The caption read 'He's got the ball at his feet', the message being that this is the same as if not better than, having the real world at his feet, ideologically reinforcing the myth of sport as a form of social mobility and empowerment. When you break it down it could of course mean any number of things or it could mean nothing, apart from: here is this (probably) working-class kid having a kick about in the park. But one thing is clear; anyone who still imagines that sport is in a league of its own as opposed to a global icon and therefore priceless marketing tool, is deluded.

Women, sport and the media

Venus and Serena Williams, arguably the most important siblings ever to have hit tennis, flummoxed the British media at first. In countless interviews journalists talked about Venus's braids-and-beads hairstyle, her shimmering silver lycra outfits, her odd name, her musculature, in short her 'otherness' (read blackness). I remember going to interview her at the women's tournament at

Eastbourne in 1997, just prior to her first Wimbledon appearance and in her dry manner, she commented on how 'everyone is so stuck on my beads'. She wouldn't have been impervious (on an unconscious if not conscious level) to the coded message that she was viewed by most sectors of the press as a freakish upstart who'd *muscled* her way into the pro circuit without really earning the right.

On Sunday 12 September, 1999 Venus's younger sister Serena made history by being the first African-American woman since Althea Gibson in 1958 to win the US Open title, beating Martina Hingis. Although, in acknowledgement of one of the most significant events in sport history, *The Daily Telegraph's* sport section led with the story, the message was completely undermined by the first line: 'Venus helps Serena to triumph over Hingis'. Further down the article the point was reiterated: '... in time [Serena] will realize how much of the work had been done for her the day before when Venus played Hingis and how Hingis had been handicapped by the scheduling demanded by CBS, which means there is no rest day between the semi-finals and finals.' The offensive idea being that Serena wasn't skilled enough to have beaten Martina without help; almost as if it takes two black women to equal one white. *The Guardian* fared little better in giving Williams' achievement the prominence it deserved, by placing the story at the bottom of the page, underneath the large photo and story of Andre Agassi's win as men's champion. Here, rolled into one, is a clear example of the way racist and sexist discourses are reflected in sports reporting.

Breaking the barriers

On the 8 February 1997 I watched transfixed, along with the other hundred journalists sitting ringside at the Las Vegas Hilton, as Oliver McCall had a nervous breakdown instead of the fight he was supposed to be having with Lennox Lewis. Vegas is weird enough anyway – I was staying at Circus Circus, a hotel with round-the-clock trapeze acts and what looked like a geriatric trans-vestite convention installed on the banks of slot machines in the foyer – but this farce of a fight was too much. McCall, clearly, should never have been allowed near the ring. A recovering crack addict who was under constant watch by drug counsellors, and under the arm of Don King; he didn't stand a chance. This bore all the hallmarks of a cynical fit-up and beyond the outrage of feeling cheated, there was a sense of pity and perhaps shame at the casualties boxing in particular seems to spit out. Watching McCall drop his arms, then stand staring into space with tears rolling down his cheeks, was a harrowing spectacle.

Ringside, after the immediate shock realization that what we were all seeing made this contest more than a fight report – it was now a story about frailty, corruption and greed – was the adrenalin-charged knowledge that I had to write it within a couple of hours. So I went back to the hotel, ordered a flask of coffee, wrote tremulously into the dawn, until I had said what I felt needed to be and in roughly the way I wanted it to be, then dictated my words very slowly down a crackling phone line, to a copytaker. When I'd finished it was 5.45 am in Las Vegas and just the right side of first edition deadline back in London.

From the moment I had been told I was being sent to cover the fight, until after the verdict from the boss, I had been terrified. It was my first live, overseas assignment and if I screwed this up the humiliation would be fairly public. So the fact that I did it, and had been judged by more sceptical male peers to have done it well, had big repercussions.

Vicariously, I had been empowered through sport. And not to put too fine a 'Rad-Fem' point on it, deep down this is what so many unreconstructed men and women still fear about women's success in sport. What else can explain put downs like this from sports journalist Jim White?

> Over the past year or so ... several leading women players have become alarmed at the arrival in their midst of what appears to be a new breed of power women, who are compromising the unique selling points of grace and skill. Venus and Serena Williams, the American sisters built like rugby lock forwards have been closely followed by French teenager Amelie Mauresmo, a woman with shoulders so broad she is rumoured to enter the locker room sideways.
>
> (*The Guardian*, May 1999)

Or this from Brian Glanville football writer at *The Times*:

> Well, they're allegedly football reporters but they haven't got a ghost of a clue what's going on on the field ... One can be a woman in print without it noticing – you can't see the lipstick or smell the perfume. But when it comes to a woman asking questions on TV ... I would find it difficult to listen to a Miss Motson banging on ... You'd never trust a woman with something as important as a football result.
>
> (*The Times*, October, 1998)

I could give countless other examples. The sight of women athletes grimacing and sweating, grunting and swearing in the course of breaking records or scoring goals, when captured by the photographer's lens is not pretty. These images have traditionally gone against preconceived ideas of 'feminine' behaviour and 'standards' of attractiveness, which has had a two-fold effect of turning many women off participating in sport, resulting in the largely minority status of women in sport due to lack of numbers and interest. As Mariah Burton Nelson argues in *The Stronger Women Get, The More Men Love Football*:

> athletic strength holds particular meaning in this culture. It's tangible, visible, measurable. It has a history of symbolic importance. Joe Louis, Jackie Robinson, Jesse Owens, Billie Jean King; their athletic feats have represented to many ... key victories over racism and sexism, key 'wins' in a game that has been historically dominated by white men.

Women like Olympic medallist Denise Lewis have done much, within the framework of sexist attitudes which exist, to re-focus the common perception held by men and women, of female athletes: namely that you can be attractive *and* win medals at the same time. From where the sponsor is standing this is great news, which is presumably why Lewis has had no trouble getting endorsements as 'The Face of Nivea', a good deal from Adidas, prime-time coverage and the accolade of front page pictures draped in the Union Jack, as well as a column in the *Daily Telegraph*. Like Bruno, though for different reasons, Denise Lewis is what is termed a good 'role model'.

So is Alyson Rudd. She wrote a book called *Astroturf Blonde: Upfront and Onside in a Man's Game*. The *Daily Telegraph*, which ran a feature in the paper's main section about Rudd, came up with the headline, 'How I scored with the boys'. Beside it was a large photograph of her with long, blonde hair. Inset in the piece, roughly one tenth the size, is a picture of Rudd actually kicking a ball. Clear as the coy smile on her face, is the sexism within and without sport which demands such a trade-off. And in just one quote Rudd undermines the notion of the worth of women playing sport in their right as opposed to being male imitators: 'I wanted to be good enough to play as a member of a proper men's side, without them even noticing it.'

As the phenomenal success in the United States, of the 1999 Women's World Cup finals proved – 90,000 filled the Rosebowl for the final game, which was the largest audience for a women's sporting event anywhere, ever – hopefully one day it won't be necessary for women's sporting achievements to be continually measured by a male yardstick. As Mariah Burton Nelson (1994) notes: 'The more women play a variety of sports, the more the entire notion of masculine and feminine roles – or any roles at all assigned by gender – becomes as ludicrous as the notion of roles assigned by race.'

Not cricket

When Jamaica qualified to play in the World Cup finals in France 1998, black people from the Caribbean and Africa were delighted – as one man I interviewed in the course of some research said, 'With Jamaica qualifying, all of us who used to automatically support Brazil, now have our own team' – but by and large everyone else thought it was a bit of a joke. The self-styled Reggae Boyz became a sort of mascot team and in the run up to the competition they got a lot of press attention. Some of it was intelligent, the worst of it played up to the most extreme right-wing bias of certain newspapers. 'Any nation which has rum as the liquid in its staple diet and a jolly chap called Percy Patterson as its Prime Minister deserves to have fun on the biggest coach outing in history' wrote one *Daily Mail* columnist.

Jamaica qualifying to play in football's greatest tournament, raised questions that no-one had really bothered asking before, like 'where did all these black football supporters come from?' as capacity crowds filled stadia in England and Wales to watch Jamaica play exhibition matches prior to France '98. Although columnists commented on the 'party atmosphere' no-one tackled the reason why black fans in any number at football grounds are the exception: namely black football fans are three times more likely than whites to avoid going to matches because of fear of violence.

Black footballers didn't have the option of not turning up in the days when racist abuse was at its worst. Considering the obstacles in the path of Paul Reaney, Cyrille Regis, Brendan Batson and the rest, where insults, phlegm, bananas and peanuts lobbed from the terraces onto the pitch was all in a day's play, the continued rise and success of black footballers is little short of a victory for Civil Rights. John Barnes, Ian Wright, Andy Cole, Dwight Yorke, and Paul Ince have re-drawn the football map. But at decision-making, boardroom level there are no bums on seats as yet. Ruud Gullit left these shores twice under clouds of dubious club politics, and John Barnes, who briefly became Head Coach at Celtic in 1999, fared little better. In 1998 during an interview I did with him at the Jamaican High Commission two weeks before the start of the World Cup, Barnes had this to say:

> Gone are the days in England when a black player could only be a forward, didn't like the cold, couldn't be a goalie or a defender or a manager. Barriers are going down because the world is getting smaller, so stereotypes about black players are receding.
>
> (*The Observer* May 1998)

Receding but not gone. And in the expectation of being called a pessimist (I have been called worse things), I don't think racist and sexist stereotypes will ever completely disappear, because the struggle for power and control is part of the game called 'human condition' which needs two opposing teams to play: the oppressors and the oppressed. All that might change would be the venue and the rules. I don't know whether my being at *The Observer* helped change anything on Planet Sport, but if, having done my best each week to provoke some sort of debate or at least a raised eyebrow, which I like to think I managed (sometimes) to achieve, then a path has been beaten through one part of the newspaper forest.

Nick Coleman and Nick Hornby write in their introduction to the *Picador Book of Sportswriting*: 'Sport does not exist to enlighten. It exists to be experienced.' I would argue the reason that sport continues to thrive is because the transforming magic inherent in the experience, is in itself enlightening, although not always in an enjoyable way. Indeed, there have been so many great, inspiring and humbling moments in sport, that an entire genre of writing has grown up around it, where the creative endeavour has been fuelled by an urge to capture and then distil the essence of those moments. It has been widely argued that achievement in sport opens the door to achievement elsewhere; certainly it attunes the mind to success. It is also true that for so many, sport has held out the promise of betterment and delivered.

At some deep level it is this redemptive notion of sport which compels people to want to promote and protect an Edenic view of it, but just as Adam and Eve made a hash of things, so do we, with our hang-ups, preconceptions and blind prejudices. It is perhaps through honestly surveying the damage, taking responsibility for wrecking it, and finding ways to move forwards from bigoted thinking, that sport could really be the oasis we all seek.

Selected bibliography and guide to further reading

Boyle, R. and Haynes, R. (eds) (2000) *Power Play: Sport, the media and popular culture*, London: Longman.

Carrington, Ben (2000) 'Double Consciousness and the Black British Athlete' in Owusu K. (ed.) *Black British Culture and Society*, London: Routledge.

Coleman, N. and Hornby, N. (eds) (1996) *The Picador Book of Sportswriting* London: Picador.

Creedon, P. (1994) *Women, Media and Sport: Challenging gender values*, London: Sage.

Hargreaves, J. (2000) *Heroines of Sport: The politics of difference and identity*, London: Routledge.

Hauser, T. (1996) *Muhammad Ali: His Life and Times*, London: Robson Books.

McIlvanney, H. (1992) *McIlvanney on Boxing*, Edinburgh: Mainstream Publishing.

Nelson, M. (1994) *The Stronger Women Get, The More Men Love Football: Sexism and the Culture of Sport*, London: The Women's Press.

Rowe, D. (1999) *Sport, Culture and the Media: The unruly trinity*, Open University Press.

Wenner, L. (1998) (ed.) *MediaSport*, London: Routledge.

12 Pitch of life

Re-reading C.L.R. James' *Beyond a Boundary*

Chris Searle

Introduction

Cricket is a sport, at its genesis a very English sport, and like all sports it is much more too. As a young English cricketer of the 1950s and 1960s who was passionate about the game, I sensed and intuited this, but it took C.L.R. James' epochal book on cricket, history and the relation of sport to social and political reality, *Beyond a Boundary*, to begin to articulate this to myself. James' narrative and reflections also brought cricket into my consciousness of anti-racist action, both in England and the Caribbean, and as his words have done for thousands such as I, made political sense out of apparent leisure, and struggle out of bat and ball.

Headingley in the cold

At the Headingley Test match during the frigid English June of 1991, I was watching the progress of the West Indies first innings. It was late afternoon, and by that time much drinking had been done around the ground. It was a cold, cold Saturday which had been warmed by two inspirational pieces of cricket from the young Ramprakash, a newcomer to the England team whose family roots were planted first in India, then on the coastal lowlands of Guyana and the streets of London. He had launched himself sideways to take one brilliant catch to dismiss Simmons, then minutes after thrown down the stumps from mid-wicket after a lightning pick-up to create another wicket from nowhere. Those two electric acts had sparked the cutting atmosphere of the iciest cricket-watching day that I can ever remember. Until, that is, about 4.30 in the afternoon – for then it was the time of Viv Richards, West Indies captain and nonpareil of Caribbean batting power. As he strode out to the wicket with his implacable gait, un-helmeted and unperturbed by climate, crowd, match conditions or apparently anything else around him, a lone and dreadlocked West Indies' supporter standing near the players' steps let out a loud cheer and Caribbean words of brotherhood and encouragement. The bond and magnetism of his cry was urgent and powerful. A group of white spectators standing near him, carrying their lager cans, slurring their words and grimacing their aggression, turned on him and Richards too with curses, racist insults and crude, provocative gestures. The black man stood his ground, as Viv always did, giving back everything piled upon him until other spectators intervened and warned off the insulters.

Now Headingley is certainly not the most friendly or hospitable ground in England for black cricketers and their supporters. Yorkshire cricket, its administrators and followers have often been as cold as this June Saturday in receiving and recognizing the talents of black British cricketers. The 'no foreigners' approach to Yorkshire cricket and its century-long refusal to allow anyone not born in Yorkshire to play for the county before it opened its doors for prestige overseas players like Sachin Tendulkar and Richie Richardson, has meant that still not one single cricketer from the squads of excellent black cricketers playing every weekend in the leagues and inner cities of Yorkshire has been selected. Many of these, disrespected, excluded and ignored, have gone to form their own teams and leagues to play against each other, and have thus been forced into a 'Jim Crow' cricket arrangement in the cities and old mill towns of northern England.

So when these drunken Headingley spectators spat out their invective at Viv Richards and his countryman, they were the worst of the cricket world insulting and trying to humiliate the best. The dreadlocked watcher was brave and full of resistance and had, no doubt, had to confront similar menaces before on the streets of Leeds or other places in England. Viv too, of course, was no stranger to such hostility, and more than once in his career took on the gibes of taunting spectators, British journalists and their press campaigns, and the violence of Australian attitudes during the 1975 tour (see Searle 1993). As he wrote in *Hitting Across the Line* (Richards 1991), 'We came up against extreme savagery in that series, what many people would call extreme racism. Now what is a West Indian bouncer compared to that?'

There is a perennial image of Viv Richards in my head, and it is of him walking to the wicket. The pride, the matchless inner confidence that shines out, the assuredness of movement, the purple cap as if an integral part of the scalp. Here were a whole proud people going out to bat and to com-bat, a ray of Caribbean nationhood and the proud individual citizen of that nation, from a small island yet knowing no smallness, only power and readiness. That is why that lone, proudly-locked black man could resist and feel no sense of impending defeat from a group of cowardly and pathetic racists. There was a rock-like compatriot before him, striding towards the struggle of his people's cricket – and no bitter or envious postcolonial word-lash or threat was going to turn him round. In his autobiography Richards (1991) wrote of the 'deep, deep love' that binds cricketers and cricket-lovers of the Caribbean, a love and solidarity which beamed out from his own cricket directly from 'that self-belief about finding that inner strength, that determination ... in the face of all manner of adversity and negative influence'. Who was ever going to make Viv Richards or his Headingley brother 'grovel'? (Before the 1976 series in England, the South African-born and accented English captain Tony Greig had boasted that his team would make the West Indies 'grovel' in the forthcoming tests. The victories of Clive Lloyd's team made a farce of his predictions.) Richards was a great innovator of Caribbean cricket insurgency, but he also inherited the insights and understanding of pioneering forebears like Learie Constantine of Trinidad who, like him, knew of the aggression which surrounded the cricket world in which he played, with its 'failing intelligence … clinging to its wars and inequalities, its racial barriers and shibboleths' (Constantine 1949).

Viv's example

I believe that this incident at Headingley crystallizes the effect of Viv Richards on his region's cricket, but also on his people. There is a parallel too with the deeds and words of Maurice Bishop, the Prime Minister of revolutionary Grenada (1979-83). Viv was a symbol for the Grenada Revolution and those who led it on their small, struggling island. They saw him, as C.L.R. James would have expressed it, 'as their man', but also the whole Caribbean's man, their living emblem and inspiration too: the anti-imperial cricketer, the free West Indian of the crease. As Bishop had a dream of 'One Caribbean!', of a world where imperialism would be 'hit for six', so Richards too manifested the region's essential unity: 'Our pride in the West Indies binds us all together. If only we could work together. Perhaps sport should be the model for all life.' And as Bishop's words and Grenada's achievement sought to repel the new imperialism, the Reaganism of the north to 'Leave Grenada alone! Leave the Caribbean people alone! Leave the Revo alone!' (Searle 1984a), so Richards declares in *Hitting Across the Line* (1991) 'I want to warn people to stop their racism. I want them to leave the West Indies cricket alone!' For there has never been a cricketer so proud and combative as Viv Richards. Before him Constantine, Weekes, Walcott, Gilchrist, Hall, Griffith and Lloyd had bought a concentrated power, Headley, Worrell, Sobers and Gibbs a certain grace, fluency and phenomenal talent, and Ramadhin, Valentine, Collie Smith and Kanhai a unique ingenuity and creative genius. But Richards brought all these with a sense of assertive dignity, self-confidence and outright challenge that made the racists boil and his own people come out with all their strength and defiance of oppression. He was a product of the Caribbean cricketing achievement that came before, but provoked its emulation in others through the Caribbean and across the diaspora. And by looking in contempt upon the South African rand and turning his back on those who sought to use cricket to buy time for apartheid, he inspired others, black and white, to do the same. The greatest prize for apartheid's upholders, along with Richards himself, was Ian Botham. But he could not look into his friend's eye if he had gone to South Africa, so thus he stayed away. As the contemporary of Bob Marley, of Bishop, of Walter Rodney, of Caribbean women like Jacqueline Creft or Merle Hodge – as well as Holding, Marshall, Roberts, Garner and Greenidge – Richards played for a generation of courage and creation too, across the many currents and depths of culture through the Caribbean.

It did not occur to me on that Headingley Saturday that it would be Richards' countryman and successor to the captaincy, Richie Richardson, truly the meta-phorical son of the father, who would do much to help break down the racism in Yorkshire cricket. For that is what he did when he became the county's second overseas player during the 1994 season. He is absolutely his own man and his own brilliant cricketer, but perhaps Richards' huge and empowering courage also moved him.

The importance of *Beyond a Boundary*

Such words of praise for Viv Richards could never have come to me without the agency of C.L.R. James and his book of sport and book of life, *Beyond a Boundary*. In this book James reaches three monumental purposes. First he identifies sport, and in particular cricket, as a vehicle of popular struggle, in his instance, of anti-imperialism, anti-racism and as an enemy of colonialism. Second he expresses cricket aesthetically, seeing the sport as a discourse of beauty and human culture. And finally, and most importantly, he sees cricket as not simply a metaphor of life but as life itself, a way of approaching the challenges of being and living in the world: 'How do men live?' he asks – or more exactly 'What do men live by?' Of course James was a man, largely speaking to other men who played and loved a particular sport which bespoke a particular culture in a specific age. In these senses *Beyond a Boundary* may be criticized as limited, even ephemeral. Yet in its ability to connect a pursuit of leisure to the mainsprings of human life's essential progress, it is a book which is peerless.

James (1969) wrote of the Trinidadian batsman, Wilton St. Hill, that 'as soon as he started to stride to the wicket everyone stopped what he was doing and paid attention.' Viv Richards had the same effect on spectators that day at Headingley. For Caribbean watchers he was their hero, their symbol of dynamic energy and progress. For white racist spectators he personified success, fearless-ness, power and therefore danger.

In 1998 I heard Gary Sobers, perhaps the greatest, the most versatile and complete of Caribbean cricketers, talk in Sheffield. After his presentation I asked him about his thoughts on Roy Gilchrist, the Jamaican fast bowler whom I had seen bowl against Essex at Ilford in 1957. I had never, and I think have since never, seen bowling so fast and fierce. In his first over to the Essex opening batsman, the cavalier 'dasher' Dickie Dodds, he bowled a ball which hurtled over the batsman and wicket keeper (who was Clyde Walcott, not a small man) and hit the sightscreen on the first bounce. I hardly saw it before I heard the crash and saw the umpire signal four vertical wides. 'Ah Gilchrist!' said Sobers. 'Now he was the most dangerous cricketer I ever played with.'

Perhaps that was why he couldn't last, why the black and uncompromising Gilchrist was so prematurely dismissed and rejected from the international game for his hostility to the last West Indian privileged light-skinned captain, Gerry Alexander – and it was only because Richards, with all his similar 'danger', arrived into cricket two generations later, that he could survive, prosper and conquer so formidably.

As he tells us in *Beyond a Boundary*, James supported Gilchrist and also mobilized and led the campaign for the West Indies captaincy to be given to the obvious and outstanding candidate – the black man Frank Worrell. For before James' victorious intervention, even the most successful and perceptive of black West Indies' cricketers had been virtually prohibited from captaining the side. It was, as he writes, a part of his commission to 'lay racialism flat and keep stamping on it whenever it raises its head' (James 1969). It is such commitment and achievement through writing, organizing and leading cricketing struggles against racism that has made *Beyond a Boundary* a classic manual and inspiration for standing up to all forms of Jim Crow segregation and prejudice in cricket, in small ways as in large. The book is a constant source of challenge for those cricketers and cricket lovers involved, for example, in the campaigning in Britain of 'Hit Racism for Six' (see Hit Racism for Six, 1996), the only existing organization nationally established for coordinating anti-racist activities within the sport. In the campaign's work to expose the ugly attitudes within powerful interests at the heart of cricket – for example in the established cricket journalism of *Wisden's Cricket Monthly* and the vicious article by Robert Henderson attacking black English cricketers – the example of James' own combative journalism and message in *Beyond a Boundary* played a major influence. The campaign resulted in major black county and international players like Devon Malcolm and Philip DeFreitas winning their High Court case against the magazine and receiving substantial compensation (a proportion of which Malcolm donated to Sheffield's Devon Malcolm Cricket Centre, established to bring coaching and other resources to young inner-city cricket enthusiasts). Piercing too, are those insights of James about the behaviour of cricket crowds – the responses to cricketers of 'the people who watch them', those too who crowd into Lord's, Trent Bridge and Old Trafford who 'bring with them the whole past history and future hopes' of their people. Such spectators can bring, as I discovered in their reactions to Viv Richards and his rastafarian comrade in 1991 at Headingley, all their prejudices and the detritus and residue of their imperial minds, if they are Englishmen.

Racism on the Western Terrace

In August 1996 I found myself in the centre of another crowd-scene at Headingley, this time sitting on the Western Terrace during the second Test match against Pakistan, and listening to the violent racist language and physical aggression of white sections of the crowd against Pakistani players on the pitch, and groups of Asian spectators who were part of the crowd. Inhuman, murderous shouts were interspersed with violent drunken outbreaks of jostling and outright physical challenge. The campaigning around exposing and opposing the outrage of this Headingley behaviour was again led by 'Hit Racism for Six', and included a strongly featured article in *The Observer* (Searle 1996a) written by myself, very much moved by the conscious spirit of James' cricketing journalism in Trinidad in the fifties:

> As the slow train between Sheffield and Leeds made its way through the blighted and jobless towns of the Dearne Valley – Bolton upon Dearne, Thurnscoe, Fitzwilliam – there came the first ominous comment. A group of young men going to Headingley for the Saturday of the test match against Pakistan were reading the ground regulations printed on their ticket supplements: 'Racial abuse is strictly forbidden,' one of them quoted. 'Ah, until tea time any road!' added his mate.
>
> Inside the ground, on the Western Terrace, I waited with my 11 year old son and his Pakistani friend for the day's play to begin. Rain had held it up for an hour. There was more space than usual; every third row of seating had been removed for better crowd control following disturbances during last year's test match. Majority support was white – with many spectators wearing football shirts. But a strong Asian contingent sat in clusters.
>
> A superabundance of stewards from a private security firm, dressed in luminous red and yellow jackets with 'Crowd control, crowd safety' printed on their backs, patrolled the terraces. For a reason no one could fathom, they blocked the main path through the bottom of the rows of seats, sending spectators to walk along the congested and narrow spacing between tight rows of seated England and Pakistan supporters.
>
> They were officious and uncompromising, and got up the nose of almost everyone there, soon becoming the butts of humour and abuse.
>
> At lunchtime the atmosphere was friendly and inter-active: someone had brought a bunch of large beach balls, which were punched and slapped around the terraces. It was good-humoured and brought the crowd together – until, one by one, the balls were captured by the stewards to a unity of booing from almost all the spectators.
>
> The drinking grew apace. A group of Yorkshire lads in front of me were stepping up the volume and with it abuse at passersby. They shredded up copies of the *Sun*, the *Star* and the property section of the *Yorkshire Post* and flung the small pieces in the air every time a section of the crowd attempted an abortive Mexican wave. A young man with long slicked-down hair become their particular target: 'Drown the witch! Drown the witch!' they chanted every time he passed by. It was an anachronism, but a vile and menacing one at that, and seemed like another omen.
>
> Just after tea, an elderly white man managed to defeat the cordon of stewards blocking the main route through the terrace. He was cheered by everybody, white and Asian. Then a youth in a Pakistan shirt tried the same tactic, failed and was held by three white stewards. Suddenly, in a second, scores of white spectators were on their feet, hurling abuse – now not at the stewards, but at the restrained Asian youth. A white youth clearly out of his head with drink, came hurtling downwards from the top

of the terrace, crashing into the held Asian youth, and punching him. Other Pakistan supporters came forward to protect their friend as a group of stewards and police descended from the upper terraces, grabbing three Asian youths including the challenger of the cordon, and pulled them back up the terrace.

In an instant it was as if a boil had been pricked and the pus of four centuries of Empire was pulsing out. White spectators behind me and the boys were screaming 'Stab the Pakis!' Abuse was coming from all directions. Spectators with a medley of football shirts from Middlesbrough to Newcastle to the Rangers were belching out insults. Beer was thrown over Pakistan supporters in the front rows. As a group of middle-aged Asians protested halfway back up the terraces, they too were pounced upon and led away by stewards and police. White spectators around them chanted their support for the police: 'Take them out! Take them out! Take them out!'

This was not blind yobbery. It was the spillage of racism, incontrovertible and putrid. My son's friend sat through it all, apparently bemused, but with who knows what happening inside him. An Asian women walked past with a small child: 'Let's have a look at yer chapatti, love,' shouted out a young man to my left, as a group of other Englishmen dressed as spoof Moslems screamed abuse and made fey bows towards the Pakistani supporters in front of them. Racism and sexism were feeding off each other, while Alec Stewart reached his century and Waqar toiled without success from the football ground end.

A Pakistan supporter, dubbed 'Omar Sharif' by the spectators in front of me, made a harmonious gesture by going around groups of white supporters with a bowl of cooked chicken pieces. Some accepted them thanking him – others took them and thrust them back at him, hostilely and insultingly.

As for me, I had seen and heard enough, as I am sure my son and his friend had too, and we made our way up the chaotic and fuming terraces onto the perimeter path that runs along the rear.

I felt angry all the way home: there was the customary racist partiality of the police and private security firms, the failure of senior England players sitting on their balcony one hundred yards away to come down and use their influence with the crowd – and the shameful behaviour of hundreds of young Englishmen.

The next day's papers criticized the 'yobbery' but there was very little about racism – only an oblique statement by Sir Lawrence Byford, the president of the Yorkshire County Cricket Club. 'Use your own eyes!' he declared, when a journalist asked if the behaviour on the terraces was caused by 'racial undertones'.

'Undertones' is the most inept word to use. There were racist overtones, right over the length and breadth of the Western Terrace that Saturday afternoon loud, clear and squalid. And these were not the voices of organized fascists – although they would have been overjoyed at these events. More like the sounds of a grotesque carnival of *Sun*-readers,

Murdoch-men, clones of tabloid chauvinism and racism, proud to be British, afraid to be human.

No other event has persuaded me so much of the imperative need not only for antiracist campaigns like 'Hit Racism for Six' to penetrate the heart of English cricket and its race and class complexes and prejudices, but the importance of reviving antiracist education among young people in schools, colleges and workplaces. Government and School Inspectors give this low regard and little importance, and resources and priorities in schools have turned aside from its necessity over the last decade.

Headingley's Western Terrace shows why such work is essential: and why any future social equity and coherence in British cities depend upon it.

In matters large and small from great stadia to public parks and school playgrounds, in the dialectic between the personal and the political, the protests of James also fired me to take up cricket-based protests in the intimacies of my own sporting and family life. When, for example, playing for my local club in the Sheffield League, an opposing player called my own six-year-old mixed-race son a 'bloody ethnic' when he accidentally stepped on one of his pads while I was in the field. I was determined to follow through this ignorance and racism to the heart of the league, which after some strong correspondence from officers of my own club, secured an acknowledgement and apology from the club concerned. I can say that without doubt, with reference to my own life – and I know the same is true for many others – that reading James has led directly to action and struggle for progress. Thus is the true work of words – words about a sport which at times may have been at the centre of our lives and affected much more on its margins.

The window

In August 1982 I interviewed James in his bed-sitting-room in Brixton, south London (Searle 1984b). At that time, I had recently returned from a two-year period working as a teacher educator and English lecturer in Grenada for the People's Revolutionary Government. We did not discuss cricket. I wanted to ask James his views on language and power, particularly how he saw the tensions and alliances between the Caribbean vernacular and Standard English. Yet all the time we dealt with these questions, he kept his television on, with a very slight volume, at the foot of his bed as he lay along it. Frequently he would look up at it. For much of the interview the English left-hander David Gower was batting, and James nodded or exclaimed from time to time as he played a handsome stroke or the bowlers gained some life from the wicket or showed their own skills. It seemed to me, watching him and remembering the early evocative passages of *Beyond a Boundary*, that in his old age, James was connecting with that view of cricket from his boyhood bedroom, stretching towards the windowsill to look out over the cricket field of Tunapuna, Trinidad. Now the window was this small, portable television screen, enabling him to watch over a world view of cricket and still shape his 'impressions of personality in society'. It was a long, long journey from the plebeian, snarling Matthew Bondman of his boyhood, now to the casual pose and batting elegance of the debonair Gower, but I remember how James described the transformation of the former when he took hold of a cricket bat: 'So crude and vulgar in every aspect of his life, with a bat in his hand he was all grace and style' (James 1969). For me, *Beyond a Boundary* was a book which itself became a window through which I could transform my own view of the world, and its expression through cricket. Thus James' work about this cultural activity that was so dear to my own early life, cut deeper into my mind than any theoretical work could ever manage.

All the time we discussed the implications of decolonizing language, James continually referred back to his boyhood, his saturation in Standard English through his early reading of the Bible, Shakespeare and Thackeray. He spoke of one great colonial cultural institution while turning his head to keep vigil on another as it was played at the foot of his bed. He spoke of power through language – not only in the sense of the acculturated power of the colonizer's language, but how the new black and Caribbean writers – from Earl Lovelace, Linton Kwesi Johnson, Wole Soyinka, to popular singers like the calypsonian The Mighty Sparrow, were bringing a new energy, dynamism and power to the language of black literature and society. His references to this new generation of writers and their bursting of language reminded me of his descriptions in *Beyond a Boundary* of the Trinidadian fast bowler, George John, and it took me back twenty years to my own days at school. Let me explain.

James (1969) describes George John as a powerful element of a 'generation of black men bowling fast' that was 'more sure of itself' than those who came before. Although they were still under the control of white colonial cricket officials and captains, they were gaining in their confidence – and sometimes suffering for their boldness. John, asserts James, never held back in making his 'cricketing anger' clear and explicit. He was the true forebear of formidable generations of cricketers who played with Sobers, under Lloyd and alongside Richards: 'Everything they were came into cricket with them' (James 1969). Their English equivalents were Trueman, Milburn or Lock. They gave all of themselves to the truth and sincerity of their art, so that their cricketing expression was wholly themselves. They wore no masks: they were authentic humans on the pitch of life.

James, having described John's particular cricket genius with great skill and a moving sense of personal remembrance, concludes his chapter by talking about the fast bowler's son, Errol. Now in 1963, when I was a Shakespeare-loving schoolboy hungry for the canon of English literature – from a cricket-worshipping lower middle-class home in the London suburbs – I encountered Errol John. As James tells us, he was an actor and a playright, whose poignant play set in the barrack yards of Port of Spain, *Moon on a Rainbow Shawl*, (John 1958) had won the *Observer* drama prize for 1957. He had appeared in Hollywood films and as the 1962–63 Old Vic season programme notes to *Othello* and *The Merchant of Venice* tell us, he was a fellow of the Guggenheim Foundation of New York. Ironically, as English teacher in Bishop's High School, Tobago in

1968–9, I sought permission of my headteacher to produce *Moon on a Rainbow Shawl* as the yearly school play. I was told that I could not – the play had too much 'spicey' and 'local' language, 'low-life' characters and its form of strong social realism would not be considered appropriate by the parents. It was also the tradition, I was reminded, that the school every year produced extracts from Shakespeare's plays, and that tradition should continue. After much persuasion, I managed to convince the Head that we should write our own play on a local theme and perform it. We did so, putting together a play about the human consequences of the 1963 tragedy in Tobago of Hurricane Flora and winning the National Schools Arts Festival with it – but that is another story (see Searle 1973). I was forbidden to produce Errol John's play in his own land, for fear of embarrassment of language and reality, and for fear of cultural shame.

But back to 1963 and the Old Vic season. John played Othello, and also had the minor typecast and 'black' part of the Prince of Morocco in *The Merchant of Venice* ('mislike me not for my complexion...'). But a black man playing Othello was still an unusual enough event, despite the huge success in the part of the American Paul Robeson both before and after the war. Errol John, however, was a Caribbean man, a Trinidadian – like those calypsonians who arrived on the *Empire Windrush* or celebrated the West Indian cricket victory over England at Lord's in 1950 with their burst of song and satirical lyrics. And although he was a trained classical actor, the Trinidadian foundation to his voice was still as strong as it was beautiful. I saw the production, looking down from the gallery over a three-quarters empty theatre, and was much moved by it, as I was at the vulnerable dignity given to the main character by Errol John, and to me, the unusually melodic and un-English intonation and cadences of his speech which contrasted with the hardness of sound of the Iago of the Australian Leo McKern. Yet when I read the reviews of the production and of John's performance I remember reacting with surprise and anger. Almost to a man (and they were all men) the reviewers condemned John for his speaking of Shakespeare's poetry. The *Sunday Times* reviewer, Harold Hobson, accused John of gabbling his lines, and his colleagues all wrote similar criticisms. A black Caribbean actor could not play Shakespeare unless he aped the English of Englishmen. Of course just a few years later when Laurence Olivier, at the very same theatre, produced a histrionic caricature of blackness in his Othello, employing almost all the conceivable clichés of black minstrelsy, sucking his lips, rolling his eyes and swinging his gait while blacked out to the nines, it was marked down by the same critics as a triumph of classical character realization. Thus black actors were waging parallel struggles to playwrights like Errol John and black cricketers like Frank Worrell and their supporters like James, for true respect and a rightful place in their particular worlds of culture.

Lessons of class

When James writes of his own lower-middle-class background in Trinidad, and that of his cricketing protagonists like Wilton St. Hill or Learie Constantine, I recognize the class terrain immediately, for it is mine too. No matter I was born thousands of miles and an ocean away in what was still the seat of Empire, the signs and symbols are still the same. Being made as a human being within the same cricket culture, every Saturday and Sunday I looked through the same window, beyond the Essex boundary, onto my father playing cricket. So when James asks me as a reader, 'What do men live by?', I can recognize similar things as the learning process for me was not so different. Cricket and Englishness were woven into me like the thick white sweaters my mother knitted for me almost every new season when I was a boy growing up in the London suburbs in the decade following the war. My parents had met during the hours and rituals of cricket. My father would walk around the boundary of Romford cricket ground during his own team's innings. Being an opening bowler and a late-order batsman he had the time often to make many a circuit. He often fielded too, on the third man boundary. My mother-to-be lived with her elder sister in a house with a garden backing onto the ground, just beyond the boundary. She would look over the fence, he would chat with her. It was the scenario of a suburban idyll made by cricket, and in time produced a cricketing marriage which eventually produced me during 1944, when cricket, like everything else, was rationed – the year of the doodlebugs, when suburban cricket grounds were as vulnerable as anywhere else in London to the potential oblivion of the Nazi flying bombs.

Cricket and war were fused for my father. As a strong and talented club cricketer, he had regularly opened the bowling for his club side with the Essex and England fast bowler, Kenneth Farnes, who was to be killed during the war on a practice flight with the RAF. In his *Cricket Crisis* (1946), the Australian opening batsman Jack Fingleton, writer and commentator (a figure my father fervently admired, despite his Australianness), wrote of the 'rugged fury' of Farnes' bowling, and described him as 'the most handsome test cricketer of his age, but better than his looks was his modest, cheerful and cultured company.' My father spoke in much the same terms of his opening partner. Like many a cricketer he missed some of his best years through the war and looked back to the two decades before it as an epic era. He had two heroes. One was Douglas Jardine, the captain of the 1932–3 'bodyline' tour of Australia. For my father the 'natural enemy' was never Germany or France. It was Australia, and Jardine and his fast-bowling noncommissioned officers, Larwood and Voce, were at the centre of his pantheon. As was the former Essex and England captain, J.W.H.T. ('Johnny Won't Hit Today') Douglas, who exerted a virtually mystical influence over my father's memories of boyhood. He told me that one evening, having missed buying the evening paper, he also missed knowing the overnight Essex score in a county match at Leyton. He found Douglas' phone number in the telephone directory, phoned the Essex captain directly at his home in Wanstead, apologized for his intrusion and asked him the score. Douglas was pleased to tell him: 'Any time you want to know, ring me, son!' he told my father, who never forgot it, and made several other late evening calls on later occasions to the Essex captain. Such were the ways of cricket that stood in his memory.

For my father and many lower-middle-class men, cricket was a bond of blood.

Right through my boyhood, to my late teens as I grew a strong right throwing arm, he would stand ten paces opposite me in the garden, and command me to throw a leather cricket ball directly at his head. He never flinched as I hurled it, and he never dropped a catch. For me, particularly as I grew older and stronger, it was a frightening ritual but seemed an organic part of being a cricketer's son, along with the Saturday and Sunday accompaniment to all home and away matches as team scorer, or the winter evenings – every Monday night – when I was despatched to Romford cricket school in the yard of the Golden Lion public house, with a ten-shilling note in my pocket, for half an hour's coaching from the Essex opening batsman A.V. 'Sonny' Avery. Even now, in my mid fifties, when I play a correct forward defensive stroke, I remember the mild commands of Avery, who opened the batting for Essex in the decade after the war, scoring 1,000 runs in every successive season.

But cricket for my father was also truly the imperial game and a way of interpreting the world and its cricket-playing peoples. His respect for the enormous cricketing abilities of Bradman, Lindwall or Miller and the generations of Australians was qualified by his doubts about their lack of Britishness and suspect morality. The Indians were definitely untrustworthy – in business they were 'twisters', crafty, liable to cheat, and this also spilled into their cricket – except the aristocratic ones, the Ranjitsinjhis, the Duleepsinjhis and Pataudis. The West Indians were flamboyant and often brilliant – he spoke warmly of Learie Constantine, whom he saw as the consummate all-rounder, and against whom he had once played and with whom he had shared a drink after the game – a 'real gentleman', he said. But they were flawed, he claimed – they were no good when they were losing, when the pressure was on. They couldn't fight back, they would 'run' like typical colonial troops, before the enemy. For the (white) South Africans and New Zealanders he had an ungrudging admiration: they were truly 'like us', he would declare, and of us too. Thus cricket rendered the imperial 'values' and caricatures perfectly in digestible assertions that were unquestioningly passed on through generations. It took me many years, many experiences and much reflection as well as much passionate and painful argument with my father, to 'unlearn' these things and build a more authentic picture of the people of the post-imperial world. Yet the mediator of that world had undoubtedly been cricket: and cricket was often to break it asunder, as the colonized peoples used the sport of Empire to assert their anti-imperial genius and creativity in those years.

But when James writes about W.G. Grace as an example of a man and cricketer who was 'strong with the strength of men who are filling a social need', so was J.W.H.T. Douglas to my father, for this cricketer represented to him a bonding in the father–son relationship which became exemplary. Douglas' own father was an athlete, boxer and cricket enthusiast who became wealthy as a City-based businessman, owning a firm which imported timber for the construction of staves used in the building trade (Lemmon 1983). My father identified strongly with this trade background, working in the Sales Department of a small city commodity broker's firm, a job he had from leaving school at 14 in 1922 until his eventual retirement in the late seventies. Finding buyers and sellers for

Chinese bristles comprised his entire professional life, broken up on summer weekends by his love and pursuit of cricket.

The younger Douglas, also a prominent amateur boxer and international foot-baller, joined his father's firm, which allowed him to play as an amateur for the rest of his cricketing life in a situation of relative privilege. In 1930, however, tragedy struck both father and son. The younger Douglas, as usual, went with his father to Scandinavia during December to purchase timber which would be delivered to Britain when the northern ports unfroze in the Spring. While returning to England in the Finnish ship, the *Oberon*, both father and son were drowned as the vessel went down in thick fog in transit from Helsinki to Hull. My father would tell me how the son lost his life in a last effort to rescue his father, trapped in his cabin, as the ship finally foundered. Of such stories too, his life in cricket was made: sons and fathers, fathers and sons. They became part of a controlling cricket mythology locked into English lower middle class life. For my father too, the cricketing family ideal was that father and son would play together – even open the batting together as we did once in the village ground of his own Essex boyhood. That too was a statement of culture, of cricket life, an essential part of what James (1969) analysed, for me too, as 'the framework of my existence', interpreting a set of 'unstated assumptions that are the well springs' of his (and my) thought.

It was a part of the class to which I was acculturated through cricket, as I was to realize only when I first read *Beyond a Boundary* in my twenties, from the Car-ibbean island where I first became a schoolteacher – a part of James' nation. The book put into lucid perspective my own education as an Englishman and a crick-eter – from the books I read as a boy, the public school 'Greyfriars' novels imbued with the cricket culture, with Billy Bunter and the colonial Indian prince 'Hurree Jamset Ram Singh', and the 'boys' own' story whose title I can never remember, about another cricket-playing Maharajah's son at an English public school, who is pursued by a gang of murderous low-class dacoits for his father's precious stone which he carries. His father had forced him into cricket as a right-handed batsman when he was a natural left-hander. It is only towards the end of the novel that the son frees himself from his father's domination, bats left-handed and scores a vital century to enable his school to win a key game over a rival team. The dacoits are captured, the jewel recovered and the father pacified by his son's cricketing success albeit as a left-hander – as well as realizing the errors of his own parenting. This and a thousand other tales in boys' books, comics and cricketing biographies sat within the motto, the moral code burnt into a block of balsa wood, that my father gave me for my bedroom wall, whereby the ethics of a cricket culture took on a quasi-divine dimension:

> For when the one great scorer comes
> To write against your name,
> He writes not how you won or lost
> But how you played the game
> (Rice, Grantland, 'Plumnus Football')

'What do men live by?' asks James. This was it.

Yet, as I was to discover – partly through my readings of James applied to real life – it was a morality surface-deep. As I grew into cricket, progressing from school to district to junior county and England sides, I saw how the elements of class prejudice dominated the culture of English representative cricket, from selection to coaching to resources to official encouragement. When James writes of the gradation of cricket according to class and complexion in his boyhood Trinidad, it seemed not so different in England. The issue of race and resources for young black working-class cricketers from the inner cities has now also become a major factor in the sport – still being largely ignored in many powerful quarters of the cricket establishment (Searle 1996b). But during my own boyhood the distinctions were often more subtly revealed, as they were in James' Trinidad. Not by race, but certainly by class, often class within class.

When I began to play regularly in Essex junior cricket, the major opportunity was the chance to play for the 'Essex Young Amateurs' team. This was chosen preferentially not only by factors of talent, but *more so* by school. It was the territory mainly of the public schools – not the most prestigious like Eton, Harrow or Winchester who had their other more powerful cricketing outlets, but lesser-known and minor public schools like Tonbridge, Felsted, Brentwood or Newport. I was a secondary moderner by origin who had made a late entry to a new suburban grammar school which had no cricketing tradition. Thus I was very soon and very effectively marginalized by the aspiring public-school ethos of the majority of the young players. I discovered that my own lower-middle-class credentials failed to suffice, and although I enjoyed the cricket – played often at county grounds, sometimes against the skilled young professionals of county Club and Ground sides – I found myself swiftly educated into the subtle violence of a class society and its sharp gradations. James had written in *Beyond a Boundary* long before I read and understood the words: 'Cricket had plunged me into politics long before I was aware of it.' I discovered them too suddenly and acutely, when I played for Essex Young Amateurs against the Essex Club and Ground – a virtual 'Gentlemen versus Players' contest. The majority of young working-class professionals of the latter (including two future international players – the leg-spinner Robin Hobbs and Essex and England captain and manager to be, Keith Fletcher) seemed socially intimidated by the confidence, sometimes arrogance, and style of the 'Young Amateurs', and were clearly expected to show a certain respect for their 'betters'. In the event, their batting collapsed, giving even me some cheap wickets and bolstering the overweening assuredness of the public-school clique. It was a clear encounter of class played out on a cricket pitch, and an early lesson for me in the way in which English society was graded and fundamentally operated. When I read *Beyond a Boundary* years later in the Caribbean, these Essex moments, astonishingly, like a sudden yorker from the past, came directly back to uproot me.

San Fernando rendezvous

I spent my entire boyhood obsessed by cricket – as a typical Essex seam-bowler, playing and watching. These were the years when England lost its imperial hegemony to the USA, shed its struggling colonies and began to fail abidingly in its cricket. The year of its greatest Ashes dominance, 1956, when the England team was captained by Peter May and symbolized by the unplayable off-breaks of Jim Laker and his nineteen wickets in one Test at Old Trafford, was quickly followed by Nasser reclaiming the Suez Canal for Egypt and the decisive lakering of British imperialism. I was schooled and played on the green Essex wickets through the massacre of protesting black South Africans at Sharpeville, and the 'D'Oliveira affair', when in 1968 the mixed-race South African all-rounder Basil D'Oliveira, who had been playing English county cricket and was in exile from the land of his birth, was selected by the MCC for their tour of South Africa. The South African government refused to accept his selection. The MCC called off the tour, thus precipitating the international isolation of South African cricket, while the mighty West Indian tradition rose to supremacy under the leadership and black captaincy of Worrell and Sobers and the genius on the field of other masters like Kanhai, Gibbs and Hall. I had no idea that such changes had been provoked by the campaigning by James and others for a signal change in Caribbean cricket leadership, as the popular struggles and anticolonial leadership of Eric Williams, Cheddi Jagan and Norman Manley had secured formal independence for Trinidad, Guyana and Jamaica. It was only when I read *Beyond a Boundary*, having worked as a teacher in James' own country in the late sixties, that a realization broke inside me: *that to play and read cricket was to read and act in life.*

In acknowledgement, and thanking James for the world of living insight that his book has offered me, I shall return to 1982, a few months before I was to finally meet and interview him. While working as a teacher educator in Grenada, I was charged by the People's Revolutionary Government to help establish a publishing initiative. Later called Fedon Publishers (after the leader of the 1795 anti-colonial rebellion, Julien Fedon) it published a number of books narrating various aspects of the progress of Grenada's Revolution. We were invited to visit Trinidad in June 1982 as part of a Grenada delegation to the yearly celebrations at Fyzabad organized by Trinidad and Tobago's Oil Workers Trade Union (OWTU) to commemorate 'Butler Day,' when the life and struggle of the migrant Grenadian trade union leader Tubal Uriah 'Buzz' Butler and in particular his part in the 1937 Oil Workers' struggle, was remembered. We were very hospitably invited to sleep at the OWTU headquarters in the southern town of San Fernando during the night before the event (Searle 1989).

At suppertime I needed to make a telephone call, and was directed to a room up the corridor from where we were sleeping, which, I was told, had a phone. As soon as I entered the room I could sense it was lived in by someone with a particular personality and strong interests. One bookcase contained the complete works of Marx and Lenin, and many other political works. The other supported what seemed to be a complete set of *Wisden Cricket Almanacs*. On a hook on the inside of the door was a wide-rimmed hat and a cape. Who else could be living in this room? Yet what suddenly rendered me breathless was the book, open on the desk of the room's resident, covered with pencil jottings, its pages heavily annotated with margin commentary. It was a book I had written a few years before, *'We're Building the New School!'* (1980) about the democratic changes in the education system in Mozambique, from where I had returned in 1980 after a period of teaching in a secondary school. I froze. Without knowing, I had met the writer I most admired. All the way from the London suburbs and the green Essex wickets, and we had met in words of print about revolutionary Africa in a trade union building in the south of Trinidad. I could only marvel. I made my call, nervously, and returned and asked, 'Whose room was that?' 'Mr. James,' said one of the OWTU officials. 'He stays here when he is in Trinidad. At the moment he is away – in England, I believe'.

At least I had the chance to meet him and thank him for his writing and his lifetime's work for cricket too, and for much more than cricket. I have probably read *Beyond a Boundary* as an adult as many times as James tells that he read *Vanity Fair* as a boy, and it is possible that it has had as similar a huge and lasting impact upon my life, as Thackeray's book had on James. For with his 'marvellous West Indian brains' that he attributed to Learie Constantine, he had in his own life, in his activism and his writing achieved what he claimed W.G. Grace had created in his own era: 'He had extended our conception of human capacity' in a culture which he had appropriated, emulated and forged again in the image of his own and all people.

Conclusion

And what does James say to us at the dawn of the new millennium, beyond his century? That sport comes from and to us all certainly, but comes with the qualities of difference and character according to our histories, tenacities and circumstances. To return to where we began and to the genius of Viv Richards, who in his 1988 coaching manual *Cricket Masterclass* wrote: 'Work at the basics, but never be afraid of doing something different.' A grounding for every human being involved in sport, as expressed by the Trinidadian brilliance not only of James, but of his friend Constantine too: 'Try to contribute something new,' the latter advised, 'and carry the spirit of your cricket into your life' (Constantine 1949). It is that very sense of difference expressed through the language and unique insight of *Beyond a Boundary*, a different courage to challenge and overcome domination, racial arrogance and injustice, that James bequeathed to his Caribbean son Richards and those men and women who come after, in many places of the world. And like Viv of Antigua we take it into our lives with the wristband of African colours swinging with the arm-whirl of the bat and the uncompromising step out to the wicket, forward ever like Maurice Bishop's revolutionary cry – towards the real and metaphorical contest in the middle.

Selected Bibliography

Constantine, Learie (1949) *Cricketers' Cricket*, London: Eyre and Spottiswood.

Fingleton, Jack (1946) *Cricket Crisis*, London: Michael Joseph.

Hit Racism for Six (1996) *Race and Cricket in England Today*, London: Centre for Sports Development, Roehampton Institute.

James, C.L.R. (1969) *Beyond a Boundary*, London: Hutchinson [originally published 1963].

John, Errol (1958) *Moon on a Rainbow School*, London: Faber and Faber.

Lemmon, David (1983) *Johnny Won't Hit Today: A Cricketing Biography of J.W.H.T. Douglas*, London: George Allen and Unwin.

Richards, Viv (1988) *Cricket Masterclass*, London: Macdonald Queen Anne Press.

—— (1991) *Hitting Across the Line*, London: Headline.

Searle, Chris (1973) *The Forsaken Lover: White Words and Black People*, London: Penguin.

—— (1980) *'We're Building the New School!' Diary of a Teacher in Mozambique*, London: Zed Books.

—— (Ed.) (1984a) *In Nobody's Backyard: Maurice Bishop's Speeches, 1979–1983*, London: Zed Books.

—— (1984b) *Words Unchained: Language and Revolution in Grenada*, London: Zed Books.

—— (1989) *Grenada Morning: A memoir of the 'Revo'*, London: Karia Press.

—— (1993) 'Cricket and the Mirror of Racism' in *Race and Class*, Vol. 34 no. 3, London: Institute of Race Relations.

—— (1996a) 'Running a gauntlet of hate at Headingley' in *The Observer*, 18 August.

—— (1996b) 'Towards a cricket of the future' in *Race and Class*, Vol. 37 No. 4. London: Institute of Race Relations.

Author index

Subject index